The Long Retreat

'Boris Kagarlitsky is a man of enormous intellect, knowledge and bravery. He has done so much for the ordinary people of Russia, including in his campaign for socialism, democracy and peace. His unjust imprisonment is a chilling attack on free speech – and his courageous words must be heard. I've always been stimulated by discussions with Boris and his relationship with thoughtful figures all around the world. Boris represents Russia's future, not that of the oligarchs and greed.'

—Jeremy Corbyn MP

'This gloomy book will depress everyone who reads it. A willingness to confront our miserable circumstances honestly and directly, though, may be exactly what the left needs to build itself into a force that can win.'

—Jodi Dean, author of *The Communist Horizon*

'Russia's foremost Marxist thinker, the imprisoned Boris Kagarlitsky, provides us with invaluable insights on how to rescue the left from the two tragic paths that have led to its irrelevance: an obsession with "political correctness" based on dogmatism, and compromising with neoliberalism on pragmatic grounds. Kagarlitsky does not hesitate to break icons in his quest to end the left's long retreat and reassert itself as a force that can again shape the future.'

—Walden Bello, founder of Focus on the Global South

'This brilliant and profound book is likely to become a classic. Boris Kagarlitsky brings his formidable, clear-eyed analytical power and immensely readable style to what may become the definitive assessment of the Soviet experiment and its aftermath. In the process he also provides insights into decaying democracy under neoliberal capitalism. A major work by this courageous and committed scholar.'

—Jayati Ghosh, University of Massachusetts Amherst

'This remarkable book tackles a formidable problem: the global crisis of the left in the twenty-first century. It explains how the contradictory tendencies of neoliberal capitalism contributed to this crisis and discusses strategies for overcoming it. As with everything that Boris Kagarlitsky writes, the book offers an impressive and deeply informed analysis, moving effortlessly between countries and continents, global perspectives and local specificities, theoretical discussions and empirical facts of everyday life.'

—Alexei Yurchak, author of *Everything Was Forever, Until It Was No More: The Last Soviet Generation*

The Long Retreat

Strategies to Reverse the Decline of the Left

Boris Kagarlitsky

Foreword by Patrick Bond

Translated by Renfrey Clarke

First published 2024 by Pluto Press
New Wing, Somerset House, Strand, London WC2R 1LA
and Pluto Press, Inc.
1930 Village Center Circle, 3-834, Las Vegas, NV 89134

www.plutobooks.com

Published in partnership with the Transnational Institute

The Transnational Institute (TNI) is an international research and advocacy
institute committed to building a just, democratic and sustainable planet.
For 50 years, TNI has served as a unique nexus between social movements,
engaged scholars and policy makers.

British Library Cataloguing in Publication Data
A catalogue record for this book is available from the British Library

ISBN 978 0 7453 5028 8   Paperback
ISBN 978 0 7453 5026 4   PDF
ISBN 978 0 7453 5027 1   EPUB

This book is printed on paper suitable for recycling and made from fully
managed and sustained forest sources. Logging, pulping and manufacturing
processes are expected to conform to the environmental standards of the country
of origin.

Typeset by Riverside Publishing Solutions, Salisbury, England

Simultaneously printed in the United Kingdom and United States of America

Contents

Foreword

Boris Yulyevich Kagarlitsky has had a torrid time with Russia's notorious carceral regime – most recently on 13 February 2024 when prosecutors allied with one Kremlin faction had him re-imprisoned for a five-year term – albeit, he would insist, not nearly as severe as the systemic torture suffered by the late liberal opposition leader Alexei Navalny, killed on 16 February at the 'Polar Wolf' Artic Circle penal colony. Since the early 1980s, Boris has been repeatedly prosecuted for articulating left-wing ideals.

Boris was jailed in July 2023 on the way to fetch his wife from the airport, on charges of 'justifying terrorism'. He was sent to a prison in the north-western city of Syktyvkar, far from his Moscow base, once home to Soviet-era gulags. His crime, committed ten months earlier, was expressing a cheeky analysis of the Ukraine war via a (self-confessed) weak joke about Mostik, a stray cat who was the construction workers' mascot for a recently built bridge linking the Russian mainland to Crimea. But the bridge was bombed by Ukrainian or allied forces in October 2022. As he recalls, 'Just on the eve of that attack, congratulatory wishes from Mostik the cat to President Putin were spread on Russian social networks [...] I joked that he had acted as a provocateur with his congratulations.' As Boris knew so well, 'Unfortunately, Leviathan has no sense of humour. I had to spend four and a half months in a prison cell.'[1]

Nevertheless, after local and international pressure – and amidst incomprehensible gyrations within competing factions of Russia's security bureaucracy – he was freed, having paid a fine of 600,000 roubles ($6,700; £5,250) raised within a day from his supporters via the Rabkor YouTube channel. The story is one he alone can tell, armed with his famous dry wit and optimism:

> The prosecutor's office stated that the joke about Mostik the cat was made 'in order to destabilise the activities of government agencies and to press the authorities of the Russian federation to terminate the special military operation on the territory of Ukraine'. While I was behind bars, a solidarity campaign was unfolding outside, in which many people took part in Russia and around the world. Moreover, it seems that the Kremlin leadership was especially impressed by the fact that a significant part of the voices in my defense were coming from the Global South.

In the context of confrontation with the West, Russian rulers are trying to establish themselves as fighters against American and European neo-colonialism, so criticism of them voiced in Brazil, South Africa, or India was received with vexation.[2]

Along with so many others from the international left, there were indeed South Africans close to the SA Communist Party who added pressure comrades with whom Boris will normally disagree on most matters of principle, analysis, strategies, tactics and alliances, since the Talk-Left, Walk-Right dance isn't one he tolerates. Still, what became evident from the episode was not only the ease with which he could proceed with sociological research on the situations facing fellow inmates. Also clear was an inexorable popularity stemming from his anti-war stance amongst both a new generation of Russian rebels and within an international independent left that for at least forty years has looked to Boris for socialist clarity at home and beyond.

But upon an extremely complicated political-ideological landscape, even where in some circuits of the left there is no critique of the Ukraine invasion, Boris attracted a broad scope of solidarity, e.g. when Manitoba-based geopolitical economist Radhika Desai made an in-person appeal to Vladimir Putin during a Valdai Club conference in October 2023: 'We found ourselves also in a bit of a quandary because we do not agree with the position our dear friend [Boris] has taken. But we also remember how much we have learned from his formidable knowledge of Russia's history and his formidable commitment to Russia. So, we just appeal to you that you take a personal interest in this case.' Putin's reply: 'You know, to be honest, I do not really know who this Kagarlitsky is – so my colleague here [Fyodor Lukyanov] even had to fill me in on that one. I will take the letter you have signed for me, I will read it and give you a response. I promise.'[3]

In fact it was at least the second time that Putin was responding to questions about the Kagarlitsky case, and he still didn't know what the issue was about. No response was given to Radhika Desai or other Valdai Club members who signed the letter. However, ten weeks later, when rumours about Putin's supposed death were widely circulating around Russia, Boris was briefly released, albeit with restrictions on his freedom of expression.

Two months later, Kafkaesque bureaucratic manoeuvres led to his re-imprisonment. Remarkably, he retained an optimistic fighting spirit, posting to Telegram: 'I continue to collect data and materials for new books, including descriptions of prison life – now in Moscow institutions. Anyway, see you soon! I am sure that everything will be fine eventually. We will see each other again both on the channel and in person. We just need to live a little longer and survive this dark period for our country.'[4]

Awareness of his plight emerged around the world once again, and even if soon overshadowed by the killing of Navalny, International Director for Russia Natalia Zviagina reminded:

This conviction, and the closed nature of his trial, provide another stark example of the treatment of political dissenters in Russia. It is an overt attack on freedom of expression with the aim of silencing critical voices through fear and repression. This case is not an isolated incident but part of a broader, systematic effort to stifle opposition and control what can and cannot be said in Russia.[5]

* * *

Boris has long directed the Institute of Globalisation Studies and Social Movements, whose fate also hung in the balance due to Putin's periodic clampdowns and the Institute's 'foreign agent' designation (thanks to grants mainly from the Rosa Luxemburg foundation). It was closed down in 2022 after failing to pay severe fines which were regularly showered on the organisation by hostile bureaucrats. Boris had earlier served on the faculties at Moscow State University, the Moscow School for Social and Economic Sciences, and the Institute of Sociology of the Russian Academy of Sciences. But it was through global-justice activists, starting when he hosted a session in Moscow in 1999 parallel to the Seattle World Trade Organisation, that many more came to know of how broadly he could apply class analysis. In South Africa, we'd hear of his courage in speaking truth to power dating back to the early 1980s. During his studies of theatre criticism at the State Institute of Theatrical Art, he was expelled as a dissident. He edited samizdat journals, which led to his 1982 arrest (and his longest spell in jail), followed by an official pardon in 1983. five years later, his book *The Thinking Reed* won the Deutscher Memorial Prize, the most prestigious of international progressive literary awards. During the early 1990s he was active in the Party of Labour (including having won a Moscow municipal electoral office), but in October 1993, Boris's opposition to the Yeltsin regime's unconstitutional power grab led to another arrest – and an immediate release after international protest.

Boris's 1995 visit to a South Africa that was then hosting scores of left celebrities, after Nelson Mandela's release from jail, left a major impression on many of us. We had many interactions in the subsequent years, especially when Boris began considering the global justice movement as his natural international home. He published (often with Pluto Press) a variety of influential books on Russian and international politics. The latter included two co-edited works, *Globalization and Its Discontents* in 1997 and *The Politics of Empire* in 2004. Sole-authored books about the world situation included a 1999 trio – *New Realism, New Barbarism; The Return of Radicalism;* and *The Twilight of Globalization* – followed by *From Empires to Imperialism* in 2014, and *Between Class and Discourse* in 2020. He benefitted from a long-running fellowship at the Transnational Institute in Amsterdam, starting in 2000. Boris played a leadership role in anti-Putin protests in 2011–2012, but a shift in perspective took place when the G20 was hosted in St Petersburg in mid-2013. Many international allies (myself included) attended the counter-summit his institute organised, but funding contributed by a faction within Putin's state may have deterred local attendees, for interest in the event was sparse.[6]

* * *

This period, from 2013 to 2017, was one in which Boris was labelled a 'pink Putinist', unfairly it seems to me, but not without contradictions worth recalling. After the popular 2014 Maidan uprising in Kiev against pro-Putin leader Viktor Yanukovych – albeit one that was Washington-facilitated with all manner of conservative features – Boris was fascinated by the opportunity a Donbas workers' rebellion and breakaway from the Ukrainian state presented for self-government and radical social policy.[7] However, hijacked by Putin's Eastern Ukraine allies, the experiment ended soon enough. In the pages below, we learn that, 'In supporting the people's republics that were proclaimed in Donetsk and Lugansk, the Kremlin rulers were mainly interested in ensuring that the protests by dissatisfied citizens in south-eastern Ukraine against the new authorities in Kiev did not turn into a social revolution. The radical-minded leaders of the revolt were almost all killed or excluded from the leadership of the movement.'

Another force loomed, as Boris had acknowledged in *Links* in August 2014: 'Over several weeks the entire leadership of the Donetsk and Lugansk republics has effectively been replaced. The most momentous, and unexpected, development has been the ousting of the military leader of the militias, Igor Strelkov [...] an obvious act of revenge on the part of those very Kremlin forces on whom [Strelkov] had inflicted a serious political defeat in early July.' Boris recognised Strelkov's 'sympathies for the pre-revolutionary monarchy and nostalgia for the Russian empire', as he wrote at the time, but was more impressed by the mass base, e.g. 'rank-and-file militia fighters demanding that the slogan of "social republics" that had been proclaimed in Donetsk and Lugansk should be put into effect, that the property of oligarchs should be nationalised [...] A law was adopted reversing the commercialisation of health care that had been initiated by the previous leaders.'[8]

The Donbas worker uprising was soon repressed, but Boris was accused by progressive allies of unjustifiably supporting Russia's Ukrainian land grabs, including Crimea. However, Kagarlitsky never sided with Strelkov, who later called Boris his most respected enemy. Boris and his comrades backed the left-leaning militia of Aleksey Mozgovoy (he was later killed, apparently by Putin's special forces or by mercenaries from the Wagner Group). for his part, Strelkov was an uncomfortable partner for the Kremlin. He was subsequently convicted by a Dutch court for shooting down the Malaysia Airlines plane above south-eastern Ukraine in mid-2014, killing all 298 passengers and crew. As the most prominent populist right-wing critic of Putin, Strelkov was arrested in mid-2023 just days before Boris, leading to suspicions that the Kremlin was attempting an incarceration balancing act.

The situation at that point was extremely fluid, with Putin obviously feeling more vulnerable than ever, having just been disinvited from the Brazil-Russia-India-China-South Africa (BRICS) annual summit by Cyril Ramaphosa due to the outstanding International Criminal Court arrest warrant for Ukrainian war crimes. The prior month, Wagner Group leader Evgeny Prigozhin tried his own quasi-coup against Kremlin military elites. Then, just as the BRICS summit began in Johannesburg on 23 August, Prigozhin was (reportedly) killed when his airplane mysteriously exploded between Moscow and St Petersburg.

The extent to which Boris had distanced himself from Russian nationalism was clear through his role in both the Belarusian anti-Lukashenko revolt of 2020–2021 and pro-Navalny activism of early 2021. In early 2022 he immediately was one of the most vocal critics of the Ukraine invasion. This we learned when Johannesburg hosted the August 2023 BRICS summit and Boris was invited to keynote the 'BRICS from Below' workshop at the University of Johannesburg Centre for Social Change. He agreed to speak on video link – but not come in person, out of concern he would not be re-admitted to his homeland. The lecture was prevented from happening, for a month before the BRICS convened, Boris was confined to a jail term some observers feared would last seven years.

What we had anticipated hearing from Boris, as occurred periodically at such sessions dating back to his own Moscow hosting of BRICS-country dissidents in 2012, was a sense of how weak we then found not only global capitalist managers but also the BRICS versions – including those in Moscow promoting Russia's desired de-dollarisation agenda (foiled in Johannesburg by conservative forces within the BRICS financial elite). But what you will read in the pages below is probably the most cogent explanation of why, alongside the empire of capital, it's been our international and local left oppositions that have weakened far more rapidly since the 1970s.

* * *

The conditions in which Boris wrote, before his arrest, provided greater confidence in elite breakdown, dating back fifteen years to the world financial crisis catalysed by US home mortgage gambles gone sour in 2007, spreading quickly across speculative European real estate markets and then across the world, requiring a G20 financial fix. Since then, he insists, global capitalism 'has been unable to restore its "normal" process of reproduction', given that all manner of money-printing gimmicks, artificially low interest rates and rising debts kept the capital-overaccumulation bubble from bursting, as all had feared would happen in early 2009. But, he warns, 'Unfortunately, at the same time as public dissatisfaction with capitalism around the planet has reached an unprecedented scale, the left movement has finished up at the lowest point in its entire history. If this is not true on the organisational plane, then it is certainly the case on the ideological and moral level.'

That weakness allows not only right-wing populist forces to fuse economic grievances and culturally reactionary politics, but at the same time, according to Boris, gives greater reign for corporate elites 'to curtail, and if possible to end altogether, the participation of the masses in politics while preserving the formal institutions of parliamentarism, free elections and other conquests of liberal democracy. This task was achieved through combining market reforms with the technocratic adoption of decisions supposedly too complex to be understood by ordinary voters.' With this force emanating from corporate centres of power in New York, London, Paris, Frankfurt and Tokyo, resistance in these sites has been timid, and the mild-mannered Western intelligentsia continually disappoints. Work by one prominent Dutch historian reflects 'the moral and methodological dead end in which the left movement in the early twenty-first century has finished up', thanks in part to 'the epoch of postmodernism, when an integrated worldview is replaced by an unsystematic pastiche of ideas, of fragmentary concepts and of arbitrarily assembled images'.

In contrast, find in the pages below a systematic socialist analysis, including important auto-critiques of Soviet legacies: 'after the collapse of the USSR, when the world communist movement no longer possessed any rallying point or shared guidelines (even if only negative), it was placed in a situation of "everyone for themself", and rapidly fell apart. The organisational and political inflexibility had turned into an appalling fragility.'

That state of fragility degenerated yet further, leaving room for far-right populists to rise with critiques of 'globalist' elites. In Russia, Boris has been writing in a context in which, as he told *Links*'s Federico Fuentes in mid-2022, 'All sorts of racist, fascist statements are made on state channels. It's an absolutely incredible flood of aggression, xenophobia and hatred.'[9] Proving his point in late 2023, Sergey Lavrov offered this extraordinary statement to *RT*: 'The goals declared by Israel for its ongoing operation against Hamas militants in Gaza seem nearly identical to those put forward by Moscow in its campaign against the Ukrainian government […] we need to be very careful about our common history with Israel and, above all, the history of the fight against Nazism. This is the main thing that unites us historically.' This comparison was 'bizarre and greatly offensive, to say the least', according to Palestinian analyst Ramzy Baroud – but offers a flavour of the ideologically surreal times we suffer.[10]

Boris's 'Letter from Prison' shortly after the July 2023 arrest was philosophical: 'This is not the first time in my life. I was locked up under Brezhnev, beaten and threatened with death under Yeltsin.[…] In the 40-odd years since my first arrest, I have learned to be patient and to realize how fickle political fortune in Russia is.'[11] The re-arrest on 13 February drove home that point. Debates over his mid-2010s positioning within Russia aside, Boris's international analysis has *not* been fickle, all these years. The humility needed today is summed up in this book's advice: 'in changed circumstances the left should learn to retreat, without succumbing to panic or losing its nerve, and should regroup its forces in order to prepare for new battles'. We're terribly fortunate Boris has updated his critique of political economy and politics with the grace and passion for which this great sociologist has long been respected, and look forward to his eventual release from another undeserved term in a Russian jail – with the greatest impatience.

Patrick Bond, Johannesburg
February 2024

Preface

In the classic work *On War*, by the Prussian general Karl Clausewitz, there is a whole chapter devoted to retreats. Analysing the experience of numerous campaigns during the eighteenth and nineteenth centuries, Clausewitz shows that organising retreats is just as important a part of strategy as achieving advances. 'Each day, a strictly measured resistance must last only long enough for the balance in the struggle to be kept in a state of fluctuation. Using this method, we insure ourselves against defeat, while yielding the space over which the battle was fought.'[1] Most important is to stop the retreat from turning into a panicked rout, to prevent the forces from falling into disorder and the courage of the defenders from being undermined. The struggle may become drawn out, 'but thanks to the change in the relationship of forces, not only do the chances of victory grow, but simultaneously with the changed position of the two sides, the significance of that victory also increases'.[2]

It has long been known that the laws of political strategy bear many resemblances to those of military strategy. Niccolò Machiavelli wrote on this topic, which is also mentioned by Antonio Gramsci in his *Prison Notebooks*. Depending on the circumstances, a struggle may be prolonged or may be settled through rapid manoeuvres, while a historical situation may create opportunities for a revolutionary overturn or else block its path. Most important, however, is that 'one cannot, as one pleases, choose this or that way of conducting a war, and still less choose to achieve immediate superiority over the enemy'.[3] Instead, one must work calmly and systematically, without falling into a panic or allowing oneself to be seized by transient enthusiasms.

Unfortunately, such lessons are rarely learned.

At the end of the 1980s my book *The Dialectic of Change* was published in Britain (though it did not appear in Russian).[4] In evaluating this work, the well-known left commentator Alex Callinicos latched onto my idea that in changed circumstances the left should learn to retreat, without succumbing to panic or losing its nerve, and should regroup its forces in order to prepare for new battles. To Callinicos, the very idea that retreat was possible appeared shocking and inadmissible. Unfortunately, events during the years that followed showed convincingly that throughout the world the forces of the left were not just retreating, surrendering position after position, but that they were pathologically unprepared to wage struggles in these circumstances; panic, demoralisation and betrayal (even if beneath the slogan of 'modernising' the movement) effectively became the norm. A refusal to acknowledge the extent to which the social changes under way required new methods of political struggle, as well as changes to the organisation and even the lexicon of socialist movements, led these movements not just to failure after failure, but to a train of catastrophes from which recovery would become increasingly difficult. To use an expression of Gramsci, the members of the left 'allowed reality to swallow them, instead of their subjugating it'.[5]

Undoubtedly, the problems of the left were in the first instance of an objective character. Nevertheless, it is not hard to see that even when we encounter circumstances that are obviously more powerful than us, we can manage various results and achieve a range of outcomes. Even if we find these outcomes unpleasant, we can still influence the scale of the defeats, and their consequences can be completely different.

Among the members of the left, three decades of such experiences have created a specific culture and psychology in which belief in the possibility of major political successes is almost absent (and when such successes suddenly occur, the left is completely unready to take advantage of them). Meanwhile, enticing utopias have taken the place of realistic programmes for changing society and the economy. The combination of morally exalted utopianism with an absolutely mundane pragmatism, which preoccupies itself not just with 'minor matters' but with the pursuit of petty short-term gains, has ensured a fatal inability to devise any kind of strategy. After all, a strategy is a concept of how to link everyday tactical matters with mid-term and long-term tasks, of how to arrive at results that are definite and completely real, but at the same time substantial and significant. Belief in a utopia might serve to maintain enthusiasm, but it cannot provide strategic reference points. At best it helps people cope emotionally with a situation in which they cannot explain the concrete political and social meaning of their own actions, since more than likely there is no such meaning.

Left-wing politicians, commentators and activists have increasingly become divided into a number of groups, all equally useless from the point of view of real social change. One group has replaced class politics with politically correct incantations on the rights of every conceivable minority. This is completely in line with the logic and demands of the neoliberal capitalism that is fragmenting society. Another group, while continuing to swear its fidelity to the working class, has replaced politics with role-playing, seeking to convince itself that nothing in the world has changed since 1917. Inasmuch as the working class imagined by this group no longer has anything in common with the actual working people who live under the new conditions (not always better, but *different*), each successive round of role-playing sees the members of the group increasingly remote from reality. Finally, a third group has ceased even to pretend to take part in politics, shutting itself away in the sphere of culture. The members of this group have built themselves the same kind of 'ivory tower' as the aesthetes of the early twentieth century, refusing to have anything to do either with bourgeois philistinism or with the crudity of the proletariat. This time, however, the tower has finished up daubed with radical slogans, and sometimes may even be decorated with red flags.

The paradox is that the decline and disorganisation of the left movement (in all its varieties from moderate social democracy to hard-line communism) has done nothing to help capitalism, and in a certain sense has even served to deepen the crisis in bourgeois society. Left to its own devices after coping with external challenges and overcoming the danger of socialist revolution, capital in a strikingly brief time span has pushed all its own contradictions to the limit, creating the conditions for the multitude of crises – social, environmental, economic and so forth – that are now heaped one upon the other.

Since the Great Recession of 2008–2010 the system has been unable to restore its 'normal' process of reproduction, and its permanent characteristics now include instability. This instability is not just growing, but is coming increasingly to be recognised by the masses. Unfortunately, at the same time as public dissatisfaction with capitalism around the planet has reached an unprecedented scale, the left movement has finished up at the lowest point in its entire history. If this is not true on the organisational plane, then it is certainly the case on the ideological and moral level.

Throughout their long retreat, the forces of the left have sought to save themselves from this disagreeable reality either through trying to adapt to the triumphant neoliberalism by espousing the ideology of political correctness (accepting the logic of the sociocultural fragmentation, but trying at every point to occupy the niche of its most radical supporters), or else through sectarian-dogmatic repetition of old slogans that bear no relation to reality. The mechanism through which a sectarian consciousness takes shape was described exquisitely by Zdeněk Mlynář in his autobiography. After reading a few simplistic pamphlets on Marxism, he and his comrades were convinced they had assimilated advanced theory in all its fullness. Ultimately, his thoughts were to be very different:

> Now, many years later, I am finding the sole answer: in people who in fact know little or nothing at all, the ideology set out in these pamphlets creates a feeling of conceit, a confidence that they know everything, and have mastered the laws of development of the world and of humanity. [...] Although as before they know nothing, they are convinced of their ability to judge everything, to decide what is good and bad for humanity – to perceive what is scientific and what is unscientific, despite never having taken the trouble to engage in scientific study. In an instant, such people become all-seeing; they are immediately elevated above the level of the unconscious masses, who wander in the darkness of ignorance and doubt. While still knowing nothing, such people acquire consciousness.[6]

It is important to note, however, that the psychological consequences of developing a cult of political correctness and those of reinforcing the traditional sectarianism are strikingly similar. In both cases the bearers of an abstract 'truth' constantly present an account of reality in which they condemn not only the bourgeoisie, capital and the ruling elite, but with no less aggression (and usually, with far more) the workers, who refuse to correspond to the truth-bearers' abstract ideas and normative values.

Of course, it happens now and then that even such a demoralised movement, bereft of perspectives and unable to understand the meaning of its own existence, may be borne aloft by a wave of social discontent. Unfortunately, every such victory ends in yet another defeat. With no idea of what to do with their good fortune, left intellectuals and politicians are easily reconciled to losing their gains, and return to their comfortable niche in a sectarian-opportunist existence that has little in common with politics.

This existence is comfortable for the members of the left, but certainly not for society, which is in need of change. The question of a socialist alternative is taking on a practical meaning, and is requiring serious thought. Not, however, in the form of utopian daydreaming, but precisely as applied to political strategy.

Fortunately, the situation is not entirely bad. History teaches us that the preconditions for social change mature unevenly, and if in various countries the demand appears for a new socialist theory, this means that there is also a chance that organisations capable of suggesting thought-out solutions may achieve a great deal. The important thing is to take the first steps, breaking with the sad ideological heritage of three decades of backsliding and defeats.

Once again, it is necessary to pose the question of the socialist perspective as a matter of practical politics.

PART I

Socialism as a Problem

1

In the Labyrinth of Ideology

Over the three decades since the disintegration of the Soviet Union and the collapse of the world communist movement, innumerable commentators have declared that socialist ideas have disappeared, have become unpopular, or are out of date. As always, reality is proving to be different from what the ideologues have assumed. During the years since the American philosopher Francis Fukuyama published his well-known essay on the 'end of history', in which he argued that around the globe no other political ideas apart from liberalism continued to enjoy mass popularity,[1] it has been found that to banish socialism completely from the sphere of public discussion is impossible. This is not even due to the convincing nature of the arguments put forward by left-wing writers (unfortunately, these arguments have very often proven no more serious than those of their opponents), but due to the nature of capitalism itself, which gives rise to numerous social contradictions, and as a consequence, to the demand for ideas and strategies different from those offered by the ruling classes.

The outstanding German sociologist Werner Sombart wrote in the early twentieth century that 'socialism is the necessary reverse side of capitalism'.[2] It was the development of capitalist society that gave birth to the modern socialist movement, which evolves and finds new forms in parallel with the reconfiguring of the bourgeois order itself.

This is why the numerous and regularly repeated attempts to bury socialist ideas and the practical movements oriented towards them have again and again been unsuccessful. The rumour concerning the death of socialism has once again turned out to be seriously exaggerated. But having stated that socialism is alive, we certainly cannot argue that it is healthy. Rather the reverse.

The development of socialism from utopia
to science ... and back again?

The political retreat of the left on a global scale began in the late 1970s, though at that time few would have guessed how serious and prolonged it was to be. The rapid rise of neoliberalism, marginalising the liberal centrism that had been considered completely natural, seemed to be a sort of ideological excess, while the slogans of Ronald Reagan and Margaret Thatcher were initially perceived as grotesque exaggerations that had little to do with practical politics. Meanwhile, a sharp ideological turn to the right seized not only the traditional elites, but also a significant section of the middle class. At the same time the Soviet bloc, having lost completely not only its earlier dynamism but also its image as an attractive alternative, was clearly in decline. The hopes on the left that the collapse of the conservative-bureaucratic system in the Soviet Union would help to liberate the creative forces of society, and would cleanse socialist ideology of the burden of moral responsibility for the crimes committed under its banner during the twentieth century, proved illusory. Even if such expectations were justified from a historical point of view (examining events on a scale of several decades), they were in no way founded on an analysis of the social, political, psychological and cultural situation in the countries of Eastern Europe. The decades that followed merely deepened the decline of the left movement. The social-democratic parties, failing in their attempts to halt the onslaught of neoliberalism, joined its adherents.[3] The communist parties either made haste to change their signage, or while retaining it, transformed themselves into social conservatives yearning nostalgically for the 'good old days' and speaking in an outdated language that was simply incapable of articulating questions of current politics.

Worst of all, however, was the fact that the retreat was not just political. It was intellectual as well. How can we fail to remember the well-known words of Lev Trotsky:

> Reactionary epochs such as ours not only corrupt and weaken the working class, isolating its vanguard, but also lower the general ideological level of the movement, driving our political thinking back to long-past stages. In these circumstances, the task of the vanguard is above all to prevent itself from being distracted by the general backward current. It is necessary to swim against the flow.[4]

This applied not only to the left, but to society as a whole. Everywhere, regardless of the peculiarities of one country or another, the bar of political discussion was being lowered dramatically. Ideas that seemed long ago to have been forgotten, to have been refuted and to have revealed their complete bankruptcy returned suddenly to circulation, winning adherents and being discussed as the last word in social thought. If neoliberal doctrines had driven economics back methodologically to the conceptual level of the early nineteenth century, the situation with the left was not much better.

During the 1840s Karl Marx and Friedrich Engels had posed the issue of the need to be done with utopian dreams and to make socialism scientific. Later, opponents of Marxism argued that the theory of social transformations that had been created within the Marxist framework was also a utopia. Now in the early twenty-first century, members of the left have not only ceased trying to dispute such assertions, but to the contrary, declare their adherence to utopias.

A glaring example of the way in which leftists themselves are presenting their programme as a utopia is provided in the book *Utopia for Realists*, by the Dutch economist Rutger Bregman. The author's programme is not so much realistic, as moderate in the highest degree. It is utopian only in the sense that the toothless, opportunist recommendations put forward in it cannot act as a key to social change, and thus are most unlikely ever to be put into practice, since they are incapable of inspiring anyone. In Bregman's view, the salvation of the world will be achieved through distributing 'free money' to the poor, introducing a universal basic income and cutting work hours, with no systemic transformations required for this even in a capitalist context. The book's author begins his narrative by mentioning:

> It is capitalism that opened the gates to the Land of Plenty, but capitalism alone cannot sustain it. Progress has become synonymous with economic prosperity, but the twenty-first century will challenge us to find other ways of boosting our quality of life. And while young people in the West have largely come of age in an apolitical technocracy, we will have to return to politics again to find a new utopia.[5]

Since the shocks of 2020–22 there has been no special point in discussing such programmes as recipes for the future progress of humanity. In this case, however, it is noteworthy that the author presents his set of benevolent wishes precisely as a new utopia, suggesting sincerely that such recommendations are capable of inspiring people. Bregman's attempt to combine a return to utopia with bourgeois practice and technocratic optimism is visible proof of the moral and methodological dead end in which the left movement in the early twenty-first century has finished up. Lacking a positive programme, and refusing to recognise the political vacuousness of their current activity, which is petty and devoid of historical perspective, many critics of capitalism console themselves with utopian fantasies. In the first half of the nineteenth century socialists needed utopias precisely because the concrete tasks of revolutionary struggle, of reforms and strategy, had not *yet* been formulated. Today, these tasks have *already* been given up as lost causes. The more that socialists set out to again become utopians, the less they remain socialists.

From the sphere of the possible and necessary, socialism is shifting once again to the sphere of the ideal and desirable, transforming itself into an ideological myth or moral principle while failing completely to provide leadership in the development of practical programmes and strategies. Of course, not all the ideas that under a given political system are deemed utopian are without practical meaning. As Karl Mannheim wrote early in the twentieth century,

> it is quite obvious that the social strata that represent the existing social and spiritual order will consider valid those structural ties of which they are the bearers, since the opposition layers in that society will orient themselves towards the fresh shoots and trends of the new social order that is the goal of their efforts, and that is becoming established thanks to their strivings. The representatives of a given stage of being describe as utopian all those concepts whose realisation, from their *point of view*, is fundamentally impossible.[6]

It is natural that the opponents of social change will always regard as 'utopian' ideas that 'cannot be put into effect within the framework of the given social order'.[7] In the present case, however, it is important to note that those who are talking about utopias are not the *opponents* of change, but its *supporters*.

In the early twentieth century many critics of Marx were already declaring that his socialism was merely claimed to be scientific, and that in reality it was just as utopian as that of his predecessors. The essence of all this criticism, however, consisted of pointing out that various forecasts or conclusions of the author of *Capital* had not been confirmed by practical experience. It is significant that the pretexts for accusing Marx of utopianism changed constantly, while all that remained unaltered was the accusation itself.

When Eduard Bernstein early in the twentieth century proclaimed the need for a revisionist approach to Marx's ideas, it was no accident that he applied a thesis drawn in essence from accountancy, and which saw him trying to separate useful theoretical 'assets' from unneeded 'liabilities' that merely burdened the social-democratic movement. This approach not only makes impossible any understanding of the mutual relationships between the different parts of the theory, but also does away with the idea of reality as something constantly changing and evolving, as a complex process that cannot be reduced to a mechanical *totality of facts*. Meanwhile, the phenomena referred to not only change their form and significance, but may also disappear, to re-emerge again under the influence of more general laws of historical development.

The authors who speculate on the utopianism of Marx refer exclusively to prognoses that have not been confirmed (at one or another moment), and to real or supposed problems associated with their concept of how a future socialist society might be organised. The scientific nature of Marx's socialism, however, and its principal difference from utopianism, does not lie in scientific thought always and unfailingly yielding unerringly precise results. To accuse Marx of utopianism on the basis of particular inaccuracies is just as absurd as describing weather forecasts as utopian because they are far from always being accurate in every respect, or as rejecting the scientific nature of mathematics and physics because a researcher has made a mistaken calculation, or has used imprecise, unverified data.

The question of the relationship between socialist strategy and utopia cannot be reduced to consideration of the degree to which various specific positions of Marx's theories are correct. This question is on a quite different plane. Before assessing the accuracy of a forecast, one must understand how the forecast was made, and on what basis. Just as it is possible at times to proceed from correct premises and to reach incorrect conclusions, correct conclusions may, by coincidence, be drawn from faulty assumptions. What is of fundamental importance here is not the specific conclusion, but the method of reasoning.

'Consciousness is utopian', Mannheim wrote, 'when it does not accord with the "being" that surrounds it. This lack of correspondence is always apparent in such a consciousness, in terms of experience, thought and activity, being oriented towards factors that are not actually present in this "being".'[8] But what are the reasons for this lack of correspondence? Does it result from our imagining things that do not and cannot exist, or from our evaluating things that currently exist, and reaching conclusions about how they can and must be refashioned?

This situation was formulated brilliantly by the German philosopher Ernst Bloch in his well-known work *The Principle of Hope*:

Everything is *objectively* possible whose emergence may be scientifically anticipated, or which at least is not excluded on the basis of a simple, partial knowledge of its outward conditions. By contrast, everything is *genuinely* possible whose traits are not yet incorporated fully in the sphere of the *object itself*, whether because of their immaturity or because new conditions, though mediated by those that already exist, prepare the way for the emergence of a new reality. A fluid, variable and changeable existence, appearing in dialectical materialist form, has this unfinished potential development, this quality of not yet being conclusive, both in its foundation and in its horizons.[9]

Strictly speaking, to criticise a utopia is pointless, since a utopia presupposes above all a belief that its basic principles are true in the abstract sense. These principles do not represent conclusions (whether correct or mistaken) arrived at on the basis of researching a problem, or procedures for solving this problem in practice, but a pre-prepared answer to the very existence of the problem, a challenge to imagine a society where this problem simply does not exist.

Socialism in utopian thinking was understood, if we use the words of Engels, as 'the expression of absolute truth, reason and justice'.[10] Meanwhile, justice was extra-temporal and extra-historical, or in the words of Emile Durkheim, what was involved was attempts to 'advance an abstract principle of ideal legislation'.[11] Developing a strategy for the systematic transformation of society thus requires the formulation of an idea of justice that is more robust than our present concepts, which at times can be extremely shaky.

Plato in his dialogues already expressed repeatedly the idea that justice is 'what suits the strongest'.[12] In the dialogue 'The Republic', Thrasymachus argues that while to enforce laws is just, on the other hand,

> every authority imposes laws that are to its advantage – democracy, democratic laws; tyranny, tyrannical laws; and so forth. Having imposed laws, authorities declare these laws to be just so far as the people subject to them are concerned, and punish violators as offenders against the laws and justice. Hence, venerable Socrates, I say that there is one and the same thing that is considered to be justice in all states, and that is what suits the existing authorities.[13]

Although Socrates does not agree with this point of view, it is clear that such a position was extremely widespread, especially since it is defended by the sophist Callicles in the dialogue 'Gorgias'. Of course, what is at issue here is the justice of laws adopted by the state – that is, laws relating to the political order. The question, however, is posed in this way precisely because the validity and naturalness of the existing social order is not subjected to the slightest doubt. From the point of view of our epoch, the socio-economic system of classical Greece would hardly be considered a model of justice.

In the book *Monday Begins on Saturday* by the Strugatsky brothers, the hero, falling into an imagined past that is an obvious parody of a Platonic dialogue, encounters individuals from an ancient utopia. One of these, the book relates,

> set out monotonously and at length the bases of the political system of the beautiful country of which he was a citizen. The system was unusually democratic, there could be no question of any compulsion being applied to citizens (he stressed this several times, with special emphasis), everyone was wealthy and carefree, and every last farmer had no fewer than three slaves.[14]

The ironic argumentation of the Strugatskys in this case is absolutely well founded from a historico-sociological point of view. The point is not simply that the people had yet to 'grow into' a modern understanding of equality, but also that technological necessity made it simply impossible for ancient society to create an efficient economy without slavery, and that as a result the conceptual horizon of justice and freedom corresponded to this fact.

The outstanding sociologist Zygmunt Bauman addresses another very important aspect of mass concepts of justice. These concepts are always conservative, and if not based on ideas of some golden age in the past, they at least reflect some established norm:

> For most people most of the time, 'unjust' meant an adverse departure from the 'natural' (read: habitual). The 'natural' was neither just nor unjust – it was, simply, 'in the order of things', 'as the things were' and were bound to be, full stop. Resisting departure from the 'natural' meant, ultimately, defence of a familiar order.[15]

Of course, this in no way signifies that the idea of justice cannot mobilise people in struggle for their rights. For the most part, however, this occurs when the social equilibrium of the system is violated by the ruling class itself, whether through efforts to raise exploitation above the levels that are customary (that is, 'just' from the point of view of the normal order of things), or else when the bosses show a preference for one group of workers to the detriment of others. In the latter case the rage may be directed both against the employers who do not provide everyone with equal and 'just' remuneration, and against the workers who have received 'unjust' privileges and benefits.

The principle of scientific socialism, proclaimed by Marx and Engels in opposition to the utopian variety, consisted in rejecting attempts to construct a programme of social change on the basis of subjective concepts of goodness, and of setting about devising a method based not on moral assessments of the existing reality, or even on criticising it from the point of view of the class interests of workers, but on analysing the dynamics and contradictions of bourgeois development. *Socialism is essential and possible not because we want it, but because capitalism itself is creating the need for changes whose implementation will, in sum, give birth to a qualitatively new society.* Karl Kautsky, summarising Marx's ideas, wrote that 'the goals of the modern social movement are the natural and inevitable result of previous historical development, and do not take shape arbitrarily in people's heads as demands for some kind of "eternal justice".[16]

What is involved here, of course, is not a rejection of the social imagination, or of efforts to construct the future. But on what basis should this construction proceed, and to what degree should it rest on our present-day concepts of 'how everything should be constructed correctly'? According to Engels, the sources of the socialist project should not be sought in ideas of justice and ethics, but in history and economics. Socialism is

> the necessary result of the struggle between two historically formed classes – the proletariat and the bourgeoisie. The task of socialism is not to construct a perhaps more perfect system of society, but to investigate the historical and economic process whose inevitable outcome has been the rise of the earlier-mentioned classes with their mutual struggle, and within the economic position created by this struggle, to find the means for resolving this conflict.[17]

The fundamental difference that distinguished Marx and Engels from utopian thinkers was not that their conclusions, forecasts and suggestions were always, in every way and in their smallest details correct (which was simply impossible in living, developing scientific research), but the fact that they developed their concepts on the basis of studying the contradictions and dynamics of capitalism as it actually existed. Their conclusions did not rest on their own ideas of what was just or desirable, but on *analysis of what was objectively necessary and possible.* It was for this reason that, even when mistaking the details or time frames of the processes they studied, they were almost always correct in indicating the trends.

With reference to Marx, Ernst Bloch wrote that 'you cannot turn abstract ideals into reality through militant optimism, but it is nevertheless possible to set free suppressed elements of a new, more humane society, that is, a concrete ideal'.[18] In political practice, of course, there is not always a clear boundary between rational cognition and the necessary ingredient of individual or collective intuition. Ideals can become reality, however, only to the degree and in the case that the dream coincides with real possibilities, expressing objectively matured social needs on the level of unconscious wishes.

The desire of the left to return to utopianism, a desire that emerged clearly around the turn of the twenty-first century, is the direct result of *capitulation in the sphere of practical politics*. A revolt might be inspired by utopian ideas, but politics, by contrast, begins only where utopia ends. Politics is obliged to be concrete and practical, for the simple reason that no other kind of politics exists. This, however, by no means signifies that politicians (and especially those of the left) must be limited by a close horizon of petty and immediate tasks. The struggle to transform society itself opens up new perspectives, though not through efforts to turn utopian desires or idealist dreams into reality, but through the work of carrying out specific tasks, which may be on a very large scale. This point was made very precisely by György Lukács when he noted: 'The working class does not need to realise any ideals, it needs only to free up the elements of a new society'.[19]

Revolution and democracy

Throughout the second half of the twentieth century socialists and communists were constantly forced to publicly explain and justify themselves, demonstrating that they were not enemies of democracy. The historical experience of the Soviet Union and of other states oriented towards it was cited as clear proof of the thesis that attempts to construct socialism would lead inevitably to a loss of freedom and to the appearance of authoritarian regimes that often became totalitarian.

The truth, if we examine the actual historical experience, is that a multitude of contrary examples show the left to have been committed to the principles of democracy. Members of the left have played decisive roles in liberation struggles and in the formation of modern democratic regimes, from France, Italy and Portugal to South Africa and Brazil. Neither this record, however, nor the numerous theoretical and journalistic texts written by Marxists criticising the Soviet experience have been able to alter the way this matter is posed. Not only are members of the left still invariably suspect so far as liberal thinkers and journalists are concerned (as is readily explained by the bourgeois interests these authors defend), but the members of the left themselves have been endlessly prepared to reproach themselves and constantly to repent, seeming as a result to confirm the justice of the accusations. Thus, in the view of the German philosopher Axel Honneth classical socialism was marked from the first by an innate tendency to undervalue the institutions of liberal democracy, or more precisely to deny the intrinsic value of these institutions, even while socialists recognised general democratic principles.

In this situation the use of the slogan 'democratic socialism' does not change things essentially, since it merely states that members of the left recognise the existing state as being constructed on democratic principles. In other words, it still articulates the same bourgeois 'negative freedom'. As a result, Honneth considers, members of the left think of their own positive programme exclusively on the level of socio-economic measures that do not affect the realm of political freedom. Honneth himself, however, does not suggest anything on the political level apart from supporting the same liberal principles, while at the same time calling for more attention to be devoted to the public sphere, which Jürgen Habermas gained fame by studying.

Why is it, however, that the events of 1917 are generally examined in the context of certain 'primordial' theoretical constructs, and not in the context of the political practice of that time? Why is the collapse of democracy in Russia under the Bolsheviks (but not under Yeltsin and Putin) explained by citing one or another utterance of Marx or Lenin, while for the dozens and hundreds of cases in which democratic institutions failed in the course of other, bourgeois revolutions no-one seeks explanations in the political philosophy of, for example, Thomas Hobbes, John Locke or Jean-Jacques Rousseau, preferring instead to investigate concrete conditions and causes on the practical plane?

History teaches us that members of the left are obliged to be consistent and principled democrats, since if they diverge from this path, they will sooner or later lose their socialist perspective as well. But if our concepts of democracy and freedom are limited by the horizon of liberal political institutions, then we risk losing both our social rights and our political freedoms.

2

Revolution as Practice

As early as 1918 the declarations and especially the actions of the Bolsheviks were arousing serious protests within the socialist movement, not only from right-wing social democrats such as Karl Kautsky but also from members of the left. The dissolution of the Constituent Assembly was perceived as a crude violation of the obligations the Bolsheviks themselves had accepted. The young György Lukács saw Bolshevism as 'an insoluble moral problem', since its methods differed little from 'the methods, rightly hated and despised, of the old world order'.[1] It was thus necessary to observe the principles of democracy in all cases, even if this required 'an exceptional degree of selflessness and self-sacrifice from the people who strive for democracy honestly and conscientiously'.[2]

In essence, this was also the position embraced by Rosa Luxemburg, who on the whole supported Lenin's policies but who criticised the Bolsheviks sharply for their dictatorial actions and for rejecting the democratic principles that lay at the basis of socialism. Hence her well-known formula:

Freedom is not freedom if it extends only to supporters of the government, only to the members of a single party, however numerous they might be. Freedom is always freedom for people who think differently. This is not because of a fanaticism about 'impartiality', but because all the enlivening, healing and cleansing action of political freedom depends on this essence. If 'freedom' becomes a privilege, this action ceases.[3]

The tragic nature of this situation lay, however, in the fact that political reality did not leave the people taking part in these events any 'good' or democratic escape from their quandary. Luxemburg herself summed up the dilemma precisely: 'However paradoxical it might sound, there simply is no correct tactic that the Russian proletariat might employ.'[4] The circumstances of the Russian Revolution were inauspicious for the success of socialism, but for the proletariat that had already won power, the refusal to implement radical changes would turn out to be an act of 'self-betrayal'.[5] Most importantly, it was not evident that a firm and undeviating obedience to the demands of democracy would in turn have guaranteed the triumph of freedom, and not the victory for authoritarian reaction of which Luxemburg herself had directly warned (and to which the history of many other twentieth-century revolutions bears witness).

The heritage of the Jacobins

Recalling his meetings with Lenin, the sociologist Fedor Stepun, later to be exiled from Russia, observed that Lenin's 'main talent was an improbable gift for simplification'.[6] It was, however, precisely the Bolshevik leader's 'gift for simplification' that allowed him to work out the optimal revolutionary tactics in the extreme circumstances of 1917, when only resolving the question of power could have stopped society from sliding into chaos. An understanding of the tragic impossibility of achieving a 'good' resolution united most of the honest critics of Bolshevism. Nikolay Berdyaev, who did not support the Communists and whom they banished from Russia as one of the passengers on the well-known 'philosophers' steamship', acknowledged that democratic variants for solving the problems of Russia in 1917–20 simply did not exist:

> Only a dictatorship could halt the process of final disintegration and of the triumph of chaos and anarchy. There was a need to give the rebellious masses slogans in whose name they would consent to organise and discipline themselves; there was a need for energising symbols. At that moment Bolshevism, prepared over years by Lenin, proved to be the sole force that could put an end to the decay of the old and organise the new. Only Bolshevism was capable of taking control of the situation; only it corresponded to the mass instincts and real relationships. And demagogically, it turned everything to its purposes.[7]

Recognising the tragic nature of the Russian political situation between 1917 and 1920, of course, led different people to varied conclusions. But while the Christian socialist and thinker Berdyaev could allow himself simultaneously to condemn the Bolsheviks from a moral point of view and to understand their correctness from the angle of practical politics, the participants in the socialist movement themselves were compelled to make a choice. It was for this reason that both György Lukács and Rosa Luxemburg, for all their doubts and well-founded criticisms, chose in favour of Lenin.[8]

By contrast, Kautsky in criticising the dictatorial measures of the Bolsheviks did not in principle ask himself how else Lenin and his comrades might have acted in the existing situation. In the concrete circumstances of Russia in 1918, should the Bolsheviks have surrendered power to the forces of counter-revolution? Should they have laid down their arms? It can readily be seen that such an alternative was unacceptable not just to the Bolsheviks, but also to the substantial part of Russian society that had come out in support of a radical break with the monarchical past.

As the guardian of Marxist orthodoxy, Kautsky honestly considered that to triumph in the dispute it was sufficient to show that his opponents had deviated from one or another point of the Marxist theoretical heritage to which they had declared their adherence. In convicting Lenin of theoretical inconsistency, Kautsky was correct. While resting on Engels, and repeatedly citing him, Lenin then proceeded to say something quite different. It is impossible not to see the divergences here. Did these divergences, however, have their sources exclusively in the views of the two men on democracy as a theoretical question, or in the practical conditions under which their positions took shape? If practice required retreats from the ready-made (and in essence, absolutely correct) prescriptions of classical Marxism, then a reckoning in theoretical terms with what had occurred had to begin precisely by assessing this practice and its implications.

Finding themselves in the situation of a real and not imagined revolution, which was occurring against the background of an ongoing war and of a vacuum of power occasioned by the collapse of the old regime, the Bolsheviks were forced to act in response to the circumstances. This did not signify, however, that in their intellectual baggage they were without experience on which they could rely for making their decisions. The English revolutionaries of the seventeenth century related their actions to those of biblical figures, the French revolutionaries a hundred years later looked to the republican traditions of classical antiquity, and their Russian successors in the early twentieth century to the ideas and experience of those same French.

Acting contrary to the accustomed ideas of Marxist socialism, Lenin inscribed himself fully into another revolutionary tradition – that of the Jacobins.[9] This was not just a matter of ideological succession, but related also to the similar practical situations in which the revolutionary regimes in France in 1793 and in Russia in 1918 and 1919 found themselves. For Kautsky with his professorial socialism there was nothing to be gleaned from existing circumstances, but Robespierre and Saint-Just provided the leaders of the young Soviet state with concrete models of political decision-making. To what extent the decisions made were correct from a socialist perspective is a different matter.

It was not the Bolsheviks but the French revolutionaries who proclaimed the principle *no freedom for the enemies of freedom*. Explaining the need for terror, Maximilien Robespierre neatly formulated the idea that Lenin would repeat in almost identical terms: 'In order to create and fortify democracy among us, in order to arrive at the peaceful rule of constitutional laws, we must wage to the end a war of freedom against tyranny'.[10] In this context it is significant that in defending the harsh policy implemented by the Soviet regime, Lenin emphasised:

> Without such a dictatorship, that is, without the systematic, merciless suppression of resistance from the exploiters, without halting before any bourgeois-democratic formulae, not only a socialist but also a consistently democratic overturn is inconceivable. Just as inconceivable are any serious measures of struggle against the crisis and destruction wrought by the war.[11]

Exactly the same logic was followed by the leaders of the French Revolution in crushing the revolt in the Vendée, and in mounting campaigns of repression against speculators and 'suspect elements'.

To a substantial degree, the revolution that occurred in Russia early in the twentieth century carried out tasks that for the French Revolution still remained in the future. The Russian Revolution not only destroyed the bourgeois order, but also the traditional pre-bourgeois relations that in practice were inextricably intertwined with it under the conditions of peripheral capitalism. Lenin stated repeatedly that the Bolsheviks had to complete the work of the bourgeois revolution that had not occurred in Russia. Hence there is nothing paradoxical in the fact that on the ideological and cultural-historical level Lenin rested quite consciously on the tradition of French Jacobinism, which he never rejected and to which he repeatedly declared his adherence.[12]

The revolutionary dictatorship

During the years of the Civil War Lenin formulated clearly the principles of the revolutionary dictatorship: 'The enemies of socialism may be deprived temporarily not just of their personal inviolability, and not just of their freedom of the press, but also of their general electoral rights'.[13] To Michael Brie this approach appears strange; he states perplexedly that 'the inviolability of the person, that is, the protection of people's physical and psychological integrity against political violence, rates lower here than the political rights associated with elections'.[14] From the point of view of the Jacobin tradition, however, this is completely logical. Within this tradition, violence against a specific person who in the view of the revolutionaries is an enemy of freedom becomes perfectly permissible, especially when bitter resistance is involved. An attack on democratic institutions as such is a quite different matter; in this case there arise numerous questions including the limits that should apply to such restrictions, which as Rosa Luxemburg warned in her writings on the Russian Revolution, sooner or later begin to affect people in the revolution's own camp. To Lenin, however, it was obvious that the exceptional circumstances of the Civil War created a basis for incursions even on these democratic freedoms, which the Bolsheviks themselves had fiercely defended not long before.

To justify their decisions, both Lenin and Trotsky repeatedly stressed the 'temporary character' of the measures being applied:[15]

> Democracy came to be restricted to the degree that the difficulties increased. Initially, the party had hoped to preserve freedom of political struggle within the framework of the soviets. The Civil War, however, brought a severe correction to these calculations. The opposition parties were banned one after another. In these moves, that openly contradicted the spirit of Soviet democracy, the Bolshevik leaders saw not a principle, but an episodic act of self-defence.[16]

There is no reason to doubt the sincerity of these words, especially in light of the fact that during the Civil War years the repressive policies of the Bolsheviks were extremely inconsistent, and were interspersed with attempts at dialogue with political opponents (anarchists, social democrats, populists and to some degree, ethnic nationalists). Far more important than the question of the Bolsheviks' intentions was that of the consequences of the decisions they took. Both in France and in Russia the implacable policies of the revolutionary dictatorship led to the mass execution not only of enemies of freedom, but also of a multitude of people who were in no sense opponents of the revolution. The Soviet historian of the French Revolution Albert Manfred, who took a sympathetic attitude to the Jacobin terror, nevertheless stated: 'Robespierre and the revolutionary government were fighting against an insuperable force, against a hydra that, when one of its heads was cut off, immediately grew ten new heads in its place.'[17] Manfred, of course, saw the reason for this situation in the fact that the Jacobins were swimming against the current, having begun waging war on the bourgeoisie in an epoch when capitalism was still gathering strength. It can readily be seen, however, that terror not only does away with enemies, but also creates them. Most important is the fact that while terror may at times be a forced and even indispensable measure, it nonetheless discredits the ideas that are used to justify it.

Almost a century after the Russian Civil War, Michael Brie noted reasonably enough that Lenin's formulations assumed the possibility, for the sake of carrying out the tasks of the revolution, of limiting the freedom and rights not only of supporters of the old regime but also of the workers themselves, adding that this diametrically contradicted the ideas of all socialists.[18] Indeed, what occurred in Soviet Russia even in the first years of the revolution differed greatly from the image of the *democratic* dictatorship of the proletariat set out by Lenin in *The State and Revolution*. Brie voices his bewilderment: 'If the proletarians themselves no longer have democratic rights, then who is it that exercises the dictatorship in their name?'[19]

The trouble was that despite the rhetoric of the Bolsheviks, the Russian Revolution could not be reduced to the class struggle, and meanwhile, the tasks before the party that had seized power were not in the first instance linked to the struggle for socialism. Initially, it was necessary to ensure the survival of the cities, to cope with hunger, to prevent the factories from shutting down and to save the country from falling to pieces. At a later stage the need would arise to carry out industrialisation, to overcome illiteracy and to create an effective army. These were among the tasks that objectively confronted the Soviet leaders, and in one way or another, any government that was at the helm of the Russian state during that period would have been forced to try to deal with them. The result of failure would not simply be the downfall of the particular party that held power; instead, the country as a whole would be threatened with total collapse. In other words, the dictatorship of the Bolsheviks, even when it took the form of a struggle for the interests of the proletariat (interests that the party at that time placed in the forefront), was nevertheless in the first instance the dictatorship of a progressive, educated elite ruling in the name of modernisation. The working class acted as a support for this regime, but in no sense as the dominant force.

For Lenin the Jacobins were a model, revolutionaries of a sort of ideal type whose sole shortcoming was the fact that they had acted in an epoch of bourgeois and not proletarian revolutions. By contrast, Marx and Engels had regarded the Jacobin experience far more critically. In a letter to Marx in September 1870, Engels provided an extremely harsh assessment of the Red terror:

If you observe how the French endlessly fall into a panic out of fear of such situations, when it is instead necessary to look the truth in the eye, you gain a far better view of a period of the reign of terror. By this latter we understand the rule of people who instil terror, but the real situation is the reverse: *the rule of people who are themselves frightened.* For the most part *terror consists of pointless cruelties, committed for their own reassurance by people who are themselves stricken with fear.*[20]

This does not, of course, mean that Marx and Engels regarded the Jacobin period of the revolution in a negative light. They simply understood the contradictory nature of the policies of Robespierre and his co-thinkers. The defeat of these policies was preordained by the natural dynamic of the revolution, and the terror, which had escaped the control of the leaders of the ruling party themselves, did not prevent their fall but hastened it. In France, however, the heritage of Jacobinism and the tragic experience of revolutionary terror *in the final instance* aided the victory of bourgeois modernisation, and did not prevent the establishing of a democratic republic. The fact that in Russia things worked out differently was not the result of the ideology embraced by the revolutionaries, or of 'errors of theory', or even of the tragic consequences of the use of terror, but flowed from the specific historical conditions under which the revolution unfolded.

The tragic path of the Bolshevik revolution

Analysing the prospects for revolution in Russia long before the Bolsheviks came to power, Max Weber regarded with scepticism the chances that democracy would emerge victorious. His scepticism had nothing to do with the ideas espoused by socialists, but with his perception that at a certain stage of its development industrial capitalism would itself begin to undermine the democratic institutions to which it had given birth. The requirement for discipline and order, without which industrial production was impossible, might coexist more or less with liberal democracy when the conditions for development were peaceful and crises were absent. A direct contradiction would arise, however, when the necessity emerged to mobilise resources in order to maintain production and preserve the social structure essential for capitalism. In the West this was discovered in dramatic fashion during the First World War, but the same problems revealed themselves on an even greater scale in Russia, where in the spring of 1917 a series of military defeats precipitated not just the fall of the tsarist regime, but also a disintegration of state authority.

The practical experience of the Bolshevik dictatorship during the years of the Civil War had nothing to do with the theoretical propositions even of such a work as *The State and Revolution*, written in 1917 at a time when its author was seriously preparing his party for the seizure of power. It was obvious how greatly theory and practice had diverged, and how much the actual events contradicted the initial plans of Lenin and the Bolsheviks.

The highly authoritarian forms that Bolshevik rule assumed during the Civil War are explained, of course, not only by wartime conditions and the cultural backwardness of the masses (to which Lenin referred repeatedly), but also by the tragedy, observable in all great revolutions, of the transition period. The 'Red Terror' and the subsequent dictatorship of the Soviet bureaucracy were not historical accidents, just as the repression of dissident thinkers organised by the Puritans in seventeenth-century England and the dictatorship of the Jacobins during the French Revolution were not accidents either. As we know, neither of the latter developments prevented the eventual establishing of bourgeois democracy, for which, indeed, they provided indispensable conditions.

The fact that in Russia everything turned out differently from in France is explained not only by the different conditions of social development, but also by the evolution of the Bolshevik Party during the Civil War years. Trotsky notes that although the Bolsheviks during the period of the revolution studiously preserved the class character of their party, they initially permitted sharp discussions within its ranks:

> In reality, the history of Bolshevism is a history of struggle between factions. Indeed, how could an authentically revolutionary organisation, setting itself the goal of transforming the world, and gathering beneath its banners courageous deniers, rebels and fighters, exist and develop without ideological clashes, without the formation of groupings and of temporary factions? The far-sightedness of the Bolshevik leadership often resulted in the clashes being softened, and the duration of the factional struggles curtailed, but no more than that. It was on this seething democratic basis that the Central Committee rested, and from it, the committee drew its boldness in making decisions and issuing instructions. The obvious correctness of the leadership at all critical junctures gave it immense authority, this invaluable moral capital of centralism.[21]

Of course, to the extent that the party concentrated ever more power in its hands, there occurred 'an extraordinary convergence, and in part, a direct fusion of the party apparatus with that of the state'.[22] Now, it was not political discussions that commanded the centre stage, but questions of administration. 'In the first years after the conquest of power, however, at a time when the party was already suffering from administrative corrosion, every Bolshevik, including Stalin, would have described as a malicious slanderer anyone who displayed on a screen what the party would look like in ten or fifteen years!'[23]

In one way and another, the centralisation of power and administration in the hands of the party altered its structures and character. The logical next step on this road was the decision by the Tenth Congress to ban factions within the Bolshevik Party itself. This, Trotsky insists, was not meant as a permanent move either:

> The ban on factions was again intended as an exceptional measure, that was supposed to be rescinded at the first serious improvement in the situation. At the same time, the Central Committee applied the new law with extreme caution, above all taking care that it should not have the effect of stifling the party's internal life.[24]

Unfortunately, Trotsky here is being somewhat disingenuous. During the years of the Civil War the opposition-left parties, despite from time to time being subject to Bolshevik persecution, were nevertheless able to operate openly within the framework of the soviets and the trade unions. When the Bolshevik leadership after a period of bans took the decision in November 1918 to legalise the Menshevik Party, Lenin expressed himself on this point with characteristic bluntness, declaring that from the petty-bourgeois parties (among which he included the Mensheviks) he expected at least neutrality:

> Not only is there nothing threatening for us at present in this neutralism, these neighbourly relations on the part of the petty-bourgeois democracy, but we find these relations desirable. This is why, looking at the situation from the point of view of representatives of the class that is enacting the dictatorship, we say: we have never counted on anything more than this from the petty-bourgeois democracy. From our part, this is enough. You will have neighbourly relations with us, and we will hold state power.[25]

In reality, the Mensheviks were not neutral. Despite their party's serious political and ideological disagreements with the Bolsheviks, it instructed its members to fight in the ranks of the Red Army against the counter-revolutionary White generals. 'We supported the Bolsheviks unconditionally in the struggle against Kolchak and Denikin', wrote the social-democratic leader Yuly Martov. 'We chose the lesser evil.'[26] Lenin thus had every reason to declare at a meeting of Moscow party activists on 27 November 1918 that the government was 'willingly legalising' the Mensheviks.[27]

In 1919, despite the continuing war, the Mensheviks were given the opportunity to run candidates for the soviets, and achieved impressive successes. Martov later declared:

> The Bolsheviks permitted us to take part in the 1919 elections, but unleashed a powerful campaign against us. Nevertheless, we gained 45 deputies in Moscow, 225 in Kharkov, 120 in Ekaterinoslav, 78 in Kremenchug, 45 in Tula, more than 30 in Kiev, Samara and Bryansk, and 20 in Tashkent. We have no doubt that in conditions of democracy we could have gathered the majority of the working class beneath our banners.[28]

It can readily be seen that these prospects brought no joy to the Bolshevik leadership, especially in circumstances where in the midst of an armed struggle, it was managing to hold onto power only at a heavy price. A systematic campaign to liquidate the opposition soviet parties began in late 1921 and early 1922, not in connection with the Civil War but with the transition to the New Economic Policy. A number of the social-democratic leaders were arrested or exiled, while many were forced to join the Communist Party. In 1922 and 1923 the Mensheviks, socialist-populists and anarchists were driven out of the trade unions.

Lenin justified this policy with references to the fact that in the conditions of the New Economic Policy the bourgeoisie would gain access to substantial resources that could be used to acquire political influence. Opposition parties in the soviets, even if they adhered to socialist ideas, would inevitably become conduits for such influence: 'They are the vanguard of all the reaction.'[29] In Lenin's view, the economic liberalisation to which the Soviet regime had resorted needed to be offset by a tightening of political control. The decision to ban factions within the Communist Party was also a natural consequence of this approach.

Returning to Lenin's views and constructs, we find that the main element that defined the nature of the political system in Russia – the justifying of a one-party system – is not present in any of his theoretical works. It is significant that this theoretical justification is not just lacking from his works of the pre-revolutionary period and from *The State and Revolution*, but is also absent from his texts written after the Bolsheviks came to power, when they were already in fact the only party in the country. Lenin quite clearly perceived this situation as the result of the specific political events of the Civil War, and in no way as a norm or principle that should be followed.

While embracing the dictatorship of the Bolshevik Party as an effective and completely acceptable tool for socialist change, he recognised perfectly the limited and problematic nature of this decision. In Lenin's texts, all the evaluations and political recommendations connected with questions of rule relate precisely to the concrete situation and have a clear *short-term* character. For the Bolshevik leader, the question of what form the socialist state should assume *in the long term* remained open and not relevant because of the *emergency* situation in which the state found itself. In his late works he revealed a painful concern at the rapid bureaucratisation of the Soviet state and party, complaining that 'we call ours an apparatus that in fact is still alien to us through and through, and that in fact amounts to a hodgepodge of bourgeois and tsarist elements. During five years there has been no possibility of refashioning it, given the lack of aid from other countries, military "activities" and the struggle against hunger.'[30] Nevertheless, we do not find in Lenin's texts any convincing plans for correcting this situation. He called for strengthening the leadership through attracting a large number of representatives of the working class, recommended that an excessive concentration of power in the hands of such ambitious leaders as Stalin and Trotsky not be permitted, and expressed hopes that the cultural development of the people would enable them to take their fate into their own hands once ignorance and illiteracy had been dealt with. But he had no political or strategic solution, since bureaucratism was already becoming not simply an ailment of the Soviet regime, but an organic process determining its further evolution.

The change in the rules of intra-party life also created ideal preconditions for changes to leadership personnel at all levels. Confirming the gloomy prophecy of Max Weber, people from the bureaucratic apparatus came to the forefront, and gradually took over political functions. These were individuals who were not just living off politics, but who 'failed to elevate themselves to the level of their own actions'.[31] In these circumstances Stalin, who had established himself as a party leader during the years of the revolution, but who in the course of the 1920s had also mastered to perfection the skills of bureaucratic management, proved the ideal chief, easily surpassing his collaborators and allies. The reverse side of this situation became, on the one hand, the use of reprisals to suppress those who tried to take over the same role by employing the same levers of power, and on the other, the further degradation of the leading ranks of the party, as became especially obvious following Stalin's death. In eliminating potential rivals, Stalin had also done away with the most promising of his would-be successors.

Drawing up a balance sheet, Trotsky was forced to acknowledge that the process of stifling soviet democracy had its internal logic. Although the dictatorship of the Bolshevik Party was a powerful instrument of social progress, it had become more harsh with each passing year:

> The forbidding of opposition parties drew in its wake the banning of factions, and the banning of factions ended in a prohibition on thinking differently from the infallible chief. The police monolithism of the party led to bureaucratic impunity, that became the source of all types of dissoluteness and decay.[32]

After transforming itself from a governing party into a central link in the apparatus of administration, not just political administration but also economic and to a certain degree also military, the communist organisation in the Soviet Union was not simply transformed but also changed its ideology, identifying itself more and more with the state. In essence, it was now a completely different organisation, operating under different rules and with different aims. This was noted by Antonio Gramsci in his *Prison Notebooks*, when he described how at a certain stage a party that monopolised power could facilitate social progress, but that once it became totalitarian and impeded society's free self-expression, it became 'objectively reactionary and regressive, even if (as is usually the case) it fails to recognise this and seeks to appear to be the bearer of a new culture'.[33] Conscious of the declining quality of the theoretical work in the communist parties, Gramsci was then forced to agree with Benedetto Croce, who was lamenting the dogmatism of Marxists. Gramsci was forced to admit: 'Many so-called theoreticians of historical materialism have finished up in a philosophical position akin to that of medieval theology'.[34]

The world party of communists

In founding the 'Third International' during the Russian Revolution, the Bolsheviks did not conceal their hope that revolutionary events in other, more developed countries of the world would help them solve their problems. Among those who wrote in this vein was Karl Kautsky; especially in the early period of the revolution, Kautsky recognised the dramatic nature of the situation in which Lenin and his co-thinkers found themselves: 'The Bolsheviks cannot be reproached especially for the fact that they expected a European revolution. After all, other socialists expected it as well.'[35] The seizure of power in Petrograd in the autumn of 1917 was in part based on these calculations. But what should be done if these expectations were not borne out?

Our Bolshevik comrades staked everything on the card of a general European revolution. When that card was beaten, they were compelled to follow the path that the unfulfilled tasks placed before them. Though without an army, they had to defend Russia from a powerful and merciless enemy; they had to create a regime of well-being for all amid universal breakdown and impoverishment. The worse the material and intellectual conditions for what they were trying to accomplish, the more they were forced to make up the deficit with the bare force of dictatorship, and the more rapidly, as opposition to them grew among the popular masses. The inevitable result was dictatorship instead of democracy.[36]

The logic of the Bolsheviks was the exact opposite. The correct course was not to wait for the European revolution, but to promote it. Victory in the 'western direction' was indispensable for reasons that included solving the problems that Kautsky had pointed out. Lenin, Bukharin and Trotsky all reasoned in this fashion. If quick success could not be achieved, however, it was necessary to construct a political strategy for the long term. This meant that the communist parties of other countries would have to be effectively controlled, and directed towards the carrying out of shared tasks connected in one way or another with the situation inside Russia.

The world communist movement was transformed, not just becoming an external wing of the Soviet party and a tool of Soviet foreign policy, but also being restructured accordingly. The absence of intra-party democracy became the entirely natural result of the tasks that had been posed, since objectively there was nothing to be discussed – all the main tactical and strategic turns of the movement were determined in Moscow.

Striving as always for objectivity, Joseph Schumpeter acknowledged:

It should not be forgotten that the Communist International was founded in that atmosphere of impending life and death struggle. Many things which acquired a different meaning afterwards – such as the centralized management that has unlimited power over the individual parties and deprives them of all freedom of action – may then have seemed quite reasonable from that aspect.[37]

The same applies to other authoritarian measures adopted during the revolutionary period, both in domestic policy and in the field of economic management.

The problem does not even lie in authoritarianism, which throughout the course of history, unfortunately, has constantly proven the quickest and most convenient method (and often the only one) for solving the dilemmas that pile up in extreme situations. The trouble is that such temporary measures have a tendency to grow into institutions that function and reproduce themselves on a continuous basis. Here it is enough to recall that the notorious Soviet state security apparatus was conceived as an 'extraordinary' commission for waging a struggle against counter-revolution and banditry, but failed to disappear following the end of the Civil War and the suppression of anti-Bolshevik revolts. Further, the use of such methods and institutions implies the existence of a multitude of people with an interest in maintaining precisely these structures of rule. *The problem with authoritarianism is not that it fails to work, but precisely the fact that such measures do work, and often, may even work very well.* So well, that abolishing them and overcoming their legacies as society moves on to addressing new tasks can prove extremely difficult.

The successes of Soviet industrialisation and the victory of the USSR in the Second World War everywhere strengthened the conviction of communists that an orientation to the Soviet experience was correct and necessary, even if doubts arose on particular questions. Zdeněk Mlynář, one of the ideologues and leaders of the 1968 Prague Spring, notes that the Soviet Union was seen not only as a force capable of social transformations on a world scale, but also as an aid in the struggle for democracy: 'In Czechoslovakia in 1945 there was no contradiction between devotion to the Soviet Union and Stalin and the general popular striving for the freedom and justice that were supposed to prevail in the new state.'[38] This was the case not only in Czechoslovakia but also in Italy and France, as well as in many other countries that had gone through the experience of resistance and popular anti-fascist mobilisation. The German communist Wolfgang Leonhard, who worked with the founders of the German Democratic Republic Walter Ulbricht and Wilhelm Pieck and who later fled to Yugoslavia, recalls in his memoirs how he and his comrades believed that with the help of the Soviet Union they would be able to 'build a new, democratic Germany'.[39] This belief filled him with enthusiasm:

> I was full of hopes that we would receive relative freedom of action in the political development of German affairs, the right to implement various measures in a manner different from that in the Soviet Union. Apart from that, I thought that in the Soviet Union as well there would be a change of regime after the war ended, a change in the direction of providing the population with greater freedom.[40]

After all, the democratic constitutions adopted in these countries had been written with the active participation of communists, and with the full support of Moscow. None other than Stalin, at the Nineteenth Congress of the CPSU, had called on communists to struggle for the political rights and freedoms of citizens as proclaimed by the liberal tradition:

> Earlier, the bourgeoisie allowed itself to play at liberalism and at defending bourgeois-democratic freedoms, thus winning popularity for itself among the people. Now there is not even a trace of liberalism left. Nothing remains of the so-called 'freedom of the individual'; the rights of the individual are now recognised only for those who have capital, and all other citizens are considered raw human material fit only for exploitation. The principle of the equality of people and nations has been trampled underfoot, to be replaced by the principle of unrestricted rights for the exploiter minority and by the powerlessness of the exploited majority of citizens. The banner of bourgeois-democratic freedoms has been thrown overboard. I believe that it is up to you, the representatives of communist and democratic parties, to raise this banner and carry it forward, if you wish to gather the majority of the people around you. There is no-one else who can raise it.[41]

Of course, Stalin in this case was referring to the communists of foreign countries, and in no way was he calling for democratisation in the USSR. It is noteworthy, however, that with his political intuition he sensed the moods that prevailed in many countries following the end of the war. For the masses, who for the first time in many years felt themselves to be a motive force of history, the Soviet experience and the victories associated with it were an inspiration. 'To the question of whose side one should fight on, and for what,' Mlynář continues, 'the epoch provided a simple answer: on the side of those who most consistently and radically acted against the past, who did not waver, who did not seek compromises with the past but who cracked down on it using revolutionary methods, and who overcame it. That force then seemed to be the Soviet Union, and the individual concerned, Stalin.'[42]

Many communists and their allies admitted in hindsight that they did not know the whole scale of the repressions unleashed in the USSR under Stalin. In this sense the revelations of the Twentieth Congress of the CPSU, which did not give a full picture of the events either, were a shock for them. But we should be honest: the use of repressive and authoritarian methods in the Soviet Union and other countries where communist parties came to power was no secret. As early as the mid-1930s, Lev Trotsky stated that the Soviet regime had taken on a 'totalitarian' character 'long before this word arrived from Germany'.[43]

The trouble was that Stalin's repressive methods were not in the least exceptional for his time, a point on which Schumpeter, who did not approve of Bolshevism but who tried invariably to be scrupulous, wrote with complete honesty. In his view, 'Stalin followed the established practice of the age. Most national governments have acted as he did and it is pure hypocrisy to profess special indignation in his case.'[44]

The specific conditions under which the international communist movement took shape left an indelible mark on its subsequent fate and on its whole political culture, determining both the strength of these parties and their weakness. Even the more or less successful attempts to overcome the authoritarian style of governance that began everywhere after the death of Stalin did not alter the situation fundamentally, since they affected neither the organisational structures nor the cultural norms that held the movement together. The result was not only and not so much the retention by the communist organisations of an authoritarian mode of leadership, as a political inflexibility that meant they were constantly late in recognising and responding to social and political events that changed society, whether these were the Cuban Revolution of 1959, the 'Red May' of 1968 in France or the 'Carnation Revolution' in Portugal in 1974. Even while criticising Stalinism and the decisions of the Soviet 'centre', and while stressing their own adherence to democratic values, the communist parties of the West continued looking on the Soviet Union if not as a model to be followed, then at least as one from which they should refrain from taking their distance. Then after the collapse of the USSR, when the world communist movement no longer possessed any rallying point or shared guidelines (even if only negative), it was placed in a situation of 'everyone for themself', and rapidly fell apart. The organisational and political inflexibility had turned into an appalling fragility.

3

The State and the Bureaucracy

Industrialism and freedom

The bureaucratic centralisation that accompanied both the establishing of Soviet planning and the development of the welfare state in Western Europe was not the product of some kind of primordial 'vice' inherent in the idea of socialism or state regulation (as Friedrich von Hayek tried stubbornly to prove), but the result of a historical contradiction between the need for planning, which had objectively matured in industrial society, and the immaturity of that society's organisational and technological possibilities, which did not allow planning to assume any but a centralist-bureaucratic form (a contradiction that Max Weber captured acutely in his forecasts). Early socialist revolutions, like social-democratic reforms, demonstrated the *possibility* of a general participation in administration, at the same time as they did not create the *conditions* for its effectiveness. Instead, they transformed the mass involvement of the population in the decision-making process from a tool of democratisation into a channel of *vertical mobility*, while creating a new bureaucracy that topped up its ranks from among the popular masses.

In its turn, the striving to construct a socialist society on the firm foundations of an efficient industrial economy not only met with criticism from certain thinkers, but was even perceived by them as the main source of the authoritarianism that prevailed in Soviet Russia and other countries where communist parties had come to power. Thus, Albert Camus complained of the development of a 'technical civilisation' on which both capitalism and socialism were 'equally dependent'.[1] In the opinion of the French writer, Marx shared his belief in technical progress with 'enthusiastic bourgeois ideologues'.[2] The result was the emergence of a society 'bowing before the cult of production', while 'the heavenly gates remained closed'.[3]

To see the roots of authoritarianism in the logic of industrialism is far more correct than to view the whole sum of events as stemming from ideology. Unfortunately, the development of industry was an objective requirement presented by the twentieth century, and as we know, it is by no means true that industrial development has led invariably to a negation of freedom. Nevertheless, the attempts by many people on the left to justify themselves and to conduct painful searches for an 'original error' or 'lost opportunity' in the ideas of the founders demonstrate not so much a need to renew socialism as an incapacity for historical and sociological thinking, and thus make no sense to those who are trying to revive the movement and go forward under changed circumstances.

If the identification of capitalism with democracy is no more than an ideological formula, arising with hindsight on the basis that modern democratic forms of state organisation became established by the end of the nineteenth century specifically within the framework of bourgeois society, then the question of whether the development of the capitalist system presupposes the maintaining and developing of democracy – or, to the contrary, creates ever new dangers to it – is extremely relevant. On the one hand, it is a historical fact that it was under pressure from below that democratic procedures became implanted first in Western, and then in other societies. As the processes of democratisation gathered strength, the bourgeois classes constantly held them back. The struggle by the Chartists for universal manhood suffrage in nineteenth-century Britain; the protests by the suffragettes demanding equal rights for women around the turn of the twentieth century; and the civil rights movement in the US in the 1960s, when the Black minority in the American South had literally to conquer the right to take part in political life, are just some of the best-known examples of how democratisation occurred through bitter conflicts with the bourgeois establishment. On the other hand, these struggles were nevertheless able to achieve victories within the framework of capitalist society. The existence of independent courts, making it possible to resolve economic disputes impartially and to defend property rights, is indispensable if the bourgeois order is to be reproduced, and this creates at least a precondition for individual freedom and civil equality. On this basis, Joseph Schumpeter reached his optimistic conclusion: 'Lawless violence the bourgeois stratum may accept or even applaud when thoroughly roused or frightened, but only temporarily.'[4]

Far more pessimistic in this respect were the views of Max Weber. Analysing the development of corporate capitalism, Weber warned that there was no reason to see in it a basis for democracy, since all the economic trends were 'leading to a growth of "unfreedom"',[5] while the organising of industrial production required an inevitable strengthening of bureaucracy 'as the heart of *any* mass rule'.[6] In this respect capitalism and socialism would be forced to confront the same problems irrespective of ideology;

a threat to democracy thus arose precisely out of this objective dynamic of mass industrialisation. Weber's thoughts led him to a tragic prophecy: under the conditions of the emerging industrial society, both capitalism and socialism were doomed in equal measure to be bureaucratic. In this situation, the main question was no longer whether socialist democracy was possible, but how great the chances were that bourgeois democracy would survive. On the other hand, was it not the case that an attempt to escape the bounds of capitalism was at the same time a chance to save bourgeois democracy from natural self-destruction?

The contradictions of victory

The psychological and organisational mechanisms preordaining defeats for the left were, unfortunately, predicted exactly by Max Weber when he observed that no fighter for the public good can get by without a political apparatus, functioning according to its own logic. The socialists of the first half of the twentieth century were mistaken in their characteristic belief that a new society could be built at one attempt, a belief that remained erroneous even if the attempt was initially successful. Proving just as ill-founded, unfortunately, were the reformist hopes of a gradual or, still more, 'evolutionary' transition to a new social order. The socialist transformation of one's own country and of the world as a whole becomes a reality only as the historical sum of numerous endeavours, of reforms, revolutions, restorations, new revolutions and conflicts that allow an accumulation of irreversible changes in the long-term perspective, while making it possible to correct past errors and to escape from dead ends. It is the sequence of these endeavours that forms the essence of the revolutionary *process*. In no way, however, does it follow from this that the question of political responsibility loses its meaning. The relative nature of any success that may be achieved does not alter the necessity to consolidate it in the form of social institutions and relationships, transforming the structures of the economy and changing the relationship of class forces.

A catastrophic chance

It is quite obvious that the *economic* basis for socialism is not falling wages, the impoverished position of the workers or a decline in the economy, but to the contrary, the development of the forces of production. This was the position of Karl Marx. The social democrats of the early twentieth century thought the same, as did Max Weber. The latter criticised the Bolsheviks and the radical wing of the German Social Democrats, rejecting the 'unreasonable' demand for the socialisation of finances under the conditions of post-war ruin prevailing in Germany and after the defeat of the Bavarian and Hungarian soviet republics, trying to dissuade his young friends Otto Neurath and György Lukács (who had been members of the defeated revolutionary governments) from taking part in more such attempts. Weber stressed constantly that when he spoke out against premature radical measures, this was 'from the point of view of the possible future of socialism'.[7] Prematurely radical politics would not only lead to defeat, but would also topple society 'into the depths of idiotic reaction'.[8] Referring to the difficult economic situation in Germany and to the backwardness of Russia, the eminent sociologist wrote to the young Lukács: 'I am absolutely convinced that these experiments can only, and will only, result in the discrediting of socialism for the next hundred years.'[9]

Weber's words turned out in a sense to be prophetic, but at the same time, it should not be forgotten that the founder of 'interpretive sociology' was quite incorrect in his assessment of the prospects of the Bolshevik regime. He was certain that the new Russian government would quickly collapse, to be followed by an inevitable Black Hundred reaction. In other words his prognosis, while seemingly accurate, was based on an incorrect understanding of the current situation.

Weber considered that the Bolshevik Party, which rested not on the organised proletariat but on a declassed soldier and peasant mass, would be unable to maintain control over the situation, and that the Marxist intelligentsia that was heading the revolution was doomed to be swept along by the moods of the mob whose support it enjoyed. The problem lay not just in the authoritarian methods of the revolutionaries, but above all in the fact that implementing any progressive agenda while resting on such a mass would be impossible. Any sacrifices that were made would turn out to be in vain.

Weber argued this position in his legendary debate with Joseph Schumpeter. Here is how the historian Timofey Dmitriev describes this episode:

In the spring of 1918 visitors to the Landmann café on Vienna's Ringstrasse, opposite Vienna University, became involuntary witnesses to a debate between a number of respectable gentlemen. After beginning quite calmly, the debate then turned into a heated altercation, and ended with one of the participants running out onto the street in great agitation. This café debate broke out between Max Weber and the Austrian economist Joseph Schumpeter. Weber arrived for the meeting accompanied by Ludo Moritz Hartmann, a specialist on ancient history, and the reason for the meeting was the need to discuss an important academic question. In the course of the conversation, however, the talk turned to the revolution in Russia. Schumpeter declared that thanks to the revolution, socialism had ceased to be a 'paper discussion', and was now being forced to demonstrate its viability in practice. To this, Weber objected that the attempt to introduce socialism in Russia, considering its level of economic development, was in essence a crime, and that the socialist experiment would inevitably end in catastrophe. In reply, Schumpeter remarked coldly that such an outcome was perfectly likely, but that Russia in these circumstances would represent 'a wonderful laboratory'. At this Weber could not contain himself, and burst out, 'A laboratory with a mountain of corpses!' Schumpeter countered, 'Like any other anatomical theatre.'[10]

The debate flared up, and became increasingly fierce. Weber began speaking 'more and more sharply and loudly, Schumpeter more quietly and sarcastically'. Visitors to the café began listening to the dispute. Finally, Weber in great agitation leaped up from his seat and with the words, 'It's impossible to endure this any longer!' ran out from the café onto the Ringstrasse. Hartmann caught up with him, handed him the hat that Weber had forgotten in the café, and tried to calm him down, but in vain. At this Schumpeter remarked phlegmatically: 'Well, how is it possible to raise such a ruckus in a café?'[11]

It is significant that the metaphor 'laboratory', applied to the USSR, was used not only by Schumpeter but also by J.M. Keynes, who saw in Soviet Russia 'a laboratory of life', recognising that in this laboratory accidents were constantly occurring, after which corpses were carried out – an inevitable consequence of a large-scale, risk-laden but indispensable experiment.[12]

It should be noted that both Schumpeter and Keynes were considering the Soviet Russia of the 1920s, long before Stalin's 'Great Terror'. In the early 1930s, evaluating the results of collectivisation and the accelerated implementation of the first five-year plan ('the five-year plan in four'), Keynes arrived at far less optimistic conclusions. In his view, the excessively rapid shift would have such grievous effects on prosperity that the new state of affairs would at first be significantly worse than the previous one, and the great experiment would be discredited.[13]

Nevertheless, the events occurring in Soviet Russia had a huge influence on the rest of the world, and most importantly, expedited social and political changes in many other countries. Comparing the experience of the Russian Revolution with that of the revolutions in France and China, the American scholar Theda Skocpol notes that such overturns stimulate changes due to the fact that ruling elites throughout the world 'are compelled to respond to the challenges or threats posed by the enhanced national power that has been generated'.[14] The threat of proletarian and peasant revolts, emerging unambiguously thanks to the rapid spread of Bolshevik ideas not only in the West but also on the periphery of the capitalist world, forced the ruling classes to implement reforms and soften their methods of rule.[15] As a result, to reduce the historical effect of the Russian Revolution solely to the discrediting of the idea of socialism, even if the defeat of the 'Bolshevik experiment' is recognised, would be a factual error.

However the views of the Western thinkers who observed the Soviet experiment in real time might have diverged, they were united in concluding that the tragic consequences of the events unfolding in Russia were not predetermined by the very nature of socialism, but by the attempt to construct it under very unfavourable circumstances, in a country with a backward economy, and beneath the pressure of extreme necessity that forced the participants in events to act hastily and to make irreparable mistakes. Ultimately, even many Soviet citizens who suffered from the policies of Stalin in the 1930s were prepared with hindsight to defend these policies, referring to the objective need to accelerate development.[16] The authoritarianism of Bolshevik policy was justly linked with these objective conditions, which were not in the least conducive to the flourishing of democracy. In sum, the dictatorial methods applied by the Soviet regime not only discredited the socialist programme, but in themselves led to an accumulation of problems that were inevitably reflected in the economic and social outcomes achieved in the USSR.

Nevertheless, and however logical such arguments might seem when voiced by outside observers, the political process develops according to its own logic. It is indicative that Weber saw problems not only in backward Russia but also in advanced Germany, for which he predicted not a shining future but the rise to power of reactionary forces (which, unfortunately, came to pass with the victory of Adolf Hitler, though not in the form which the eminent sociologist had in mind). Where the German situation was concerned, it was Weber's sworn adversary Rosa Luxemburg who proved to be correct, when she predicted that the defeat of socialism would automatically mean the victory of a new barbarism.

More than socialism

It is impossible not to agree with the following observation by British economist Alec Nove:

> Quite evidently, a democratic socialism is only conceivable on condition that a majority of the population desire it. At present they do not, despite depression and unemployment. So it seems to follow that only a more complete breakdown of the existing order would convince our fellow-citizens of the need to accept some fundamentally different alternative.[17]

Unfortunately, the *political* and *psychological* condition for the beginning of radical transformations is precisely a systemic crisis, accompanied inevitably by a decline in production, a fall in living standards, and sometimes too by real economic devastation. Socialism becomes *potentially* possible due to growth of the productive forces and the development of society, but a transition to it becomes *actually* possible when both the economy and society are in extremely severe crisis (which inevitably includes the destruction of productive forces and the disintegration of social ties). This contradiction arises inescapably from the very logic of capitalist development, and to a significant degree predetermined the tragic nature of the events of the Russian Revolution of 1917, as well as of other revolutions during the twentieth century. It cannot be reduced to the question of the level of development of the economy, supposedly 'insufficiently mature for socialism', since even in countries where the level of development is high, radical changes begin when the previous system has finished up in ruins.

Summing up his own revolutionary experience, Lenin did not deny that events had developed in a fashion quite different from what the theory and programme of the socialist movement had anticipated. Nevertheless, 'the complete hopelessness of the situation, by multiplying tenfold the efforts of the workers and peasants, opened up for us the possibility of finding a way to establish the basic premises of civilisation that was different from the one followed in the states of Western Europe'.[18] Hence the matter on the agenda could not be reduced to the construction of socialism, and still less of democracy. The task was to preserve and safeguard the minimal conditions for a civilised existence and for social development.

The practical problem that confronted the Bolsheviks was formulated perfectly by Karl Kautsky when he pointed out that the communists, who sought to demonstrate the need for socialism on the basis of the development of the forces of production, had come to power at the very moment when these forces were subject to the devastating impacts of a crisis, and precisely as a result of this crisis. In Kautsky's view, however, at precisely the moment when the socialists had the greatest chance of taking power, it was categorically wrong for them to do so:

> Ultimately, general well-being depends on an uninterrupted development of production. The destruction of capitalism is not yet socialism. Where capitalist production cannot be transformed immediately into socialist production, the former has to remain in force. Otherwise, there will be a break in the productive process, and with it, mass poverty, which the modern worker fears just as much as unemployment.[19]

At first glance this might appear completely convincing, in the early twenty-first century just as in the early twentieth. The problem, however, is that destruction of the productive forces, crises and periodic spasms of mass impoverishment are also products of the development of the productive forces under capitalism. Further, it is precisely the fact that such events will inevitably occur, and repeatedly, that is the most important argument in favour of socialist transformations.

There is a standard contradiction that has been noted repeatedly both by left- and right-wing commentators. When capitalism works, we do not need socialism, and when capitalism fails to work, we cannot allow ourselves socialism.

Although Kautsky does not say so directly, the logic of his thinking is that gradual reforms will prepare the conditions for the rise of socialist society, and will then just as smoothly and painlessly bring about the transition to it. This was the line to which European social democracy adhered, in the epoch when it was still capable of working out a political line. The history of the late twentieth century, however, not only showed that reforms can be reversed, but also demonstrated that even if the productive forces are raised to a new and unprecedented level, capitalism will again bring down society through a new crisis accompanied by destruction and social disorganisation.

It is this that makes revolution inevitable. But what about the contradiction to which Kautsky pointed?

The experience of the twentieth century leads us to the conclusion that we simply cannot separate off a socialist agenda from an agenda of democratic reforms oriented to goals that are far less ambitious, but no less important for society. *Socialist transformations will be successful precisely to the degree to which they solve not only the tasks of constructing a new society, but also the tasks of preserving and stabilising society as such.* Meanwhile, it is not only a real economy existing in the particular sense (in a given country and at a given moment) that acts as the objective basis for a socialist transformation, but also *the entire potential of the productive forces and scientific knowledge attained at a given moment by humanity as a whole.* It was the ability of the socialist experiments of the past to rest on this general world potential that ensured their success, even if this was only partial and reversible, and it is this potential that will provide the main basis for conducting any successful left politics in the future. This does not by any means signify that there is no chance of achieving significant results within the context of each particular country. But the key to success is not reliance by the socialist movement in each country on its own forces, not attempts by these movements to shut themselves off from the world, but to the contrary, a readiness to make use of global experience and a striving to influence the outside world.

PART II

The Revenge of Capital

4

From Nomenklatura to Bourgeoisie: The Evolution of the Soviet Elite

The first discussions of the degeneration of the Soviet bureaucracy began occurring during the years of the Civil War. This theme was later developed by the left opposition, voicing the complaint that the ruling stratum in the USSR was becoming bourgeoisified. It will be understood that conducting such discussions in Stalinist times was a dangerous matter. Nevertheless, it may be noted that in 1954 the Leningrad Bolshoy Drama Theatre presented the play *Guests* by Leonid Zorin, which dealt with precisely this topic. The play had been written in March 1953, immediately after Stalin's death, and immediately drew the attention of producers and the public. The premiere was an extraordinary success, with Zorin stating, 'that evening the audience let out their collective soul after thirty years of silence.'[1] The play began to be staged in many theatres, but almost immediately after this success the performances were cancelled, the play was banned, and in the official press, a stream of devastating criticism poured onto the author.

The painful reaction to the play, which the dramatist himself was by no means convinced was among his best works, testifies to how delicate its topic was for Soviet society.

Following the episode with *Guests*, authors when writing for legal publications sought to avoid the theme of the social and cultural degeneration of the Soviet elite, despite the revelations at the Twentieth Congress and a noticeable broadening of the area in which free discussion was allowed. For a certain time it was possible to write about the Stalinist camps (Aleksandr Solzhenitsyn's novella *One Day in the Life of Ivan Denisovich* was even nominated for a Lenin Prize), and it was possible to hint at the lack of freedom and to remark ironically on the wretchedness of Soviet daily life. Nevertheless, to criticise the Soviet elite on a social plane was extremely ill-advised. It cannot be said, of course, that this theme never saw the light of day anywhere during the years of the 'Thaw', but the tendency was uniform overall. The authorities were prepared to recognise certain problems with their past history, and even with their current policies. But not the existence of social contradictions within Soviet society.

The main Soviet secret

When discussion was forced out of the legal field, it naturally migrated to that of the illegal. Infiltrating the Soviet Union were the books *The New Class* by Milovan Djilas[2] and *Nomenklatura* by Mikhail Voslensky,[3] which described the privileges of the elite and in which the authors argued that the top ranks of the Soviet party-state (and of other countries belonging to the Soviet bloc) had transformed themselves into a collective owner of the means of production, and by virtue of this, into a collective exploiter. It is noteworthy that despite their obvious anti-communist passion, both writers sought to operate within Marxist categories, and even within the dogmatic interpretation that had become established within the framework of the communist movement of the time.

From the deft hand of Voslensky the term 'nomenklatura' entered into mass circulation, becoming a sociological denomination for the top Soviet elite, which stubbornly concealed from society the very fact of its existence as a particular privileged group. But hidden behind the high fences of the state dachas and the featureless doors of the 'closed distributors', this privileged group merely demonstrated to the entire population that it had not simply separated itself off from the people as a whole, but that it also suffered collective tortures of impure conscience, since it was not prepared to reveal its way of life publicly and openly.

Incontestably, the painful necessity to conceal their own wealth and privileges became one of the psychological mechanisms that later contributed to the open shift by former members of the nomenklatura to the camp of the restorers of capitalism. Not only that, but it helps explain the bacchanalia of upmarket conspicuous consumption in which the social elites of our society have immersed themselves during the post-Soviet epoch. The problem, however, is far more complex than it might seem at first glance. The very fact that the members of the nomenklatura could not admit publicly to society that their stratum even existed testifies to the presence in the USSR of a whole series of mechanisms that limited the nomenklatura's opportunities. This was true not only on the level of propaganda, ideology and culture, but also on that of institutions.

The privileges of the nomenklatura were, of course, significant compared to the benefits available to ordinary Soviet citizens, and thus extremely annoying. Compared to those enjoyed by the ruling classes in the West or in Asian countries, however, these privileges were quite insignificant (which, moreover, also became an annoyance to the Soviet elite itself, which had begun to experience an inferiority complex with relation to its foreign partners). The joys of the Soviet nomenklatura appear all the more pitiful and ludicrous compared to the lifestyles of the post-Soviet oligarchy and even the middle bourgeoisie. The impossibility for the members of this stratum of legalising their position, and of making their prestige consumption open and public, blighted their lives increasingly as the flow of information in Soviet society grew more and more open. Despite all the bans and limitations, the ties between the USSR and the outside world steadily broadened over the whole post-war period, including during the years of the Brezhnev 'stagnation'.

Nevertheless, the causes of the degeneration of the nomenklatura must be sought not in its lifestyle or levels of consumption, but in a far more profound contradiction. The structure of Soviet society and the organisation of state institutions were such that the bureaucratic elite, despite possessing a monopoly over decision-making, almost limitless power, and the instruments needed to control the political life of society, was at the same time forced to rule and to make its decisions in the interests of the development of society, and not in its own interests, individual or collective. Of course, the nomenklatura did not forget about itself, which appeared not just in its privileges, but above all in its consistent blocking of any attempts to improve the effectiveness of administration through debureaucratisation.

However the Soviet elite tried to fence itself off from society, the structure of power was nevertheless such that it did not permit rigid discontinuities. Vertical mobility was gradually diminishing, but the higher organs and their personnel interacted constantly with those further down, and could not ignore them. The critical-minded intelligentsia spoke of the lack of a reverse connection within the administration, but this reverse connection did in fact exist; it was simply that it operated through completely different channels, and using different means, than in the democratic West.

Class or non-class?

Under capitalist conditions, owners possess full sovereignty within the framework of their enterprises, just like a feudal prince in his domain. However this right might be restricted by various legal constructs, it not only remains 'sacred', but is also defended by the same laws that in various respects limit it. Of course, in the epoch of general democratisation during the 1960s the dominance of the corporate elites in Western countries was under constant threat, not only from the lower orders of society and from elected state organs, but above all from the middle and lower strata of the managerial bureaucracy, whose participation in the decision-making process diluted the sovereignty of the property owners. In this lay the essence of the notorious 'managerial revolution' of which the outstanding American economist John Kenneth Galbraith wrote in his book *The New Industrial State*.[4] Power become dispersed and redistributed, transforming management from a means of serving the private or collective interests of the owners (above all, their interest in growing rich) into a directly social process, though not one that was fully democratic.

Paradoxically, it was the democratisation that began advancing after the Second World War that made Western society not only less bourgeois and more technocratic, but in many respects increasingly similar to its Soviet counterpart. Not by chance, it was at this time that the 'theory of convergence', which promised an ultimate convergence of the two competing models of industrial society, gained wide currency in the West. This theory was promoted by John Kenneth Galbraith, among others. Among its initial adherents was the academician Andrey Dmitrievich Sakharov, who became the mouthpiece of the Soviet dissident movement.

The power of the ruling elite in the USSR was limited not by the will of a popular assembly, and not even by laws protecting the individual and property as in the West, but by the structure of the governing system itself. This did not allow a single official or even group of officials to acquire full sovereignty in their organisation or enterprise, and these bodies were so closely linked among themselves that they could not operate without taking account of one another's interests, and also of the interests of overall economic development. At the same time the official ideology, which was codified in extremely rigid fashion, fulfilled approximately the same regulatory role in Soviet society as constitutional legislation did in the West. While legitimising and defending the existing order, this ideology simultaneously imposed certain restrictions on the ruling group.

In this situation, there was no basis for speaking of the bureaucracy as a collective owner, since *this owner was not distinguished from non-owners*, from the mass of ordinary Soviet citizens. These citizens were constantly demanding that attention be paid to their interests, participating in a multitude of indispensable if also formal procedures, drafting complaints about the authorities and one another, negotiating on petty matters with the heads of their institutions, and constantly, even if indirectly, involving themselves in the process of making decisions.

Also making its effects felt here was the nature of Soviet planning, which was oriented towards ensuring comprehensiveness and consistency. Despite its monstrous and constantly growing bureaucratisation, this system was oriented towards the interests of the work at hand, towards the interests of development. These interests were not formulated at the apex of the party-state elite, but found expression as a result of the collective efforts of lower-ranking technical experts, managers and state functionaries on many levels. The planning rules were extremely strict; for example, any decision to construct a factory set in motion a whole train of other decisions – on the construction of housing, the opening of shops, schools and kindergartens, the building of railway stations and the setting up of new train and bus routes. As can readily be seen, this always transgressed the framework of questions affecting only one department or even of the territorial organs of power. The Gosplan system gave rise to long chains of agreements, creating the need to link social and economic decisions to one another in complex fashion.

As in the West, the complex system of vertical and horizontal negotiations was by no means free of conflicts. Along with contradictions between departments and agencies, it inevitably revealed contradictions between its topmost and middle levels. The more complex the system grew, the less effective became the centralised management that had been established during the time of forced-draft industrialisation. In essence, the USSR in the 1960s approached its own version of the 'managerial revolution', expressed in an initial project of economic reform that is usually associated with then President of the Council of Ministers Aleksey Kosygin. The reformers were prepared to grant enterprise managers broad autonomy, while at the same time allowing them to establish horizontal ties. Meanwhile each individual enterprise, which in the words of historian and sociologist Pavel Kudyukin now resembled an 'industrial commune',[5] was transformed if not into an island of self-management, then at least into an independent collective with shared interests.

It is not hard to see that this course of events not only failed to strengthen the position of the nomenklatura as a (still only potential) collective owner of the means of production, but to the contrary, undermined its chances of consolidating its dominance. The reform begun in 1964 was wound up in 1968–69 in parallel with the crushing, by Soviet tanks, of the democratic changes in Czechoslovakia. The coincidence was far from accidental, since the economic reform begun in that country had not only placed on the agenda the question of political democratisation, but had also provoked a transformation of the Communist Party of Czechoslovakia. The party had become an organisation that enjoyed the support of a majority of the population and was capable of winning elections, but that was not involved directly in questions of economic activity, local government or raising the milk yield of cows.

Assessing the significance of the economic reform, which in Czechoslovakia had been prompted initially by impulses from the USSR, Zdeněk Mlynář noted that it 'created favourable conditions for changes in the political sphere'.[6] The decentralisation and debureaucratisation of administration inevitably had a series of political and social consequences:

> Above all, the need vanished for a colossal state apparatus issuing directives that governed every step of economic activity. It now became possible to gradually transform this apparatus, except for the organs dealing with long-term planning, into an administrative apparatus of enterprises and combines, and to detach it from political and state organs. Closely linked to this was the prospect of separating off the ruling party from the decision-making management of the economy, which in turn would bring cuts to the swollen party apparatus, whose involvement in economic matters accounted for the lion's share of its activity. As a result of such changes, the Communist Party as a social organism would start occupying itself more with its own political, programmatic work.[7]

The combination of political democratisation and the decentralisation of administration would affect the lower level as well. Employees would receive 'the right to establish organs of workers' self-management of the productive process'.[8]

Workers' councils were in fact set up, and continued to develop their activity until 1969 (these events and the associated struggle for workers' control in the enterprises received the name 'the second Prague Spring').[9] The islands of productive democracy were only abolished finally by 1970, in the course of 'normalisation'.

Initially the Czechoslovak reformers, like their Soviet colleagues, hoped that in raising the question of improving the quality of management they were not undermining the system but improving it. 'A democratic system', Mlynář continued, 'would not have required the liquidating of the bureaucracy as such, but to the contrary, would have improved the position of many administrators through removing the criterion of "political reliability". Linked inseparably to the totalitarian regime were only the privileges of a narrow stratum of the political apparatus, strong precisely because of its power and not because of its importance for the normal functioning of society."[10] Unfortunately, the reformers were soon forced to recognise that the matter was being played out on a completely different level. It was now the *question of power* that was central, not only on the ideological and political but also on the social plane. Beginning with reforms to management, the proponents of change had without recognising it created the conditions for forming a socialist democracy, one that was spared not only from dominance by the nomenklatura but also, in an important sense, from the power of professional politicians as well. The shifting of practical questions to the operation of democratic structures and technocratic professional teams stripped the nomenklatura of the remnants of its economic sovereignty, without which its political power, limited by strict legal norms, lost much of its meaning.

Stagnation as a solution

The course proclaimed during the years of Leonid Brezhnev, of orienting towards stability as an alternative to reforms that would undermine the position of the bureaucracy, corresponded entirely to the hopes and strivings of the Soviet nomenklatura. Around the beginning of the 1960s Milovan Djilas stated that the 'new class' he had described wanted to 'live peacefully' following the death of Stalin; its ideal was not to continue the revolution, but to enjoy 'a peaceful and prosperous life'.[11] The hectic activity of Nikita Khrushchev and the reformist initiatives of Aleksey Kosygin disrupted this calm. The curtailment of the reforms in the early 1970s removed the threat of a spontaneous democratisation of management, but did not solve the problem with efficiency. This problem was resolved after a fashion (or more accurately, pushed onto the sidelines) in 1973–74 thanks to a new strategy introduced by Brezhnev and his team. This strategy had two main components.

On the one hand, the abrupt rise in oil prices following the Arab–Israeli war of 1973 created the conditions for a dramatic expansion of Soviet participation in the global economy. Trying with the help of an oil embargo to force the West to refrain from supporting Israel, the Arabs achieved a quite different result, radically changing the structure of world markets. The USSR now entered into the system of the world division of labour as a supplier of raw materials. Meanwhile the stream of petrodollars that was pouring into the Soviet economy, together with the possibility of obtaining cheap credit from the West, created the illusion in Soviet ruling circles that reforms were not needed. If the USSR could not produce something itself, it would buy it. The only sector that as before needed its own technological innovations and efficient management remained defence production, which was maintained at a high level by centralised efforts, a constant flow of money, and infusions of the most valuable resources and the best personnel at the expense of other sectors.[12]

On the other hand, the problem of management still needed somehow to be solved. While the policy of decentralisation was rejected, a sort of 'split centralisation' was introduced to replace it. Once again authority and resources were redistributed, only not from the top down, but directly at the top.

Anyone who attempts to trace the evolution of the Soviet system of administration in the 1970s and 1980s will be struck by the rapid growth in the number of branch ministries and departments. Every branch and even sub-branch of production sought to obtain its own administrative structure, concerned exclusively with its affairs. If powers could not be devolved to lower levels, it was necessary to strengthen specialisation at the top to the maximum degree possible. These new departments, however, were now transformed into increasingly insular, self-sufficient institutions, working for themselves. The nature of planning gradually changed. Instead of concerning itself with the technical coordination of decisions, Gosplan had now to try to satisfy the ambitions of a growing number of sectoral lobbies, each of which used a full range of administrative and corrupt instruments to strengthen its position. The party chiefs, meanwhile, did not see their power decline; it was precisely to these people that the sectoral lobbyists appealed for support as they sought to achieve their goals.

The disproportions that remained in the Soviet economy gave rise to a play of interests within which the possession of resources or products that were in short supply became a condition for exerting influence and even, within certain bounds, for wielding power. Although the often-repeated thesis that comprehensive shortages of everything prevailed in the Soviet economy is an ideologically motivated exaggeration, it cannot be denied that deficits of various items (not only consumer goods) were a constant factor, and one that played a significant role in decision-making at various levels. The historian Aleksandr Shubin writes:

> The state-owned, planned economy rested on the production either of a mass of standard (though poorly standardised) goods, or of unique

examples of complex, high-quality technology. As a result, a proportion of demand finished up not being satisfied, and production came to be divided into normal and 'deficit' categories. 'Deficit' goods came to act as a sort of natural 'hard currency', that made it possible to counterbalance various interests in the absence of a universal monetary equivalent.[13]

This 'hard currency' was more valuable than money, with which not everything could be obtained, or not always (this also affected relations between enterprises amid increasingly frequent interruptions to planned deliveries). The upshot was the formation of a black market, in which clandestine entrepreneurs and speculators played substantial roles. This was a market of informal connections, obligations and power.

On this basis, corruption grew rapidly among the top leadership. At the same time, the structure of the elite was changing. The party-state nomenklatura was no longer a cohesive grouping, and still less was it the notorious 'order of swordbearers' of which Stalin had dreamed. It was now a conglomerate of groups and clans, each of which had its own ties and mutual obligations to its 'own' group of economic bosses and regional chiefs.

Moving along such a course, the Soviet economy by the mid-1980s was already completely ready for privatisation. Not only had the corporate structures more or less taken shape and become self-sufficient, but integration of the USSR into the world market was a growing phenomenon. As a result, a transition to an open economy of a capitalist type seemed already to many of the enterprises linked to the raw materials sector not just to be perfectly possible, but also an attractive prospect. In essence, the trajectory of development that Russia would follow right through to the end of the Vladimir Putin epoch was already fully formed in the late Soviet years.

At the same time, a process was unfolding in the West that was to receive the name 'shareholder counter-revolution'. While in Eastern Europe the threat of a democratic convergence had been warded off by the Soviet intervention in Czechoslovakia and by the curtailing of the Kosygin reforms, in the US and Western Europe the elites were acting less crudely but just as decisively. A general change in the structure of capitalist corporations was under way, and would lead to the more or less unified structure of management being split. Through obtaining large packets of shares, top managers became integrated into the class of owners, while the mass of rank-and-file administrators and bureaucrats lost control over their levers of influence on strategic decisions and were transformed into ordinary hired employees, well paid and submissive.

It is noteworthy that the emergence of a so-called 'people's capitalism', in which more and more people owned shares in companies, not only failed to make the system more democratic and socially oriented, but to the contrary, strengthened the stimuli from the market for obtaining short-term gains at the cost of long-term goals. This paradox is well described by the British economist Alec Nove:

> The 'owners' may be thousands, even millions, of small contributors to these funds and trusts. It is not just that the bulk of them neither know nor care just which shares in which companies have been bought and sold during the year. The essential point is that the 'owners' and the fund managers have only the shortest of short-term interest in the firms they 'own', since they may hold the shares for just a few weeks, or even (as one Wall Street dealer put it) for ten minutes.[14]

As a result, the long-term prospects for the development of specific companies (and still more, sectors) have finished up being subordinated to the performing of two interlinked tasks: securing increased profits and raising share prices on the stock markets. Investors often buy shares not in order to hold them but to resell them, and this in turn means that the growth of industrial capital is subordinated to the tasks of expanding financial capital. Production, that remains *objectively* the foundation of the economy, is transformed into a secondary question for those who control the resources, and the public interest also disappears entirely from their field of view.

On the political level the same process found expression in the triumph of neoliberalism, when first the government of Margaret Thatcher in Britain and the Ronald Reagan administration in the US, and then the leaderships of other countries (including social democrats) not only began implementing measures to privatise the state sector and dismantle the welfare state, but also consistently limited the opportunities for democratic institutions to influence any decisions at all. This was done under the pretext of defending the market and business from bureaucratic interference, but as events proceeded the army of bureaucrats only expanded, while the democratic institutions were emasculated and withered away. Increasingly, democracy was transformed into a façade embellishing the relatively ugly edifice of the corporate state.

Not only was the Soviet elite by the late 1980s ready to implement privatisation, but the West too was prepared to embrace its former rivals. The convergence took place, but in a fashion completely different from what Galbraith and Sakharov had dreamed of during the 1960s. Rather, what occurred was a negative convergence, in the course of which Soviet society was to lose its social conquests, while Western society became less and less democratic.

In the Soviet Union, however, the problem of ideology remained unresolved. The problem lay not only in the fact that the existing ideology accorded poorly with privatisation and the definitive transformation of the nomenklatura into a corporate bourgeoisie (though this problem was being solved in China). Since communist ideology in the USSR played approximately the same organising and (with relation to official arbitrariness) restraining role as, for example, constitutional law in the US, it provided the basis for a system of checks and balances, together with feedback channels and a degree of vertical mobility. Like the law in the West, ideology in the USSR legitimised the hegemony of the ruling elite and restrained its ambitions. Ideology permeated the daily lives of Soviet citizens, regulating their social behaviour and making it predictable. This ideologically based order could not, of course, provide a genuine substitute for democracy, but for most of the population it more or less compensated for the lack of democratic mechanisms.

Communist ideology in its Soviet variant also required the authorities to present constant achievements in the fields of social and economic development. The regime had not only to come up constantly with something it could share with the people, thus proving its legitimacy. Also important was the fact that socio-economic progress was inscribed firmly in the dominant system of values. Soviet-type bureaucracy had taken shape in the course of industrialisation and modernisation, and was obliged to serve the goal of further development, or at least, to give the impression of serving it. Not only was this burdensome, but with each year the outcomes were worse. The declining dynamism of the Soviet system thus undermined its legitimacy.

The ideological transition

It is not surprising that the transition to capitalism began with a decisive dismantling of the ideology and of the institutions connected with it. In many people who were nostalgic for the USSR, this created in hindsight the idealist illusion that it had been the rejection of ideological dogmas that caused the collapse of the system, but in reality (and in strict accordance with Marxian theory) the reality was the complete reverse. The evolution of the system created the need for the ruling circles to rid themselves of the fetters of ideology.

The nomenklatura had always nourished the secret collective dream of transforming itself into a bourgeoisie. In the years from 1989 to 1991 this dream came true. Freeing themselves from their ideological shackles (and at the same time from those of morality), the ruling stratum succeeded in becoming a genuine class, privatising not only property and power, but to a significant degree also the state itself. Not only did a rupture finally emerge between the elite and society, but it also took on the character of an insurmountable opposition, sharpening the contradictions of society to a degree that in the developed capitalist countries had not been seen in many years (though there too, these contradictions were growing rapidly).

Like any complex process of social transformation, the reconfiguring of the nomenklatura into a bourgeoisie could not of course take place without incurring serious losses (which the victors themselves incurred as well). Since the entire Soviet state machine was not just closely tied to the dominant ideology, but also directly integrated with the system of planning and administration, the dividing up of property was naturally accompanied by the disintegration of the country. The liquidation of the USSR in December 1991 not only untied the hands of the new 'national' elites who split up the heritage of the superpower among themselves, but also brought the definitive destruction of the ideological structures, which lost their ties to the state tradition and history. No longer could history be lived through as a part of one's own past, connected directly to the present; instead, history had to be invented afresh.

The destruction of economic ties placed no less a stress on enterprises than the opening of markets to foreign competition, and probably even more. Nevertheless, this catastrophe aided the implementation of specific plans for privatisation. Property was transferred to private hands at a discount, and was easy to divide up.

A significant number of enterprises never recovered from what occurred, and many new owners ultimately received assets that were far less valuable than they had counted on, though this was the result of their own policies. The economy became primitivised, with raw materials production gaining greater weight. In the long term this was to make raising efficiency practically impossible within the framework of the existing structure of interests.

In changing its class nature, the elite was forced inevitably to alter its personnel too. New people emerged, individuals who had not just succeeded in attaching themselves to the ruling class as it had taken shape, but who had also actively influenced this process to serve their own interests. The new bourgeois elite never managed to separate itself completely from the traditional bureaucracy, but nevertheless changed the nature of state administration radically, making it dependent on corporate management.

The structures of state coercion, in demand during the transition process to play the role of its defenders, themselves turned into something resembling business corporations, often competing with other such bodies.

Nevertheless, the greatest change undergone by the national elite as the nomenklatura turned itself into a bourgeoisie lay in the fact that it completely lost its stake in the development and modernisation of society.

The Soviet bureaucracy had taken shape in the process of industrialisation; its structures had been formed in order to carry out the corresponding tasks, and to a significant degree its legitimacy had been based on the fact that in one way or another these tasks had been performed. Now, the oligarchy had freed itself from these obligations just as it had freed itself from the old ideology (which the older generation of bosses sometimes recalled nostalgically on the dates of Soviet holidays). Neither the structure of the regime, nor its ideology, nor its direct interests dictated to the new masters that they needed to change, develop or even improve anything. They had achieved their golden age once and for all. Their dreams had come true.

As a result, the authorities and the oligarchy in Russia in the early twenty-first century were profoundly conservative and hostile to any kind of progress, regardless of whatever words they inscribed on their banners.

Peripheral capitalism and the deficit of democracy

The restoration of capitalism in the states that arose on the ruins of the Soviet Union was in no sense simply a return to the past, or even a mechanical transfer to new soil of the institutions, practices and productive relations characteristic of the bourgeois societies of the West. Such a transfer is impossible in principle. What is fundamentally important, however, is the fact that capitalism has not only returned to the expanse where it suffered a collapse in the early twentieth century, but has returned in the form it acquired as a result of the reforms, revolutions and restorations that occurred in the course of a whole historical epoch. Here once again we may recall Max Weber. Describing the events of the first Russian revolution, Weber came to the conclusion that attempts to copy ready-made models that had been established within the framework of Western society would not bring Russia closer to political freedom:

> It would be completely ridiculous to hope that today's mature capitalism (this inevitable sum of economic development), as it evolved in America and has been imported into Russia, might somehow be combined with

'democracy' and still more with 'freedom' (in whatever sense). The question is quite different: what, in these circumstances, would be the chances of 'democracy', 'freedom' and so forth surviving in the long term? They would be able to survive only if the nation displayed a decisive willpower in its refusal to be a herd of sheep.[15]

While true with relation to the early 1900s, this thought is still more correct with regard to Russia at the end of the twentieth century. At the same time, it should not be forgotten that the bourgeois order did not take shape here on an empty space, but was superimposed on already existing social and political practices. Capitalism came to Russia and to the other states that arose on the ruins of the USSR not just as a ready-made system, one that most people at all levels of society considered did not need to be *created* but could simply be *copied*. It was also imported *in its neoliberal form*. This regime, with all its specific economic, political and cultural peculiarities, including the absence of ties between the accumulation of capital and the development of national industry, offered nothing in the way of free competition, and still less of democracy. The ideological mantras concerning the advantages of the free market, heard constantly both in Russia and the West, had as their exclusive aim the liberating of already existing and *economically indispensable* monopolies from state regulation and social burdens.

The reduction of state intervention, in the circumstances of an economy that (as Weber had shown) was unable simply for technological reasons to operate according to the laws of the classical market of the eighteenth and nineteenth centuries, meant an inevitable strengthening of corporate monopolism, and aided the imposing of oligarchic rule in both the economic and political fields.

The problem faced by the Western corporate elite in the late twentieth century lay in its need to curtail, and if possible to end altogether, the participation of the masses in politics while preserving the formal institutions of parliamentarism, free elections and other conquests of liberal democracy. This task was achieved through combining market reforms with the technocratic adoption of decisions supposedly too complex to be understood by ordinary voters. As Boris Kapustin notes, this led to the banishing of the *majority* as a political subject, and to the formation of a 'regime of exclusion of the "people"/demos as a specific form of political subjecthood'.[16] The fundamental difference between East and West lay, however, in the fact that in countries with established democratic institutions rule by the corporate oligarchy came up against a multitude of limitations, while society had the possibility and resources to effectively resist it. Even if capital managed repeatedly to overcome the resistance of developed civil society, this was achieved at the cost of lost time, a weakening of pressure and inevitable concessions. In the conditions of the post-Soviet countries the same tendencies acquired a far greater scale, and importantly, had at first an all-pervading character, taking the form of an almost 'natural' and thus irresistible process.

The anti-democratic reaction that was unfolding in the West combined with the results of the degeneration of the Soviet nomenklatura, forming a sort of synthesis. As the British economist Vincent Barnett has observed, 'the post-Soviet economy was in reality constructed through the superimposing of a Western understanding of market processes and imported technology on the existing bureaucratic order and on the remnants of the collapsing institutions of the planned economy', resulting in the rise of 'what is described as mafia capitalism'.[17]

Of course, if we compare the still-extant democratic practices in the West with what is occurring on the territory of the former USSR and of various other countries, it is easy enough to conclude that the cause of all these misfortunes lies in the nomenklatura past of the new ruling class. Nevertheless, the similarity between the processes occurring on both sides of the former 'iron curtain' is all too obvious, as is the mutual influence these processes exert on one another. The negative convergence has become a reality.

The remnants of the decayed and degraded Soviet social and political structures, along with the practices that characterised them, became combined in their own organic fashion with the relationships and practices peculiar to late capitalism. The consumption boom typical of post-Soviet society – a boom that was not just quantitative (people began consuming more, though the goods they obtained were not always better), but also qualitative (the range of offerings, and the demands catered to, expanded rapidly) – was also prepared by the late Soviet period with its paradoxical combination of quickly developing consumer society and of chronic shortages arising not only from the inadequacies of centralised planning, but also from the disproportionate growth of wages during the 1960s and 1970s. Nevertheless, it was the transformation of consumer activity into a crucially important aspect of life, shaping not only people's daily existence but to a significant degree their individual identities as well, that caused Russians to become still more dissociated. While industrial production brought people together in large collectives, consumption atomised them, causing them to perceive themselves primarily as individuals or at best, as members of families and households.

Meanwhile, large industrial plants were being shut down on a massive scale, or were sharply reducing their number of workers. Further, the work collectives were growing older; amid mass layoffs, there was no point in hiring young people. Of course, new factories appeared during the economic upturn in the 2000s, but these were most often assembly plants. They did not require such large workforces as earlier enterprises, and needed fewer skilled workers, people who could have created around themselves a new mass culture of labour.

The triumph of consumption, together with the disintegration of the Soviet industrial system, radically altered both individual and mass consciousness. For the left, which historically had rested on the strength of organised workers, the consequences were catastrophic. Although this process could be observed to one degree or another in all the 'old' industrial countries, on the territory of the former USSR it developed especially quickly and dramatically, bringing vast changes. In Western countries the transition was rendered less abrupt – though still painful – by the survival from earlier times of such institutions of civil society as trade unions and political parties.

As a result of the social shifts between 1990 and 2010, people grew dissociated from one another to such a degree that speaking of 'society' became possible only in relative terms. Horizontal ties between individuals, solidarity, mutual interaction and trust were reduced to a minimum. The communities that arose were not only formed on a relatively casual basis, but also proved extremely unstable. Outside of technical systems and formal organisations (a shared apartment block with a common heating system, or joint work under a single boss), there was nothing to unite people.

This recalls the ancient Asiatic despotism described by Marx (the well-known 'potatoes in a sack', unified from without by the strict boundaries of the state), but here too there are huge differences. Under Asiatic despotism the basic unit was the village commune, within which personal ties, solidarity, hierarchy and rules were all very distinct. Not only is the commune absent from present-day Russia, but its modern analogues (such as labour collectives in the later years of the USSR) are also lacking. Meanwhile, Asiatic despotisms featured not only a fierce and pitiless authority, but also a precisely operating, disciplined and organisationally monolithic bureaucracy. The state systems concerned, which had not 'germinated' in the depths of society, readily collapsed if they suffered an external shock (whether an enemy invasion, or a falling-out at the topmost level of the elite). But so long as everything was peaceful, their functioning was stable and exact.

In the post-Soviet countries, by contrast, the apparatus of power has finished up resembling the society itself. It consists of numerous individuals and groups with nothing to unite them apart from formal official instructions. Those who staff it are thoroughly corrupt and incompetent, with no need even to demonstrate an ability to perform their jobs in order to keep their positions and advance their careers. The Asiatic despotisms were basically non-market systems; by contrast, everything in Russia and other post-Soviet countries is not only subject to the market, but the state itself, its functions and its instruments have been privatised both formally and informally. The 'sack' in which the 'potatoes' are supposed to be stored is completely rotten and falling apart.

The neoliberal reforms in Russia resulted in the formation of an elite that clings desperately to power, but that has no need whatsoever of power as such. The key to this paradox lies in the fact that power is viewed solely as a technical resource – that is, as a means of gaining access to an unlimited amount of money, to a sort of *corruption rent* that constitutes the essence of government and the main point of exercising it. Money, privileges, every imaginable luxury and pleasure, everything that can be obtained for oneself personally with the help of an official position – this is what power is used for. Hence the members of the ruling oligarchy display no striving for power as such, and lack the sense, of which Max Weber spoke, that they hold in their hands 'the nerve of a historically important process'.[18]

The question inevitably arises: how can a revolution occur in such a society, and how is it possible to implement reforms, not only progressive reforms, but reforms of any description? Equally, however, it is obvious that maintaining even a medium-term stability in a system that is destroying itself spontaneously and irreversibly is impossible. Inevitably, the weakness of society is turning into disproportionate opportunities for any group that is united, organised and conscious of its strategic tasks. In the case of success, such a group will itself be transformed into a new centre not only of political but also of social 'crystallisation'. In a certain way the Bolshevik Party, surviving the shocks of the First World War and the Civil War, played such a role in Russian society. In the early twenty-first century, however, the conditions that made possible that type of 'vanguard party' (the product not only of a revolutionary ideology, but also of the rapid though brief industrial expansion of the years from 1890 to 1910) are absent.

How might a new social force, able to restructure and consolidate society, come into being in Russia? And will this force be left-wing, or even progressive at all?

5

What Remains of the Welfare State?

In the mid-twentieth century radical-left ideologues in the West condemned the working class for preferring consumption to revolution. Meanwhile, consumer society was viewed as depersonalised and spiritless, a triumph of alienation and commercial manipulation. Indeed, as the living standards of workers had risen, political life had grown increasingly dull, radical parties had become reformist, and the reformists had transformed themselves into moderates. Everywhere the same 'jaded indifference', of which Georg Simmel had once spoken prophetically with relation to the daily life of large cities, had come to prevail.[1]

While radical leftists assailed the petty-bourgeois degeneration of workers, among social democrats the conviction grew that the historical mission of socialism lay not in overcoming capitalism, but in reforming and humanising it. Developments in the 1990s and the first two decades of the new century, however, completely dispelled these illusions. The experience of the twenty-first century has shown that despite their undoubted correctness, the critics of consumer society had missed the main point: the well-being of workers, achieved as a result of the struggle for social reforms, had given rise to a new consumer psychology that undermined people's will to resist at the very moment when not only the results of the reforms, but also the well-being itself was under threat.

The fragile prosperity of the proletariat

In analysing the programme of the German Social Democrats, Engels turned his attention to the thesis according to which the numbers and poverty of the proletariat were constantly increasing, and voiced his firm objections. 'The organisations of the workers and their constantly growing resistance will, depending on the possibilities, create a certain barrier to the *growth of poverty*. But what is definitely increasing is the *insecurity of the workers' existence*.'[2] The events of the twentieth century confirmed this observation in full. Under capitalism, the well-being of working people is under constant pressure from the market, despite the fact that simultaneously, the market also creates opportunities to increase this well-being. In the absence of political and economic struggle, all gains are reversible.

During the 1970s Jean Baudrillard showed convincingly how closely linked consumer society was to the welfare state. 'Consumer society', he wrote, 'is characterised not only by a rapid growth of individual spending, but also by a rise in third-party spending (especially by the administration) to the advantage of particular individuals and with the goal of reducing inequality in the distribution of incomes.'[3] Collective expenditures and collective consumption, for all their 'non-market' nature, not only lifted a significant part of the burden from households, *freeing up their resources for market demand*, but also guaranteed the basic conditions for the reproduction of society, which capital, resting on its own logic of accumulation, was unable to fulfil *automatically*. Baudrillard noted further that the welfare state overcame (or at any rate, mitigated) the problem of cultural inertia, which was not reducible to inequalities of wealth. Access by the lower classes to education, knowledge and culture did not depend solely on their incomes, but 'other, more subtle mechanisms than those of an economic nature' were also at work.[4] Administrative and political measures adopted by governments under the influence of left ideology in turn allowed the situation to be changed substantially.

The limits placed by Western governments on capital after the Second World War, reflecting the influence of the ideas of J.M. Keynes and pressures from the labour movement, not only brought humanity unprecedented progress and well-being, but also stabilised the capitalist system, at least in the countries making up the centre of the world-system. But as noted by the American political scientist Geoffrey Antonio Carmona Báez, this policy inevitably ran up against new contradictions: 'Keynesian economics became the victim of its own success. It raised production and the standard of living of workers considerably in the industrialised countries and caused corporations to go beyond national boundaries to find more markets and cheaper labour.'[5]

At the same time, the social structure of bourgeois societies was changing radically. Reviewing the experience of the welfare state in the countries of the West, Paul Krugman concludes that these reforms were instrumental in bringing about the rise of a modern, mass middle class that was obliged for its prosperity not in the first instance to the market, but on the contrary, to non-market policies of redistribution.[6] Neither the dominant ideology nor, in most cases, middle-class people themselves viewed this as an obvious fact, for the reason especially that in bourgeois society people are inclined to explain their successes and well-being as due to their individual achievements.[7]

In the late 1970s capital managed to transform the middle class into its ally, promising to relieve it of the bureaucratic and taxation burdens associated with maintaining the welfare state while at the same time pledging to preserve the consumer society. This is the essence of the social policies of neoliberalism, the reason for their initial success and logical collapse.

The long-term impossibility of resolving the difficulties involved here is obvious, and the unsustainability of neoliberal policies revealed itself in full measure during a global crisis – the Great Recession of 2008–2010. In the short term, however, dealing with the problems was possible. The dismantling of the welfare state did not occur all at once or in full, and the contradictions accumulated only gradually. In addition, the reverse side of breaking down the welfare state was the *financialisation* of capitalism. Accompanying the cuts to state spending on social welfare was an increase in household debts, as people were forced to borrow in order to pay for services they had earlier received cheaply or free of charge.[8] At the same time the financial sector was also expanding, creating jobs, new technologies and stimuli to economic growth. The commercialisation of various aspects of life earlier guaranteed by the state also created new markets, employment and career opportunities for people who joined in the process of change.

As early as the years before the First World War Nikolay Bukharin wrote:

> According to Marx, included in consumption by the masses, in the level of this consumption, and in the value of labour power itself, is also the aspect of class struggle. In the whole mechanism of the unfolding contradictions between production and consumption, between the growth of production and the relations of distribution, this contest between classes is already *implicit*, even while it *wears the cloak of economic categories.*[9]

Ultimately, and despite all the specific peculiarities that characterise different but regularly recurring crises, these crises all arise out of the same fundamental contradiction between the ever-increasing development of the productive forces of capital and the 'narrow basis on which the relations of consumption rest'.[10] The welfare state, the regulation of markets and the consumer society that arose along with them not only transformed and humanised capitalism in developed, democratic countries, rendering the system less harsh in relation to working people, but also allowed the fundamental contradiction within capitalism to be mitigated for a period. The reforms not only transformed hired workers into active buyers in the marketplace, but also made the state itself a large and vitally important purchaser. The success of these measures, however, was attained at the cost of doing systematic violence to capital, of limiting its opportunities and freedom. During a significant part of the twentieth century the ruling class was prepared to reconcile itself to this situation, since it was the price, for the rulers, of their own survival. This was true, however, only to the degree and to the point that the class found itself under direct and mortal threat of revolution and political annihilation. As soon as the global relationship of class forces started to change, the conditions of the social compromise began to be re-examined as well – gradually and stealthily at first, but later, more and more radically and aggressively.

The attack by neoliberalism on the welfare state and on the regulation of economic life proceeded beneath the slogan of defending individual freedoms from bureaucratic interference. Politicians and commentators argued unremittingly that state institutions had proliferated to an intolerable degree, and were now present in a multitude of areas of life that earlier had been closed to them. It was no accident, however, that this 'enlargement' of the state had gone ahead in proportion with its democratisation, an effect that could be traced not only in the West but also in the Soviet Union; there, it was precisely in the period of the Thaw, and simultaneously with the dismantling of the repressive apparatus built up in the Stalin epoch, that a massive programme of housing construction was rolled out, along with ever-broader social provisions. The above paradox was noted as early as the 1920s by Carl Schmitt:

> The pluralist party-state is becoming 'total' not as a result of its vigour and might, but because of its weakness; it intervenes in all areas of life because it has to fulfil the demands of all interested parties. This is especially so in the field of the economy, previously free of state interference, even while the state refuses to exercise any leadership there or to exert political influence.[11]

Ultimately it was not capitalism, demonstrating its vitality, that appeared to refute Marx's prediction of the necessity for socialism, but *the effectiveness of socialist measures applied in order to overcome crises* that proved the decisive factor allowing the survival of capitalism through the twentieth century. The rejection of these socialist 'crutches', which capital discarded as unnecessary following the collapse of the Soviet Union, then had the effect of restoring the contradictions to their original level, particularly when combined with the defeat of social democracy and other anti-capitalist forces. In paradoxical (or more accurately, dialectical) fashion, it was the *political* defeat of Marxist socialism that re-actualised Marx's *theoretical* prediction.

In the course of its history, capitalism has repeatedly had need of the state in order to appropriate new spaces – both geographical, and also technological and social. Massive state investments have allowed the rise of new technologies and sectors that simply could not have been created by the private sector, both for lack of the opportunity to make quick profits, and also due to the absence of the market space from which these profits might be extracted. It was only after the state sector in the US, the USSR and Western Europe had spent a half-century developing it that the space industry acquired the scale needed to make possible the activity of Elon Musk and other 'entrepreneurial geniuses'.[12] The same applies to the internet and in a broader sense, the information sector. It is still more true of education, health care, housing and transport, which due precisely to the social policies of the state have become large sectors suited to market exploitation.

Despite the appeals to curtail the role of governments in the economy, the neoliberal transformation around the turn of the twenty-first century not only failed to reduce the size of the bureaucracy or to lower the level of state compulsion, but to the contrary, increased their influence on the life of society. As the German political scientist Ulrich Beck has observed, in most countries the authorities have conducted a 'systemic transformation under the heading of self-destatisation'.[13] Further, this counter-reform has been carried out – from above, through compulsion and often, violently – by governments acting in the interests of transnational concerns.

There is no doubt that to a certain degree privatisation, the dismantling of the welfare state and the commercialisation of the public sector in themselves became factors of growth. Meanwhile members of the middle class, while acting as consumers, at the same time acquired a whole series of short-term advantages. This served to dampen the negative consequences of the neoliberal policies, which did not make their effects felt immediately or everywhere, and which most importantly, were not felt by everyone. Accordingly, the supporters of the neoliberal *revanche* retained the possibility not just of retaining their positions in society, but also of broadening their offensive. This course, however, would inevitably come up against its objective limits. When this happened, the bills would need to be paid. All the problems and contradictions that had accumulated over decades would suddenly, all at once, come to the surface. Even if the masses did not grasp the essence of what was occurring, the emotional discomfort they were experiencing would reach such dimensions that a succession of social explosions would become inevitable.

This emerged most rapidly in the area of housing policy. Early in the twentieth century, when mass urbanisation was still only beginning, Georg Simmel stated: 'Within the cities, an increase in real estate values is occurring that has no connection to the investment of labour. Rents are rising of their own accord, due simply to the growth of business activity and to the profits that the rents bring to property owners.'[14] One result of this situation was constantly increasing inequality in housing availability not only where rich and poor were concerned, but also between generations, and between groups of 'old' and 'new' city dwellers. Municipal housing policy in the mid-twentieth century had made it possible not only to improve the situation of workers, but also to prevent this spontaneously developing contradiction from deepening and growing more massive the more successful the economy became. The privatisation of municipal housing, conducted throughout Europe from Moscow to London, had the effect of once again creating acute differences between those who already owned real estate and those who had come on the scene too late to benefit from the division of property.

The same process emerged, in somewhat different forms, in the US as well. It became apparent that various social groups who had managed to purchase housing on relatively favourable terms were unable to keep it, since their incomes did not cover the inevitable and constantly growing costs. Especially in the US and Eastern Europe, a generalised housing crisis arose in large cities. An answer was found in a vast expansion of mortgage credit. This in turn led to a growing debt crisis, with the sums owed by households reaching catastrophic proportions and with millions of people losing the ability to accumulate indispensable monetary savings. The banks, which earlier had been able to exploit their debtors, were now themselves hostage to the situation, since they could maintain the solvency of their clients only by issuing them ever-greater unsecured credits. In 2007–8 the US real estate and financial markets collapsed, while in European countries and especially on the territory of the former USSR the banking sector, now completely ineffective, finished up totally dependent on state guarantees for its survival.

Capital flight

One of the key reforms that had changed the face of capitalism in the late twentieth century was the renouncing by the state of control over the capital markets. According to the logic of liberal thinking, money would always find the best use for itself, and if investors were granted the freedom to shift their funds at any time and to any point on the globe, the maximum efficiency of investment would be assured. This, of course, was quite true, but only on two conditions. First, it would need to be understood whom this efficiency served, and what purposes. Second, it was necessary to remember that maximum efficiency is not only quite different in the short and long terms, but often presupposes mutually exclusive decisions. The financial markets, oriented towards securing rapid and tangible gains for investors, naturally chose in favour of short-term decisions, on the principle of 'a bird in the hand is worth two in the bush'. In essence, liberal thinking arrived at a curious self-justification in which it claimed that *any* use of money that occurred on the market was the best possible simply for the reason that it had taken place, and had taken place in line with market principles.

In practice, the main consequence of setting the capital markets free was to bring about a massive transfer of funds to offshore zones where additional income could be obtained not through investing in the production of goods and services, but simply as a result of lower tax costs. The quantities of money available to the real sector diminished, and credit became expensive. Long-term projects stagnated or required ever-greater expenditures, while the businesses that engaged in them again appealed for help to the state, which had fewer funds as a consequence of its reduced tax base.

The economist Brooke Harrington, who worked for many years in the field of investment management, has shown that tax evasion turned long ago into a large-scale business resting on the activity of a highly paid professional elite. Further, the managers who help their clients to shelter from the tax authorities and to export their money to exotic islands honestly believe they are benefitting society. 'So many of us, if not all, see our work as primarily about helping people – not just our clients, but more generally by helping maintain capital flows for investment and economic growth. But we can't get this message out effectively.'[15]

Naturally, the problems associated with capital flight are distributed unequally between the centre and periphery of the capitalist system. Both have suffered from the development of offshore business, but in countries such as Russia the bourgeoisie has needed both 'safe harbours' where their assets can be hidden from taxation, but also 'respectable jurisdictions'[16] where dubiously acquired capital can be legalised and where a firm legal basis can be ensured for carrying on dealings. True, the Russian–Ukrainian war that erupted in 2022 showed how risky it can be to store money in Western banks where governments may confiscate it at any moment, but this became clear only in hindsight. Further, the regularly repeated histories involving Iranian, Iraqi and Russian funds, however instructive, have not altered the general politico-economic logic of the world-system: transferring capital from the periphery to the centre is not in any way viewed as evidence of a lack of patriotism on the part of the investors, but simply as part of the general logic of accumulation.

The offshore funds, accumulating capital both in the countries of the centre and in those of the periphery, have in turn created a new financial infrastructure, a global network for money transfers that operates by its own laws and has few ties to the needs of human beings (unless, of course, we count the owners of offshore capital and those who manage these funds).

Harrington's analysis of the activity of the offshore funds leads her to the pessimistic conclusion that a system has arisen that guarantees the existence of financial dynasties divorced from society, and most importantly, ensures the systematic maintenance and expansion of an inequality that has nothing to do with rewards for business success. This rupture can scarcely be put right without a revolution.[17]

Market destabilisation

The Great Recession, accompanied as it was by bank failures and a collapse on the US real estate market, revealed at a stroke the extent to which *market reforms had become a factor of chronic market destabilisation*. Neoliberal economists would, of course, repeat their usual mantras concerning 'mistakes by the regulators', the 'greed' of individual financial operators and the chain of 'unfortunate accidents' that had derailed a system that until then had worked impeccably. Meanwhile, governments and state banks resorted to their usual panacea, massively buying up the debt that had been created by private corporations. Very soon, however, it became clear that unless policies were changed there was no reason to hope that the crisis could be overcome. It might be possible to lessen its acuteness and revive falling demand by flooding the market with public money. Such nostrums, however, could do no more than alleviate the symptoms of the disease, while causing numerous side effects that would have to be coped with separately. The crisis of private indebtedness was replaced by a rapid increase in state debt, which in turn spread from one country to another, transforming some states into bankrupts and others into aggressive creditors.

A new blow soon followed: the global pandemic of Covid-19, which along with causing economic losses brought about tectonic shifts in mass consciousness. The pandemic demolished the familiar world of obvious ideas and practices, forcing millions of people to confront not so much a new reality as formerly concealed aspects of the reality in which, sometimes without realising it, they had previously lived.

A society that had grown used to mass consumption had come to perceive it as something self-evident, supposing, in the words of Baudrillard, that citizens enjoyed a 'natural right to abundance'.[18] As a result, abundance had

become something everyday and banal, experienced as an everyday miracle to the degree that it did not appear to be something produced, seized or conquered as a result of historical and social effort, but as something distributed by beneficent mythological authorities whose legal heirs we were: Technology, Progress, Growth, and so forth.[19]

The illusion had taken hold in society that the capitalist order, in the form in which it existed at the given moment, in and of itself ensured the consumer prosperity that with the light hand of Baudrillard could now be criticised and challenged. This prosperity was not understood as the result of the development of a whole series of class and political conflicts that had led the system to enact social reforms. To the contrary, it was perceived as a natural right that would, in the view of ordinary people, be preserved for them irrespective of how the further evolution or degradation of capitalism might proceed. Worse still, the worker masses were being drawn into a race to consume, a race with its own logic, momentum and scale, in which they were beginning inevitably to lay claim to a 'normal' way of life which they also viewed as natural and modern, but which was beyond their means.

Up to a certain point, this contradiction was resolved through the granting of massive credits to the population, enslaving them to financial organisations. These now appeared as the most obvious and fearsome oppressors, since *they no longer exploited the producer, but the consumer.* Workers did not feel the exploitation they suffered in the workplace to be as painful as the financial obligations beneath which they now laboured; work for a boss was becoming simply a means to provide financial capital with the opportunity to exploit them. Meanwhile, people who in any case chronically lacked the resources to maintain their consumer equilibrium found their situation especially painful when their accustomed world of consumption collapsed – as happened during the Covid epidemic of 2020–21.

In essence, the collapse of production and the cuts to consumption that resulted from the quarantine measures meant the breaking of the customary chains of reproduction that were indispensable for consumer society. Faced with this situation, the state was forced to maintain equilibrium artificially, through payments of all kinds. As became apparent, it was possible to employ financial resources while producing nothing, or at any rate, while sharply reducing output. This not only showed the flexibility of the modern economy, able to calmly endure a large-scale breach of market equilibrium, but also demonstrated that for the ruling class, preserving financial and consumption chains at least in a certain form was even more important than the market and production. The fact that this was purely a tactical decision was another matter entirely. In this case, moreover, the tactic was aimed at postponing for as long as possible the solving of far more profound, systemic contradictions.

In supporting consumers, the state in the first instance was rescuing financial and commercial capital, which would otherwise have been forced to bear the burden of the crisis. This was in line with the usual neoliberal principle of *the socialisation of losses and the privatisation of profits*, but at the same time created new structural disproportions, in this case between various factions of capital – notably, those that had gained and those that had lost in the course of the crisis. A further aspect of what was occurring was a large-scale *resort to non-market methods of distribution in order to save the market*. Once again, elements of socialism were being rolled out in order to stabilise capitalism. Nevertheless, the escape from this situation created a new problem, in the form of an unavoidable choice between returning to the pre-crisis 'norm' (with the guarantee of a swift return to crisis in some new form), or the further development of these trends to the point where they began to change the nature of social and productive relations. This in turn was to become the terrain of a political struggle.

A moment of truth

Early in the twentieth century György Lukács, analysing the response of economists to crises, reached the natural conclusion:

> For the bourgeoisie it is vitally important on the one hand to view their own system of production as if it was formed from categories with a timeless significance, that is, as if it is destined by eternal laws of nature and reason to exist forever, while on the other hand it is important to interpret

the constantly intensifying contradictions not as inseparable from the essence of this system of production, but merely as surface phenomena and so forth.[20]

Every crisis is declared to be the result of a chain of fortuitous events, just as each crisis is presented as unlike its predecessors, so that it becomes impossible to understand what unites these developments and what causes the crises to be repeated so regularly. Ultimately, the question of theory becomes one of class interests. The problem does not lie in the weakness of the methodology employed by the researchers, and not even in the ideological bias of the authors of such texts; it is simply that 'a theory of the economy in which crises are seen as a necessity must simultaneously involve a rejection of capitalism.'[21]

At the same time, the regular succession of crises, demonstrating the weakness and contradictions of society, is not bringing us any closer to social changes. In a time of crisis, the bourgeois economic order breaks down. The trouble is, however, that after each crisis the ruling class proves able once again to set the economic process back in motion on more or less the same basis, while perhaps correcting a few technical details that were the direct (though not the underlying, systemic) cause of the downturn. Overcoming crises on the systemic level requires addressing the alignment of social and political forces.

The Great Depression of 1928–32, whose consequences were finally overcome only after the Second World War, culminated in profound reforms enacted under the pressure of the labour movement and left forces *within* the countries of the capitalist centre, and against a backdrop of *external* pressure from the increasingly powerful Soviet Union. Conversely, the Great Recession, despite the deep shocks that accompanied it, not only failed to bring about a rejection of the neoliberal model of development, but to the contrary, provoked a new wave of antisocial reforms and attacks on the democratic rights of citizens in most developed countries. The reason is obvious: this time, capital was not under serious *political* pressure either from within or without. The Soviet Union ceased to exist long ago, and China, despite officially still adhering to a 'Red' ideology, is a thoroughly capitalist power. Unlike the USSR, the Chinese leadership has not sought even on the ideological level to present its social model as a global systemic alternative that can and should be reproduced in other parts of the world. Consequently, the increasing stand-off between the West and China has turned into a completely traditional form of competition for markets and resources.

Unlike the Cold War between the 1940s and 1970s, this confrontation has not only failed to assist in strengthening democracy and the development of the welfare state in the West or the processes of decolonisation in Asia and Africa, but to the contrary, has created the conditions for a more ruthless assault on the rights of working people in the most diverse parts of the world. The Chinese entrepreneurs who act as exporters of capital have insisted aggressively on rejecting high wages, long holidays and guarantees of employment. The opportunity for harsh and pitiless exploitation of workers is seen by the young Chinese bourgeoisie as a crucially important condition that any country counting on their investment should have to meet.

Marx observed that when workers' organisations and parties struggle against exploitation, they become a force able to 'do away with or mitigate the destructive consequences for their class of this law of capitalist production'.[22] In conditions of crisis, however, the stakes increase dramatically. As Lukács noted, during such historical periods workers need to shift from 'delaying, weakening, restraining actions' to active efforts to change society.[23] This, however, signifies not only the need to renounce the familiar, 'pre-crisis' rules of behaviour, but also a readiness for harsh confrontation. The more objectively pressing the indispensable measures become, the more seriously the ruling elites will resist them, since at this stage it is impossible to alter the situation without infringing on their interests:

> The measures through which the bourgeoisie hopes to overcome the dead point of the crisis are, speaking in the abstract, available to it even today (if it could take its mind off the meddling of the proletariat), and just as during previous crises, are becoming the arena for open class warfare. Violence is becoming the decisive economic force in the situation.[24]

The dismantling of social reforms that took place during the last two decades of the twentieth century and the first two decades of the twenty-first not only created the preconditions for a diverse series of conflicts and crises. It also turned every new decision by the ruling classes into the source of fresh difficulties of ever-greater magnitude, giving rise to a sort of global revolutionary situation.

6

A Kaleidoscope of Problems and Opportunities

In the late twentieth century appeals for radical reforms and criticism of capitalist globalisation had been perceived as a clearly marginal discourse. But by the 2010s, after the Great Recession, such reasoning had become part of the mainstream. It was another matter entirely that in describing the symptoms of the unfolding crisis both the radical critics of the system and also many representatives of the establishment sought to avoid discussing the contradictions between labour and capital or analysing social processes, preferring to shift attention onto other problems that while very important, were viewed on a fundamentally different plane.

There was a whole bouquet of such topics, which while undoubtedly pressing, were far less painful in their ideological and political respects. These included the climate crisis, as well as questions linked to the implementation of new technologies, the hypertrophic development of financial capital, and the growth of new social needs in developed countries. All of these issues formed a natural accompaniment to the evolution of the capitalist world-system in the latest phase of its history. The only question was whether a full resolution of these problems could be achieved without affecting much more fundamental elements of the existing order.

The climate crisis

By the beginning of the 2000s climate change had come to be perceived as the main challenge confronting humanity in the twenty-first century. The overwhelming majority of scientists and politicians supported the conclusions of the researchers who insisted that the main reason why atmospheric temperatures were rising was the large-scale burning of fossil fuels. It is true that a few holdouts in the scientific community disputed this conclusion, but one way or another, climate change was occurring. The reasons for taking the problem seriously were indeed compelling, but discussion on the social transformations that were required by the changing climatic situation, and that were now overdue, soon entered a dead end. Overall, the discussion focused not on social and economic reforms but on technologies and scientific theories, and moreover, was conducted largely by dilettantes who had little knowledge of either technology or science.

In any case, and regardless of the climate science, the discussion finished up essentially confined to ways of transforming the structures of capitalist society. As Eve Croeser notes, left activists were divided into those who considered that capitalism could not be reformed in the ways needed to solve the climate crisis, and more moderate elements who argued that partial reforms were nevertheless possible, and who sought to 'use such reforms as a platform for more radical and fundamental change'.[1] The critical problem, however, had to do not with the climate but with the economic interests that in one way or another were affected by the environmental agenda. Whatever technological decisions might be taken, the obvious question arose: 'Who is going to foot the bill?'

By the mid-2010s a rapid change in the dominant discourse, from denying the existence of a climate problem, to transforming it into the theme of international summit meetings of heads of state and governments, indicated that the ruling class had more or less decided on its agenda. The essence of this approach lay in mobilising public opinion to support measures aimed at solving environmental problems through a sharp reduction in the use of fossil fuels – in practice, solving the problems associated with restructuring the economy in ways that left the interests of corporate capital fundamentally intact. The corporate environmental agenda required working people to make sacrifices in order to maintain the effectiveness of capital. In other words, it amounted to *expropriating the middle classes and intensifying the exploitation of workers in the name of 'saving the planet'.*

Reviewing the environmental agenda as set out in presentations by Greta Thunberg and other popular activists, the economic journalist Nikolay Protsenko has concluded that this movement is 'fully and organically incorporated into the new aims of the corporations'.[2] The implementation of new technologies, indispensable not only for solving environmental problems, but also for stimulating economic growth within the framework of such an agenda, has to be funded from the public purse and is required to serve the interests of big capital. As Protsenko observes, the oil and gas corporations are willingly reducing their investments in profitable resource projects and in the refining of hydrocarbons, while at the same time demanding huge subsidies from the state in order to undertake loss-making 'clean' energy programmes. Where governments cannot cope with the strain, global financial markets come to their aid. Hence the European Union Recovery Instrument, founded in 2020, set about financing investments of 750 billion euros, needed to ensure the energy transition, on the condition that the funds would be obtained through borrowings on the international financial markets.[3] As Protsenko notes, those who will have to pay back the loans will be the generation of Greta Thunberg, people who support this agenda enthusiastically but show no inclination to discuss its financial component.

An important aspect of the decarbonisation policy is the introduction of a carbon tax, or more precisely, of penalty duties to be imposed on goods and services imported into the European Union in proportion to the size of their carbon footprint. For several decades, whenever concerns over the environment have mounted in Western countries, European and American corporations have systematically transferred 'dirty' production into poorer countries that are now in addition compelled to pay the costs associated with the new climate agenda. This policy might aid indirectly in securing the return – on a new technological and environmental level – of a proportion of industrial production to historically more developed countries, but in any case what is involved is the reproduction and even deepening of global inequality. 'It is obvious', Protsenko concludes, 'that such an approach simply reproduces the established relations between the centre and periphery of the world capitalist system, reflecting the inequality of opportunities within the process of capitalist accumulation.'[4]

It does not, of course, follow from the above that members of the left should refrain from showing concern about the environment:

> The problem is simply that such goal-setting totally contradicts the nature of capitalism, a dynamically imbalanced system that engages constantly in 'creative destruction', and that is based on the principle of endless accumulation distributed unequally between its core and periphery. The much-celebrated energy transition is precisely a new cycle of creative destruction. To lend capitalism new stimuli requires liquidating its earlier technological platform, based on fossil fuels, and replacing it with 'green' technologies. All the losses will normally be levied on the state (and ultimately on taxpayers), while the profits will be privatised by the corporations.[5]

The 'yellow vests' movement in France has already shown the reverse side of this agenda, with the latest 'environmental' tax on fossil fuels hitting hard at the budgets of the poorest provincial families, and naturally provoking massive protests. Uncritical acceptance of the environmental discourse in the form in which it is advanced by the ruling circles and the non-governmental organisations that are financed by them (and that are united in supporting the impassioned speeches of Greta Thunberg) is drawing the left into a strategy of seeking a renewal of capitalism. Not only does this strategy fail to propose any serious concessions to the lower ranks of society, but to the contrary, it promises a still more radical division and segregation of society, on both the national and global level. Meanwhile, the poorest and most vulnerable layers of society are not just falling victim to the structural reordering, but also appear 'guilty' of environmentally irresponsible behaviour, while their resistance is viewed as amoral.

To what extent this strategy is able in principle to be applied, either on the social or on the organisational and technical level, remains an important question. It is obvious, however, that the environmental agenda does not have a genuine answer to the crisis of capitalism, and merely provides a pretext for unleashing a new and bitter struggle, in the course of which all the systemic contradictions will appear in full measure. Implementing environmental reforms in the interests of the majority of humanity (or even while taking their interests into account) is impossible in principle so long as the bourgeois order survives in its present form.

The technological transition

The crisis suffered by the left around the turn of the twenty-first century was by no means solely the result of ideological factors, but also reflected objective changes in the economy and social structure of capitalist societies. Paradoxically (or dialectically), these processes on the one hand undermined the positions of the traditional left, rendering many of its habitual approaches irrelevant, while on the other hand they created problems and contradictions that bourgeois politics proved unable to resolve.

While environmental activists heaped criticism on industrial production that poisoned the natural surroundings and that contradicted the logic of nature, large companies installed new technologies that radically altered the situation in this area. It is true that these changes were enacted only after lengthy delays, if we take into account scientific and engineering developments that anticipated these shifts by almost half a century.

The widespread installation of robots and radical changes to the labour market had begun to be predicted in the late 1970s, and even then many technologies had provided a basis for warnings that in the near future robots would force workers out of their jobs on a massive scale, not just in industry but also in transport, and later in the area of services as well. During this period, however, capital placed its stake not on automation but on the use of cheap labour power. It was only rising wage costs in China and other Asian countries, combined with the exhaustion of consumer demand in the old industrial countries that were suffering from the loss of 'good' jobs and from capital outflows, that forced a turn to employing technological solutions that had been available several decades earlier.

The new equipment not only altered the structure of employment and transformed the labour market, but also brought changes to economic geography, shifting production from some regions to others depending on the availability of resources, the location of sales markets, and whether transport infrastructure was optimal for particular technologies or types of production. As has been seen, the question of the relationship of class forces and the price of labour power in various countries is not simply one of the factors bearing on this process, but also plays an ever more important role within it. While capital in the late twentieth century shifted production from Europe and other developed countries to Asia, undermining the position of the working class in the old industrial countries, the growing cost of labour power in the newly industrialising states now meant that little by little, production began returning to Europe and the US. During the first stage 'cheap' Asians had blocked the introduction of robots, but now, the increasingly expensive Asian workers were at risk from the advance of robot technology. Shifting between markets and implementing one or another productive solution on a global level, capital simultaneously provoked problems on local labour markets and gave rise to social crises.

It was quite natural that the advent of robots and the growing productivity of industrial equipment would prompt a further outburst of discussion on machines forcing people out of their jobs. This discussion had gone on since the nineteenth century, first flaring up and then dying down as each time economic growth caused the question of disappearing jobs to vanish from people's attention. This time, a special alarm was inspired by the fact that economic modernisation had started to affect sectors, from the banking industry to the management of warehouses, in which living labour had earlier played the decisive role, while mechanisation had stayed minimal. Driverless vehicles and automatic transport systems threatened to leave large numbers of transport workers jobless. In the mid-2010s reflections on a happy 'world without work', or alternatively, a society struck by chronic and almost total unemployment began once again to agitate numerous sociologists and futurologists. The actual course of events, however, has since shown that the real processes are developing in a quite different fashion.

Each time labour-saving technologies are applied on a large scale, this is accompanied not only by the appearance of a multitude of new specialised jobs, but also by growth in the economy. Under capitalism no-one implements technology simply in order to lighten people's workloads or to allow them access to new opportunities. Technologies are applied in order to raise profitability, to increase the volume of production and to expand sales markets. Cheapening production makes goods more affordable, and their production takes on more of a mass character. This growing production again creates a demand for labour power, but now with different skills. At the same time, it becomes clear that people who do something unique or individual (from making video blogs, to fashioning distinctive craft products) remain irreplaceable. In this situation the nature of management changes as well. As labour grows more individualised, management using traditional methods becomes less productive. *Management as organisation* comes spontaneously to be replaced by a struggle for loyalty, by *management as monitoring*. The manager is transformed into a supervisor, including with relation to the people who are engaged in creative work. New sectors and types of activity emerge. Mechanisation and automation come to affect the sphere of services, while at the same time increasing the demand for services and the corresponding total employment.

Historical experience has shown that despite the whole range of social problems created by technological progress, Marx and Engels were nevertheless correct *on the whole* when they saw in the development of the productive forces a stimulus to social change and an objective basis for workers to advance new and more radical demands. On each occasion, however, technological shifts have not simply created new forms of exploitation, control and resistance, but have also altered the character of work itself, while at the same time transforming the tasks of the struggle for its liberation.

As in the early stages of the Industrial Revolution, the new technologies have not only sharpened social contradictions, placing many old professions in jeopardy or even doing away with them entirely, but at the same time have also created a rapidly growing demand for new categories of workers, a demand that often outstrips supply. Just as the Industrial Revolution created the conditions for an upsurge of workers' struggle, the new wave of automation and the emergence of information technologies have given rise not just to new conflicts, but also to a situation in which professional groups that previously have not taken part in serious conflicts, or that simply did not exist, have been drawn into a struggle for their rights. Meanwhile, the conflicts involved have mostly taken on forms quite different from those that characterised the activity and behaviour of the proletariat in the classical industrial epoch. Consequently, the methods of the left and the forms of trade union organisation that took shape during those times have proven inadequate to the new reality.

The problems that have arisen in the labour markets of many countries since the Covid pandemic have shown that at least in the immediate future, and despite all the technological innovations, there is no need to talk of workers being supplanted by robots. In many countries, the economic rebound that has followed the pandemic recession has led to shortages of labour power. The crisis in the US labour market since the pandemic has put a full stop to discussion of the 'disappearance of work'. This crisis has seen workers, taking advantage of their emergency aid packages, begin to quit their jobs in massive numbers. While citing the emergence of new medical risks, people have meanwhile demanded higher pay that can compete with the increased level of social benefits. These developments, unfolding in the US from late in 2021, have come to be known as the 'Great Resignation'.

Millions of people have refused to return to their jobs, demanding wage hikes. In the US there were more than four million such cases. The economist Robert Reich, who worked in the Ministry of Labor during the administration of Bill Clinton, has admitted that people 'don't want to return to backbreaking or boring, low-wage, shit jobs. Workers are burnt out. They're fed up. They're fried. In the wake of so much hardship and illness and death during the past year, they're not going to take it any more.'[6]

For the first time in half a century, the situation that working people are encountering in the labour market is on the whole to their benefit, and is changing the relationship of forces in their favour. But even though workers have sensed this at an elemental level, left-wing politicians and activists have grasped it only to an insignificant degree, instead remaining captive to their outmoded ideas.

Leisure time

Discussing future possibilities and the chances of progressive social change, the British sociologists Nick Srnicek and Alex Williams write that despite the political weakness of the left, the technical opportunities for realising its agenda during the twenty-first century are extremely favourable: 'Many of the classic demands of the left – for less work, for an end to scarcity, for economic democracy, for the production of socially useful goods, and for the liberation of humanity – are materially more achievable than at any other point in history.'[7] It is hard to disagree with this. But to what degree is the left itself able to formulate a radical agenda, and to grasp the opportunities that are opening up before it? This is particularly evident in the discussion that has unfolded in the early twenty-first century on cuts to the working week.

The demand for a reduction of work hours, in itself, is nothing new. As the Swiss economist Stefan Liebig has noted, 'the struggle over work time is as old as capitalism itself'.[8] Marx wrote in *Capital* that ultimately, every economy can be reduced to an economy of time. In the twenty-first century, however, this topic has come to the forefront after a lengthy period during which a more or less stable system remained in place. This system was established early in the previous century, when in most countries the struggle for an eight-hour working day, and later for a five-day working week, was crowned with success. It was at this time that the principle of '8-8-8', of an equal distribution of time each day between sleep, work and leisure, came to be formulated.

In the twenty-first century the demand from the left for a shorter working week has been based on the growth of labour productivity and social wealth. Hence the influential German trade union IG Metall has put forward the demand for work hours to be reduced to twenty-eight per week. There was also talk of providing workers with multi-month holidays. No less important, however, was the fact that the reforming of the 'economy of time' was being undertaken by capital itself, and in a very practical and effective fashion. New technologies, distance work and working from home, the use of ever more individualised and intellectual labour, and numerous other innovations not only ensured flexibility in the distribution of work tasks among the hours and days of the week, but also dissolved the boundaries between work time and leisure, making the normative regulation of time meaningless in many cases. The demand for a shorter work week, however, remained relevant for traditional industrial employment and for the swiftly expanding number of office jobs. Here too, however, serious questions arose, and with astonishing consistency, were ignored by the left.

The most important of these questions was: what was leisure time needed for anyway? A shorter work week would free up time for 'social communication, family and culture', the Swiss feminist Anna Lindmeier declared.[9] In other words, for private life outside of society and production. But even if we accept such a conventional, middlebrow view of life, it is by no means obvious that people with more free hours at their disposal will use this time more sensibly. Meanwhile, it is clear that on the economic level, modern bourgeois society will reduce 'social communication, family and culture' to consumption. Here, as people used to say in the early twentieth century, is 'the nub of the question'.

The economics of time is subject to the general logic of development of the productive and social relations that take shape within a given system. Despite the fact that the ruling class in every epoch has sought to increase the efficiency and intensiveness of exploitation, its interests have never been confined simply to increasing the length of the working day. Further, in a capitalist market economy work time and leisure are inextricably interlinked.

During the period of classical industrialism in the nineteenth and twentieth centuries the politico-economic function of leisure consisted in the reproduction of labour power, in the restoring of the capacity of hired workers for labour. In late industrial society, however, consumption has become a no less important matter. To develop and reproduce itself, capital needs the consumer no less than the worker. Increased leisure and paid holidays for workers made it possible to expand the sphere of services, and created the conditions for the development of consumer society. At the same time, the significance of the 'economy of time' for the elites and for the lower ranks of society has always been fundamentally different. While for workers the question was of the right to rest (indispensable, as we have already seen, for reproducing the very possibility of the exploitation of labour), for the elites since ancient times leisure has meant the opportunity for creativity, and for participation in civic affairs and government. In other words, *the social meaning of time for different classes has been fundamentally different.* In a society with limited resources, it was precisely the separating off of a certain number of people who were not burdened by the need to ensure their survival that created the possibility for the development of science, culture and art, and for the improvement of various social practices.

If we are to understand management not simply as the mechanical reproduction of routine bureaucratic functions, but as a creative activity aimed at mutual interaction with other people, then it is the freedom to allot one's time that becomes a critically important factor of success. Meanwhile the ruling classes, apart from possessing a large number of leisure hours, have also lived since time immemorial under a 'flexible' regime. After all, no-one can precisely determine whether, for example, the hours spent by a company boss with business partners in an expensive restaurant are part of their work time or leisure.

The German sociologist Andreas Reckwitz notes an increasing gap that has appeared between two types of workers in the labour market in the early twenty-first century. On the one hand we see representatives of the new creative professions devising unique and singular products meant to satisfy a growing need, painstakingly stimulated in society, for individualised consumption (which is itself transformed into a means of demonstrating one's individuality). The members of these professions make up a creative middle class, consisting of people equipped not just with high qualifications but also with certain personal characteristics and possibilities, with cultural capital and simply with personal ties that allow them to occupy a certain niche. The use that an entrepreneur is able to make of such employees is not limited by their work time, since it is the individual personality of the worker that becomes an object of exploitation and of competitive advantage in the labour market.

On the other hand we have the 'new poor', not just engaged in routine drudgery for low wages, but also subject to constant cultural pressure.[10] The labour of this class, and the attributes of its members, are devalued amid the universal hunt for individual achievements. Often, these people are involved in directly serving the creative economy. 'Highly successful and prestigious professions enjoying international appeal thus coexist in the creative economy with middle-class professional groups employed on standard work conditions, and also with groups whose terms of employment provide them only with low pay and unstable jobs.'[11] As a result, the impossibility of limiting work time to a set number of hours is evident at both the high and low levels of the social and employment hierarchy. In some cases work time simply cannot be divided from time spent on personal development, while in other cases there is simply no such thing as stable work with set hours.

The events of 2020 and 2021, when as a result of the Covid-19 pandemic multitudes of people had to work from home or from a distance, brought a serious rethinking of the economic significance of leisure time and work time. It also revived a number of practices characteristic of medieval dispersed manufacturing, when each craftsperson worked independently using their own equipment, at the same time as remaining subject to control by the owner of capital. Twenty-first-century dispersed manufacturing has reproduced the relations typical of the earliest forms of bourgeois production, but on a new scale and on a new technological level. Among employees of large companies, the transformation of freelancers into hired workers (both de facto and officially) has been combined with the simultaneous spread of working from home. This tendency, noticeable even before the pandemic, increased sharply once a wide range of restrictions, meant to limit the spread of the disease, came to be imposed throughout the world. Economists wrote of 'serious shifts in the preferences of workers', involving not only a readiness and wish to work from home, but also a desire on the part of workers to ensure for themselves 'a formalisation of labour relations', which in essence meant 'both increased rights and social guarantees'.[12] What was involved, of course, was not just the 'desires' of workers, but the fact that the changes in the labour market had placed them in a stronger position. Thanks to the new conditions – in which, unexpectedly for both sides, a new relationship of class forces had begun to take shape – the workers now had the chance to turn their desires into demands. As noted by the British economist Joseph Choonara, the companies in turn made use of the shift to working from home in order to enforce the intensity and duration of labour.[13] As a result the new conditions of production, creating new opportunities both for workers and for their exploitation, in themselves became a new space for class and political conflict.

The Russian sociologist Konstantin Gaaze has observed that the new forms of exploitation and the transformation of the worker's dwelling into part of the productive and technological expanse are also giving rise to new types of resistance. These include protests against 'the attack on leisure, on the remnants of the autonomous diversity of life-styles'.[14] In the twenty-first century the problem of the alienation of the individual, a problem created by capitalism and that in the twentieth century mostly remained philosophical and psychological, is becoming directly social and even part of daily life. At the same time, however, the merging of productive and personal space, of economic life and everyday activity, of hired labour and people's personal existence is also creating the potential for a 'capture' of the organisational and technological expanse by working people, who project onto it their own personal needs. This is once again placing on the agenda the question of productive self-management and economic democracy.

In the words of Gaaze, 'the pandemic removed the last barriers, inherited from the industrial epoch, between work time on the one hand and leisure and idleness on the other. It did away with the autonomy of private space that ensured this boundary.'[15] This situation has created new opportunities for control and exploitation, in essence forcing the worker to subsidise the firm (with their own premises, electrical energy, computer equipment and programs, and most importantly, time), while at the same time demonstrating how much they have become an independent, self-sufficient unit within the system of productive organisation. Horizontal coordination between workers becomes technically possible, as does the creation by them of independent associations on the basis of already established links.

Modern technological conditions, and the growing level of education of the population, are making it possible to undermine the monopoly of the ruling classes on managerial power, to change the nature of the social division of labour, and ultimately, to make the bourgeoisie unnecessary to the reproduction of the economy. This approach, however, does not presuppose a mechanical reduction of the working day, but a quite new attitude both to work and to leisure, along with overcoming the gap between them and integrating them into a *unified creative process*. For free citizens, time is indispensable not in order to permit an endlessly prolonged 'leisure' filled with consumption, computer games, dim-witted television serials, drunkenness and family squabbles, but for taking part in administration, and for participation in the making of political, social and productive decisions – in other words, for ordinary citizens to have access to the most important and socially significant types of activity, which earlier were reserved for the ruling classes and for specialised elites. The key question here is not how time is distributed between work and leisure, but altering the social nature, cultural-psychological meaning, character and content of work itself. We do not need to work less but to *work differently*, overcoming alienation through combining work with creative activity. Modern technologies allow us this possibility. For it to become a reality, however, a different politics is needed, and above all, a completely different left agenda. That is, an agenda aimed not at a moderate redistribution of resources within the framework of the existing system, but at its structural transformation.

Money for everyone (universal basic income)

Together with the rapid growth in importance of the financial sector, the appearance of new technologies and the need to reorganise the labour market, the crisis of the neoliberal economic model has inspired a number of innovative projects that offer society answers if not to all of its important questions, then at least to many of them. The most popular and widely discussed of these projects are universal basic income (UBI) and modern monetary theory (MMT). The more cautious adherents of these concepts, of course, stress that neither of them offers a means of solving all problems, but this is nevertheless how popular consciousness at times perceives them. In particular, everyday consciousness often misses the fact that these two concepts not only fail to supplement, but clearly contradict one another.

At first glance, the concept of 'universal basic income' seems almost a realisation, under capitalist conditions, of the communist utopia of universal guaranteed well-being. After all, this idea proposes that all citizens, regardless of whether they work (and of how useful to society their work might be) will receive from the state a guaranteed income that allows them to exist above the poverty line. To critics who object that in those circumstances no-one would work at all, the supporters of UBI quite reasonably reply: the people who are interested in their work will nevertheless keep doing it. Productive activities and the provision of services to the fortunate population will be carried on by people who like what they do, along with robots, immigrants and residents of poor countries whose governments cannot or do not wish to implement the prescription for universal happiness.

It was not by chance that the idea of a universal basic income (sometimes presented as a 'citizens' income') arose simultaneously with the triumph of neoliberalism. The concept represented one of the versions of the program-matic adaptation by the left to this triumph. As a proposition, UBI achieved its greatest spread during the 2010s, later taking on a renewed popularity in connection with the massive payments to the population and to busi-ness that governments were forced to make during the Covid pandemic. Despite the fears of orthodox economists, the providing to the population of this 'helicopter money', which according to journalists was handed out to all without distinction, did not bring down the economy. Meanwhile, it inspired the supporters of UBI to vigorously canvass their ideas. In reality, however, these ideas were not especially new. In 1994 David Purdy put forward this concept in the pages of *New Left Review*, presenting it as a basis for consensus between socialists and liberals, while at the same time arguing that this practice might become a 'modern, dynamic and emancipatory successor to the welfare state'.[16] If we dispense with the eloquent progressive rhetoric, the main essence here is a belief in the necessity, and inevitability, of annulling the welfare state with all its conquests and institutions.

The readiness with which all the proposals for a UBI advanced by the left have found support among members of the right is clearly to be explained on the basis that this concept reproduces the ideological principles of neoliberalism, breaking not just with the traditions of left thought, but also with the ideas of classical liberalism.[17] The concept of the welfare state originated in the idea that there were *public goods* that should not only be *accessible to all*, but should be utilised by people *jointly* (and primarily on a non-monetary basis). Neoliberalism, by contrast, postulates that society as a unitary organism does not exist, and that there is only a totality of physical and juridical persons acting as agents of the market and as needed, obtaining for money – in proportion to their income – everything essential to them.

Among the supporters of neoliberalism, the only difference is that radical adherents are willing to reconcile themselves to the view that beggars and vagrants of various kinds who are incapable (again, on a market basis) of earning the money they need should not lay claim to assistance of any type, while more moderate and reasonable political figures have been prepared to support the poorest layers of society through state philanthropy in the form of *targeted help* or *free-of-charge services*. That these services should be acquired on the market (even if the direct recipient does not pay for them out of their own pocket) is not in this case subject to doubt.

The supporters of state philanthropy, meanwhile, have not been guided solely by a love of humanity, since monetary compensation payments (monetised benefits) expand the client base of the corporations engaged in providing services, and stimulate the market when it suffers from a narrowing of demand. Properly speaking, stimulation of the market using government funds, which ultimately are redistributed to the advantage of the private sector, is a common element in all such projects irrespective of how they might be formulated in ideological terms.

If presented to us in progressive packaging, the concept of a universal basic income has of course greater chances of winning support (or to put it more simply, of being sold to society) than if put forward in its 'bare' economic form as a means of sustaining demand under conditions in which social reforms are invariably rejected. Here we find another attempt if not to resolve, then at least to mitigate the contradiction between rejection of the welfare state and preservation of the consumer society. This attempt has scant chances of being successful, but it testifies to the growing understanding of the problem at least among experts close to the elites. Why, however, should members of the left promote this idea? One can only recall the words of Baudrillard:

> Would it not make sense to accept as objective social progress (inclusion as 'rights' in the table of the law) something that amounts to progress of the capitalist system, that is, a gradual transformation of all concrete and natural values into productive forms, and specifically, into the sources (1) of economic gain and (2) of social privilege?[18]

In this case the ideologues of universal basic income proceed from the same postulates as all the other fighters against the welfare state, failing to understand (or pretending not to understand) the meaning of collective consumption and of the corresponding organisation of public goods (which, in essence, is an objective necessity not only for socialism, but for any modern society). While the left tradition proposes a broadening of this field through the *decommodification* of numerous areas of life, the concept of UBI proposes an expansion of commodity-market relations to more and more practices that earlier were protected from the market.[19]

From the point of view of economic efficiency we are of course faced with an obvious absurdity, since supplying people on an individual basis with everything that might be organised and guaranteed collectively would involve monstrous waste, with a rapid growth of transactional costs. This is confirmed by the whole experience of privatising social services both in the West and in Eastern Europe. In this case, public goods would fall victim to private interests. The question of how, by whom and on what the famous basic income would be spent actually means little. What is important is the fact that the state, through mobilising its funds, would have to support activity on the market amid a crisis of demand caused by neoliberal reforms.

Further, the concept of UBI does not in fact assume in any way that people will curtail their labour activity. To the contrary, the essence of the concept lies in once again reorganising the labour market to suit capital and the bureaucracy. In circumstances where the dismantling of the welfare state over decades has led to a weakening of demand from the groups within the population who are poorest and who are increasingly worried about their survival, the new concept suggests simultaneously stimulating the economy and simplifying social policy, principally on a market basis. In place of many different benefits there will be one general benefit, greatly simplifying the work of bureaucrats. Instead of citizens concerning themselves with the practical performance of a range of social tasks, organising themselves to provide numerous public goods and running socialised investment programmes, they are to be supplied with particular sums of money to obtain the various goods and services on the market. Instead of joint work on shared tasks, we are offered the guaranteed possibility of buying everything we need.[20]

Of course, such a scheme would not work, since it would encounter all the 'market failures' that were studied by Schumpeter, as a result of which the need has arisen for the deliberate creation of public goods even under capitalism. In this case, however, it is not the practicality of the model that is fundamentally important, but something else: diverting discussion away from the question of how to restore the welfare state while socialising diverse areas of human activity and production, and directing it onto consideration of the practical possibilities of implementing the latest utopia. The purpose of the propaganda surrounding UBI is not in the least to implant elements of communist distribution in a bourgeois society saturated with the ideology of extreme individualism and the market. As Konstantin Gaaze has correctly remarked, this concept is 'a scenario for slowing down capitalism to the greatest extent possible'. The bourgeois system should 'become unnoticeable while remaining all-powerful, and while transforming itself into a natural force akin to the movement of continents'.[21]

Money for everyone (MMT)

Unlike the market utopias that propose to achieve happiness through distributing money to individual sufferers, the concept of modern monetary theory (MMT) aims to secure active state financing for diverse programmes regardless of the limits accepted by orthodox monetary theory, which presents state finances as an expanded version of a family budget.

It is not surprising that the active supporter of MMT Randall Wray has sharply criticised the idea of a universal basic income. The degree to which the concept embraced by Wray and his colleagues is able to solve the accumulated economic problems of the modern world is not in fact particularly important. The key issue lies elsewhere: if MMT, which is one of the modern versions of Keynesianism, addresses the question of how to restructure the economy, ensure universal employment and create stimuli for increased output, then UBI, whatever the eloquent words in which it is cloaked, is about how to reconcile as many people as possible in wealthy countries to a passive existence under the conditions of a stagnating neoliberal system.

For some three decades the representatives of the neoliberal economic mainstream have sought to convince their audiences that there is no fundamental difference between household finances and those of the state. Although this idea is obviously absurd – households cannot print their own money, change the sources and dimensions of their income through political decisions, and most importantly, restructure and stimulate the economic environment in which they operate – this logic is perceived by public opinion as perfectly natural.

In their day, Marx and Engels mocked theories based on simplistic models of the interaction of market subjects acting as if outside society and outside any technological, cultural and political context. In these models, it was as if economic processes were played out on an island uninhabited except for Robinson Crusoe and his 'Man Friday'. The analogy between a state and a household is simply an extended version of this storyteller's fantasy. According to this approach, the only danger with which the state has to contend is that it will begin living beyond its means, and having fallen into debt, will stimulate inflation. The main danger with inflation, in this version, is that it will lead to a devaluation of money savings and thus create problems for financial capital.

The supporters of MMT, in their turn, begin by explaining to their readers the elementary truth that 'the federal budget is fundamentally different from your household budget'.[22] On this basis, they show that a state budget deficit is far less dangerous than is commonly supposed, and most important, does not automatically cause an outburst of inflation. Everything depends on how state spending is directed, and what economic effect this spending creates.

The rise of this new theory of money is tied up inextricably with the general processes of the financialisation of capitalism, playing out around the turn of the twenty-first century, and with the contradictions of these processes. The MMT theoreticians reject the warnings of liberal economists who suffer from a paranoid fear of inflation (with which, in any case, they are incapable of dealing despite all their efforts). The limitation of the market is that it 'sees' only effective demand. Social needs that are not supplied by monetary flows (and accordingly, by current demand) remain seemingly outside the bounds of the economy, unless the state itself acts as a centralised customer and client. To liberal thinkers, however, this latter is in itself a violation of the 'natural' order of things (despite being welcomed by practical-minded bourgeois politicians during times of crisis). Not only do the countless needs that do not figure as 'demand' remain unsatisfied, but significant resources for whose development the financial means are currently lacking remain unused. The result is a crisis in which there are both people who are prepared to consume goods and goods that are not finding consumers, but in which the two sides cannot 'meet' for lack of a financial intermediary at the necessary time and place. The situation with labour is directly similar. Under the conditions of modern capitalism, it is easier for the governments of developed countries to pay people benefits or a 'universal basic income' in order for them not to work than it is to create jobs that would allow them to engage in useful and meaningful activity. There are people who are prepared and anxious to work, just as there are numerous economic and social tasks that can be fulfilled through their labour. But there are no jobs that correspond to these tasks, since the financial flows have not been set up.

Theories in the area of MMT have been put forward by a whole group of economists who base themselves on the ideas of J.M. Keynes, and who along with others include Warren Mosler, Randall Wray, Pavlina Tcherneva and Stephanie Kelton. It is important to note that the theoretical approaches of this group of researchers have almost always been at the epicentre of fierce political discussions. For example, Stephanie Kelton was an advisor to US Senator Bernie Sanders, and took part actively in his election campaign.

MMT insists that how money functions depends in the first instance on the tax policy of the state. One of the founders of this theory, Randall Wray, stresses that it is the tax system that ensures the effective circulation of money in the economy: 'The government cannot easily force others to use its currency in private payments, or to hoard it in piggybanks, but government can force use of currency to meet the tax obligations that it imposes.'[23]

Unlike orthodox economists, who see the levying of taxes simply as a means of funding the budget, the supporters of MMT are more inclined to view taxation as an instrument for managing the economy. The aim of a progressive tax is not to redistribute financial resources, but to stimulate particular economic processes and behaviour. 'For those with low income, policy needs to create jobs and raise wages. At the upper end of the distribution, policy needs to be directed to curtailing the practices that generate excessive rewards.'[24] But contrary to orthodox economists and some members of the left who see in tax policy only a means of redistribution, the MMT theoreticians propose that it be viewed as a means of regulating social and economic behaviour, stimulating some actions and curbing others:

> We can use taxes to discourage 'sins' – in which case the purpose of the tax is to eliminate 'sin' so the optimal sizing of the tax would eliminate sin and hence raise no revenue at all. We can even view excessive riches as a sort of 'sin' that we want to tax away. Some have argued that high tax rates on high incomes in the early postwar period 'worked' by discouraging corporations from paying high incomes to top executives. Exactly! That is how sin taxes are supposed to work. The goal is not to raise revenue, but to reduce sin.[25]

In a market economy, money aids in bringing together vendors and purchasers, supply and demand, goods and those who need them. The problem, however, is that money in reality not only unites these elements of the economy, but divides them. In bourgeois society the market, subject to the logic of accumulation of capital, constantly redistributes resources, polarising wealth and poverty, restricting demand and opening a breach between needs and the ability to pay. This has nothing to do with limits to the availability of material resources, which are used inefficiently (or not used at all) if financial resources are not to be had.

If there is a social need, and the resources exist to satisfy it, the state can and should direct money into that area. If this approach is adopted, tax policy can also become a factor of redistribution. This should not, however, occur in the customary form, in which money that has been taken by the state from particular social groups is transferred to other, poorer groups, but as a means of directing funds into precisely those spheres where development of the public sector is indispensable.

Consequently, it is not just a matter of printing money. During the period of the Great Recession, and also during the Covid pandemic, governments that were completely wedded to orthodox concepts unexpectedly set about pumping the market full of money, in quantities that previously had never entered the heads of followers of J.M. Keynes. The difference was that liberal administrations did this under duress, and had no idea how to use this 'extra' money to restore economic growth. Still worse, substantial sums of money poured into the financial markets, stimulating speculation and price rises while making credit more expensive. This situation was aptly described by Wynne Godley in a report published even before the beginning of the Great Recession:

> A sustained period of stagnation or recession, through its adverse effect on the national income, could drive the budget back into deficit without there being any relaxation of policy, yet to counteract an endemic recession, it will be necessary to relax fiscal policy, making any emerging deficit even larger. Further relaxation of monetary policy could not sustain the expansion, except temporarily and perversely by giving a new lease on life to the stock market boom.[26]

During 2008–10 and 2020–21 events unfolded precisely according to this scenario, demonstrating not only the correctness of the forecasts made by critics of the free market, but also the bankruptcy of 'reasonable' conservative politics.

This situation was far from accidental. According to representatives of the liberal mainstream, 'the government is a market participant like any other, its main distinguishing feature being that it can print money'.[27] From the point of view of these thinkers social problems have no independent significance, and cannot by definition have their origins in capitalism and the market economy, except as a result of various errors and diversions from the 'true' path. 'The only way in which unemployment can be reduced permanently, according to this view, is by making markets work better, say, by removing "rigidities" or improving flows of information.'[28]

Randall Wray also complains about liberal economists who 'believe that full employment and price stability are inconsistent. Indeed, unemployment is seen as a tool to be used to promote price stability.'[29] It is, however, quite unclear why restraining inflation through stifling demand is better than regulating prices and stimulating the economy through state investments that create jobs. The presumption is that markets by themselves will not only solve the questions associated with the appearance from some unknown source of the investments needed for development, but will also create demand and ensure equilibrium. Meanwhile such events – inherent parts of real life – as natural disasters, environmental and technogenic catastrophes, epidemics, and social and military conflicts are simply annoying accidents that prevent the 'normal' functioning of the market. In such 'anomalous' situations liberal economists, central bank governors and finance ministers are not merely prepared to acknowledge the necessity for 'unorthodox' solutions, but when doing so generally fall into a panic and transform themselves from stubborn misers into hysterical spendthrifts.[30]

It would, of course, be extremely rash to present the monetary system as something endlessly flexible. Marx stressed quite correctly that money does not exist separately from the whole complex of social and economic relations. Hence the ideas of those economists who believe that rejecting the budget deficit 'scarecrow' will of itself allow the building of a 'people's economy' are naïve in the extreme.[31] When *taken in isolation* monetary policy, whether neoliberal or Keynesian, will not solve the problems. Worse still, the financial principles of neoliberalism, for all their theoretical unsustainability and the obviously catastrophic consequences to which the corresponding economic policies have already led, provide better answers to the needs of modern bourgeois society than the recommendations of MMT. The point is that it is *society*, not *financial policy*, that is in crisis and has to be reformed. On this level the ideas of the adherents of MMT can be effectively used as *part* of a general strategy of social and economic change, but they cannot replace it.

As the Swiss economist Basil Oberholzer has observed, the positive essence of the MMT concept lies not in its contention that the state can now spend money freely, but in the fact that this theory restores to the agenda the question of ensuring full employment (*Jobgarantie*):

Although many of the theoretical positions of MMT are not new, the service it has performed has been to lead discussion out of its accustomed niche. Most important here is the understanding that it is not money but real resources such as labour and technology that are the limiting factors of economic growth, while money is no more than an instrument with which to mobilise and expand these resources.[32]

Here, however, the theory runs up against a practical consequence of capitalist accumulation: finances that are required at the local level are centralised by corporations (through the concentration of capital and profits) and by the state (through the tax system). If the indispensable funds finish up finally where they are needed, this is only after long delays, and by way of a cumbersome bureaucratic machine of redistribution (including private and corporate mechanisms). Most important, however, is the fact that a whole series of objective needs cannot be expressed at all by a specific market or even social 'agent'. What particular group of consumers, or even social group, is interested in a comfortable and aesthetically pleasing urban environment? Who acts as a consumer in the solving of problems that arise in connection with climate change? Who exercises demand for objects and practices that have not yet been devised, but that might be created if money were to be invested in research? It can readily be understood that in each of these instances we are dealing with a direct social interest perceived first of all by specialists, and then by the majority of the population only in the process of open discussion. Even under capitalism, the state sooner or later begins to recognise these tasks, at least in countries with democratic systems. At first, however, it does so only after lengthy delays, when the latest 'market failure' takes on the scale of a full-blown crisis, and then, since it is hostage to corporate capitalist interests, it responds with great difficulty, sometimes proving incapable of adopting the necessary measures.

Like all technical instruments, financial policies worked out on the basis of MMT are perfectly able to function for the good of society and to stimulate the development of the economy. But these policies realise their full potential only when they are incorporated into a system of institutions of social self-government and democratic planning, becoming part of the process of socialist reconstruction of society.

This applies not only to MMT but also to a number of other initiatives aimed at correcting the situation in the financial field. Thus, calling for a struggle against the egoism of the financial aristocracy, the Swiss economist Marc Chesney suggests strengthening democratic control over the banking sector, and using legislative means to curtail some kinds of banking operations (for example, imposing strict limits on the indebtedness of financial corporations).[33] It is not hard to see that these measures will not only prove insufficient to solve the accumulated problems, but will simply not be adopted, since on the one hand they contradict the interests of the financial aristocracy described by Chesney himself, and on the other, do not undermine its power in any way. *Partial* measures, however reasonable in themselves, will have a significant effect only when combined with *radical* changes that create a new political situation, a new economic reality and new rules. In the case of large-scale financial capital, the only solution is its expropriation; in essence, the practices of the leading banks prepare the way for this, since these institutions constantly appeal to the state for help, and receive a wide variety of benefits from it. If the operations of such enterprises are in fact indispensable in systemic terms for the survival of the economy as a whole, and if they cannot develop without regular direct and indirect state support, then the nationalisation and subsequent restructuring of the financial sector is not just a natural and overdue decision, but also flows logically from the economic arguments addressed to society by the bankers themselves.

In raising arguments of this type, unfortunately, we move beyond the bounds of economic discussion, and inevitably cross over into the domain of politics. The well-known British historian and economist Adam Tooze laments the inability of politicians since 2008 'to offer an adequate response to the crisis'.[34] The reason for this situation plainly does not lie in a lack of fantastic schemes. The measures needed are obvious, and the key obstacle is not a lack of ideas or even of the political will required to implement them, but the fact that every attempt to genuinely solve the problems that have led to the crisis inevitably affects the dominant private interests. Since such attempts cannot be implemented exclusively within the sphere of finance or even of economic policy, they require changes to the balance of class forces in society. Mere changes of government are insufficient for this; what is required is a change to the system of power itself. In other words, a revolution.

PART III

Neoliberalism: Long Goodbyes

7

A Sick Society

The Great Recession that shook the world in the early twenty-first century was not a one-off event, and nor was it simply the latest (though undoubtedly massive) shock in a series of other such crises. It was the beginning of a drawn-out period when any resolution of specific economic and later political problems simply raised the stakes, thus deepening the general instability. In conditions where the underlying reasons for the difficulties not only defied efforts to deal with them, but could not even be publicly acknowledged, the situation could not be different.

When combined with neoliberal wage restraint policies, the anti-crisis measures adopted by governments created large quantities of 'excess' money, which could not be invested profitably in production due to the lack of demand. Although the global economic slump was overcome, this was not accompanied (unlike the case between 1932 and 1936) by even limited structural reforms, and hence none of the causes that had given rise to the Great Recession was removed. Industry in the developed countries was being stifled by competition from cheap labour on the periphery of the capitalist world-system, but there in turn a sales crisis broke out due to the cuts to employment and reduction in the number of 'good' jobs in the countries of the 'centre'.

Throughout the period from 2008 to 2010 the crisis was simply 'smothered with money'. In line with Keynesian prescriptions, central bank interest rates from 2008 were kept extremely low, and supplies of credit to corporations became cheap. But under conditions in which states continued to reduce their direct participation in the economy, and while workers and small businesses lacked spending power because of low wages and the dismantling of the welfare state, investing money in establishing new production or in the large-scale expansion of existing businesses made no sense. The excess capital poured into the 'digital sector'.

Permanent crisis

Marc Chesney states that since the first half of the 2000s the development of the capitalist banking system has been in a state of 'permanent crisis', accompanied by the growth of an irresponsible financial aristocracy. 'The financial markets are no longer able to function normally. They are not fulfilling their role of assigning capital and risks in optimal fashion.' Now exercising huge political influence, the financial sector 'instead of *serving* the economy, is *subjugating* it'.[1] The largest banks, having made themselves essential in systemic terms to the functioning of the economy, are becoming able to blackmail governments and societies, demanding to have their losses covered whenever their unrestrained thirst for profit, by causing them to take on unjustified risks, creates difficulties for their business.

The neoliberal policies of the late twentieth century transformed financial capital not only into the main force determining the development of markets, but also into the key factor in economic growth. Nevertheless, the events of the first two decades of the new century showed how limited and unstable this dominance was. The Great Recession of 2008–10 revealed that even the most powerful banks could easily become the victims of their own speculative expansion, dragging a multitude of other enterprises into insolvency, after which it was necessary to seek salvation in the government intervention whose ineffectiveness had just been declared axiomatic. A decade later, in 2020, financial capital with all its developed infrastructure, advanced information technologies, impressive global networks and political might was to prove impotent and useless before a tiny adversary – the Covid-19 virus.

Analysing the events of 2008–10, Adam Tooze wrote: 'One might be tempted to conclude that the crisis of globalisation had brought a reaffirmation of the essential role of the nation-state and the emergence of a new kind of state capitalism.'[2] However, this diagnosis was 'partial at best'.[3] Even though states have everywhere acted to save collapsing markets, it is still transnational corporations that are the moving force of world trade and finance. Nevertheless, Tooze acknowledges that the problem is not the mythical weakness of national governments, but the fact that in the course of neoliberal reforms they have transformed themselves into tools for the realisation and defence of corporate interests. The three decades preceding the crisis had been dominated by the idea of the 'market revolution', and governments had been assiduous in ending 'state interventionism'. In reality, state regulation had not disappeared, but was now delegated to 'independent' institutions, above all to 'independent central banks' whose tasks were to maintain discipline and to lend order and predictability to spontaneous economic processes.[4] Meanwhile the problem, in Tooze's view, was that 'there were rules for some and discretion for others'.[5] In essence, two or three dozen of the largest banks determined the workings of the financial markets of the whole planet, acting at their own discretion and paying scant attention to rules and norms. Meanwhile, governments were forced to cope with the consequences of the banks' errors and failures:

In fact, neoliberalism's regime of restraint and discipline operated under a proviso. In the event of a major financial crisis that threatened 'systemic' interests, it turned out that we lived in an age not of limited but of big government, of massive executive action, of interventionism that had more in common with military operations or emergency medicine than with law-bound governance. And this revealed an essential but disconcerting truth, the repression of which had shaped the entire development of economic policy since the 1970s. The foundations of the modern monetary system are irreducibly political.[6]

Unfortunately, this problem in turn is merely a consequence of a far more massive shift, one closely connected with the reassertion (under new conditions and with new force) of the class nature of the capitalist state. Under capitalism, the institutions of the state were established from the outset to defend definite corporate interests. The rules governing these institutions were drawn up to this end, and the 'independence' of central banks and of other financial bodies linked to the state has served not just to ensure direct control for the largest corporations over these institutions, but also to free them of any control on the part of the public, or of responsibility to the mass of the population. It should be noted that Tooze also acknowledges the 'political' nature of the decisions that are adopted. Nevertheless, the question is not simply one of politics, but relates to the fact that the dismantling of democracy is a critically important condition for realising the power of the financial elites in present-day circumstances. The reverse side of this process is the illusion of independence not only from the people, but also from objective circumstances, which inevitably make their reality felt through crises that each time take on a more catastrophic nature.

Covid as a social challenge

The salvaging of the banking sector during the 2008–10 crisis not only failed to solve the accumulated long-term problems of the neoliberal system and mitigate its contradictions, but to the contrary, allowed these problems and contradictions to continue accumulating, while the crisis took on a drawn-out character.[7] In 2020 the situation became still more difficult, when the pandemic of the Covid-19 coronavirus superimposed itself on the problems of the global economy.

The resulting huge production cuts and lifestyle changes, affecting millions of people on all continents, gave rise to new social contradictions, altered the economy and caused numerous problems on both national and international levels. Not long before the beginning of the Russian–Ukrainian war in 2022, the American scholar of international relations Joshua Busby argued that the pandemic might be 'the most consequential event of the early 21st century'.[8] While dealing a blow to globalisation, the pandemic simultaneously demonstrated its consequences, which to a significant degree were proving irreversible:

> States […] cannot meet their own needs for dealing with the crisis through domestic production alone. Globally integrated supply chains mean that they will depend upon imports for medical supplies, masks, pharmaceuticals, and machines. Some countries lack the wherewithal to tackle the disease on their own, and few if any states can collect necessary information on the trajectory of the disease all over the world or invest in the novel therapeutics and vaccines that are required to treat the sick and ultimately stop the virus.[9]

The worldwide situation proved once again that market structures are incapable of ensuring an effective reaction to global challenges that require international cooperation. What occurred was the direct opposite of this. The disorganisation of the markets, the panic and the inability of states to collaborate contrasted sharply with the manner in which governments in 2008–10 had actively coordinated their efforts in combatting the financial crisis. This, in turn, reveals the system of institutional priorities that had become established throughout the world by the beginning of the twenty-first century. 'Given limited medical equipment and pharmaceuticals at the moment and various countries simultaneously fighting outbreaks, we have seen competitive efforts by countries to lock down supplies for themselves rather than consider global solidarity.'[10]

With hindsight, it may be stated that the panicked measures adopted by most governments on the basis of the recommendations by the World Health Organization not only weighed heavily on the social situation and consumer markets, but also proved relatively ineffective from a medical point of view. The way in which events developed, however, was the outcome of established economic and political practice, not the result of incompetence or of some secret conspiracy between medical experts and bureaucrats.

Despite the serious damage to health brought about by the new virus, it was far less dangerous than many of the other diseases that medicine has confronted throughout human history. Although the death rates and the scale on which the infection spread substantially exceeded those for seasonal influenza, the figures were not such as to pose a threat to the existence and reproduction of society. Covid was not to be compared with the epidemics of 'Spanish flu' and typhus that had raged a century earlier. The damage dealt to the world economy and to the majority of national economies by the shutting down of whole sectors and the huge reduction in demand due to quarantine measures was obviously greater than the direct harm caused to society by the virus. Even if a correction is made to take into account the absolute value of human lives, the answer is still not obvious – it remains to be calculated how many people in developed countries ended their lives as a result of the stress of loneliness, and how many people died of hunger in the countries of Asia, where whole regions were deprived of the means of survival as a result of the curtailment of export orders.

It is quite logical that the disproportion between the scale of the medical problem and the absolutely unprecedented quarantine measures imposed in the majority of countries should have given rise to conspiracy theories. Under conditions in which a rational picture of the world had been undermined in the heads of millions of people by decades of ideological reaction (including the systematic extirpation of Marxism), such versions of events spread with irresistible force, like a prairie fire, in all corners of the planet.

Despite many predictions, the Covid pandemic did not change the world, but it dramatically sharpened all the world's contradictions, drawing a line beneath a whole historical period. The pandemic clearly demonstrated not only the crisis afflicting the socio-economic and political institutions of modern society, but also their inability to cope with ensuring even their own current reproduction in the face of so dire an objective challenge.

The more pronounced the market nature of an economy, the less prepared it is for the challenges created by wars, epidemics, natural disasters and at the same time, for sudden technological shifts. In the words of Schumpeter, social needs as they emerge reveal 'market failures', whose scale increases the more sharply and suddenly these needs manifest themselves. The neoliberal system has proved to be fundamentally incapable of reacting quickly and adequately to sharp changes in the internal or external conditions of its own existence, but at the same time has effectively resisted any remotely significant reforms.

A crisis of mass consciousness also developed hand in hand with the crisis of the social system. The epidemic undermined trust in institutions that earlier had been considered absolutely indispensable, but did nothing to help people grasp the necessity for a radical transformation of the world.

In the case of the coronavirus, the problem was not even so much the scale of the challenge as the suddenness with which it appeared. The cuts to the social sector and the dismantling of the welfare state removed essential insurance mechanisms without which reacting quickly to such threats became impossible. It was not the virus that caused the medical crisis, but the generally degraded state of health care that transformed a dangerous but quite ordinary epidemic into a global catastrophe. So long as vaccines against the coronavirus did not exist, shortages of medical staff meant it was impossible to help all the sufferers equally, providing them with essential care, alleviating symptoms and treating complications so as to guarantee a low death rate. Meanwhile, the concentrating of all efforts on the fight against Covid meant that millions of patients suffering from other illnesses were denied essential help, causing large numbers of additional deaths.

The system of universal free health care had been set up on the basis of non-market principles, and its functioning was interconnected with other elements of the social sector that were also suffering as a result of neoliberalism. Twentieth-century health care, which had developed as one of the institutions of the welfare state, had its shortcomings. The medicine of that time was not especially attentive to the individual peculiarities and feelings of patients. Nevertheless, its dismantling in favour of a 'client-oriented approach' was a catastrophe not just on the medical level, but also in economic, social, ethical and even political respects. Health care in most developed countries, Russia included, proved unprepared for the struggle against the pandemic not because of a lack of facilities or medicines, but because of the changed organisational structure, which in turn gave rise to shortages of medical personnel, beds and protective equipment for staff.

Lack of financing and the market reorganisation of health care had led to a worsening of outcomes even before the Covid-19 pandemic began. The British press reported in October 2019, before the coronavirus began its spread, that 62,000 people had died in the country from ordinary influenza, a figure inconceivable in the late twentieth century.[11] In Russia, the number of hospitals halved in the period from 2000 to 2015 alone, falling to the level of 1913, while over the same years the number of hospital beds fell by 27.5 per cent (in rural localities by 40 per cent). Between 2017 and 2019 the number of hospital beds per 10,000 of the population declined from 80.5 to 78.4.[12]

The tragic paradox is that in most developed countries funds continued as before to be assigned to health care, and remained very significant. Nevertheless, the structure of the spending was changing. Even in the public sector, the effectiveness with which funds were employed was coming to be assessed purely according to market criteria. During the twentieth century health care had developed as a system designed to meet *social needs*, not the health of individual 'clients' but that of the population as a whole. Precisely for this reason, the organisation of national health care systems was fundamentally 'loss-making' from the point of view of the market. By contrast, the neoliberal conception of economic development presents medicine as one of the branches of the service sector. Since the market orients management towards current demand, there is no point in keeping extra beds 'in reserve', in paying 'extra' medical personnel or in training specialists. As governments set out to optimise their budgets, they cut expenditures they considered 'ineffective'. Throughout the world, this optimisation led to a squeezing of health care systems. Current measures of medical prophylaxis were done away with as 'loss-making' or 'cost-ineffective', as a result of which health care systems everywhere finished up unprepared for dealing with large-scale epidemics.

The curtailing of the public sector, of course, had to be made up by the development of commercial medicine. It too, however, was oriented towards current *effective* demand, and hence finished up super-specialised and incapable of being rolled out quickly in a crisis. Although extraordinary sums were assigned in many countries to specific projects (most often in the fields of oncology or cardiology), unsystematic financing of particular areas unconnected to other elements within the health sector merely brought disorganisation. Notwithstanding the scope of particular programmes, institutional financing for health care declined. The ability of health systems to respond flexibly to new problems and challenges was reduced to a minimum, and self-regulation became impossible.

Sanitary authoritarianism

The main economic consequence of the pandemic was not the financial damage it caused, and not the changes to labour organisation linked to the spread of working from home, of remote services and internet commerce, but the obvious change in the general rules of the game, of the relations between society, business and the state. In reality, the pandemic once again provided a typical picture of *market failure*, demonstrating the need for planning in medicine and in the social sphere more broadly. Further, this planning now needed to be coordinated on an international level. None of this, of course, was attainable without national and regional planning institutions. The Turkish medic Ertuğrul Oruç wrote:

> The fact that the commercial rights for the production of vaccines belong to a handful of firms results in an insufficient quantity of vaccines brought to the market and the markedly high prices charged by the pharmaceutical companies for the vaccines together lead to a situation in which the poor countries of the world barely have any success in accessing the vaccines they require for their population. The rich countries, on the other hand, have already acquired a hoard of vaccines that go way beyond their reasonable needs.[13]

Governments were, of course, obliged to take steps to correct the situation. The historian Aleksey Sakhnin describes the dramatic strengthening, from the spring of 2020, of state intervention in the lives of citizens as 'sanitary socialism', by analogy with the 'war socialism' introduced by European countries during the First World War.[14] But when state intervention in the life of society has not been associated with fundamentally rejecting a course meant to perpetuate an antisocial policy, the result has not been an increase in the level of solidarity and an expansion of social rights, but the rise of new conflicts and contradictions.

The American sociologist Charles Thorpe characterises the methods that arose as a result of the pandemic as an attempt at normalising an abnormal world, a sort of 'post-normalcy'. The reason for what occurred in this case should not be sought in the spread of the virus, but in the destruction of the welfare state:

> This should be understood more broadly as the end of the precarious normalcy of the period of Fordism-Keynesianism, which lasted only a quarter of a century from the end of World War II and was also the period of peak modernity. The origins of post-normal times, which have marked the experience of the Covid-19 pandemic, must be sought in the 1970s. It was then that the political-economic roots of post-normalcy began to develop.[15]

The sharp reduction in the functions and potential of the welfare state did not have the effect of reducing bureaucracy and government interference in private life, or even in market processes, but it altered the thinking in the institutions of power. For these bodies organised violence once again became, as in the mid-twentieth century, the basic and most organic function. As a result, *the state carried out its social and regulatory functions through violent and repressive methods.* Everywhere, the authorities resorted to quarantines and prohibitive measures of the sort practised in the Middle Ages and until the seventeenth century. It is true that experience of organising quarantine measures had to a significant extent been lost. Hence the state not only combatted the epidemic mainly through the use of bans and other repressive measures, but also did this very ineffectively. The social and economic damage wrought by the quarantine measures was, for the most part, roughly proportional to the degree in which the institutions of the welfare state had been undermined in one country or another. The virus also tested the 'quality' of the government bureaucracy, and revealed disturbing results.

Even in countries with relatively robust democratic institutions, it emerged that the structures most able to cope with the situation were not social services, but the military and police forces. The latter complex was the only sector of the state system that had not only remained exempt from large-scale cuts and 'optimisation', but that had actually expanded in virtually all countries. This can be explained on the basis of completely rational considerations. Unlike health care workers and teachers, who were constantly forced to justify their existence in market terms, military personnel and police were free of such strictures. They were able at any moment to establish the need for their existence and even to accumulate reserves. Even in peacetime an army must prepare for war, and generals, unlike scholars, cannot be transferred to other work on a project principle, or sent off to work on a remote basis. Funds spent on the police and military can always be justified by real or imaginary dangers – terrorism, international tensions or mass disturbances. The more 'market' the nature of one or another society, and the more acute the competition, the sharper the conflicts and contradictions.

Possessing weak health care but strong police forces, governments did not have a choice. These services continued to operate on the basis of their usual funding. Similar arrangements were introduced in the most diverse countries, including the most democratic, and any city that was under quarantine came to recall a territory under occupation by a hostile army.

As the political scientist Gleb Kuznetsov has observed, 'the pandemic enabled a concentration of powers in the hands of the executive authority, and also served as a pretext for limiting the possibilities of anyone who sought to raise objections'.[16] Everywhere, alongside the quarantine measures and the protection of citizens' health, limitations were placed on freedom of speech and association, and no-one was prepared to abolish these restrictions abruptly after the disease had been defeated. The bans that were introduced in Russia were duplicated in striking fashion in Western democracies that condemned 'Putin-style authoritarianism'. Even on the purely medical level, the task of governments everywhere became *'administering Covid under the guise of struggling against it'.*[17]

In most countries the political and administrative classes tried to exploit the possibilities that the pandemic opened up for them, but meanwhile, were unable to devise a strategy for operating under the new conditions. From the moment when the coronavirus appeared, Gleb Kuznetsov writes,[18] these classes 'concentrated on introducing states of emergency and on spreading fear among citizens. This allowed them to introduce restrictive measures out of proportion to the existing threat.'[19] The Italian philosopher Giorgio Agamben went even further in his conclusions, declaring that in principle, the epidemic was no more than a pretext for introducing extraordinary police measures, the need for which was dictated not by the dangers associated with the spread of the disease, but by the general logic of the development of modern capitalism. A new political order was taking shape, one that did not formally abolish democracy, but that replaced it with a state of emergency.[20] In contrast to Agamben, the Swedish geographer and ecologist Andreas Malm viewed the experience of the emergency measures undertaken by states in the course of the Covid epidemic as a recipe for the future salvation of the planet. A state of emergency was needed to open the way for radical environmental reforms in the spirit of Soviet war communism.[21] The key question, however, remained unanswered: which state would make use of the state of emergency to implement these measures, and which social groups would win or lose as a result? For the moment, political control remained in the hands of the old elites, and the efforts at mobilisation, even when justified by the best of intentions, were being turned against the rights and interests of the majority.

Meanwhile, there was no such thing as an exit strategy; states did not have the slightest notion of what to do when all this ended. Of course, the ideal would have been to retain the existing rules indefinitely, but even the most authoritarian governments understood that managing this would not be possible in practice. At the same time, moods of weariness and irritation were spreading in society. In a passive response to this objective challenge, the ruling elites kept postponing a decision, attempting to draw the situation out and to put off ending the emergency regime until some ever more distant point. This, however, merely provoked a further growth of social tension that ultimately spilled over into a whole series of mass protests, and then into a genuine popular revolt that in Canada took the form of the 'Freedom Convoy 2022', when with broad support from the population, the drivers of tens of thousands of trucks demanded an end to the restrictions introduced by the government.

It was soon discovered that such restrictions could not be introduced for lengthy periods in virtually any part of the world. Contrary to the expectations and fears of many, the readiness of the repressive structures to employ the mechanisms they had been given for use in controlling the population turned out to be limited. Instead of a 'digital concentration camp', what often transpired was a 'digital shambles'; the restrictions were breached on a massive scale, and numerous means emerged for circumventing them. The bans and quarantines proved successful and lasting only to the degree to which they rested on the support and cooperation of society. Proving more effective than the administrative prohibitions was the propaganda, but the possibilities of this were not limitless either.

The pandemic and social contradictions

The universal failure of attempts to impose total control had other causes as well. In most countries, of course, the traditional elites were not opposed to strengthening controls over the population. Measures to install electronic tracking of citizens were widely practised in even the most 'free' of countries. The 'digital concentration camp', however, not only presumes the use of a particular set of technical means, but also requires a redistribution of power from the current elites to the forces of coercion (at the same time as inevitable shifts also occur within the repressive apparatus, with the distribution of influence, power and authority changing radically). In the spring of 2020 the ruling groups in most of the world's countries simply had no alternative but to turn for help to the police, the military and the repressive elements of the bureaucracy. Once the acuteness of the crisis had begun to decline, however, the governing bureaucracy and the elites close to it found themselves in a sort of political trap. They vacillated between a desire to revoke the unpopular measures, at times even sacrificing the effectiveness of the quarantines, and a fear of losing control over the situation – not so much on the medical level, but on the political one. Consequently, all of 2021 and part of 2022 were marked by uncertainty and inconsistency, until the situation was abruptly altered by the Russian–Ukrainian war, compared with which all the problems associated with Covid suddenly appeared insignificant.

Meanwhile, *Covid and the war were simply manifestations of one and the same global crisis.* The 2020 pandemic occurred precisely when the global economic and social system was in any case encountering extremely severe problems. The model of development that had dominated the world throughout the preceding thirty years had reached its historic limits, exhausting its possibilities. In essence, the blow dealt by Covid-19 was merely the catalyst for an inevitable collapse, all of the conditions for which had been prepared by the developments of the two preceding decades. In 2020 economists were already stating that the pandemic was 'being used as an opportunity to solve accumulated economic problems under the pretext of "the onset of *force-majeure* circumstances".'[22] In a certain sense the war was a logical continuation of the epidemic, though to use the terminology of Clausewitz, 'by other methods'.

'The quarantines', Gleb Kuznetsov notes, 'replicated and even reinforced the classical forms of inequality.'[23] People who were living in the worst of social conditions now encountered still more serious problems. On the emotional level, however, the main victim was the middle class. 'Though well off, and surviving quarantine with fewer losses and in greater comfort, the members of the middle class were now in an unequal position compared to rednecks and other proletarians. They were more vulnerable, and more easily frightened. They were literally neuroticised.'[24]

The crisis of the middle class had begun long before the pandemic, having been remarked on by numerous scholars as early as the first years of the twenty-first century.[25] Because of Covid, however, all the accumulated contradictions had come to the surface, and in an especially painful form.

'Because of the pandemic, inequality has become more noticeable', state the Swiss economists Hans Baumann and Robert Fluder.[26] The Russian political scientist Konstantin Gaaze makes the same point: 'The pandemic has now reconfigured social time in such a way that the contrast between the lifestyles of rich and poor will once again be obviously deliberate, as in the times when people were persecuted for idleness.'[27] Counterposing the lives of rich and poor creates an effect of 'aesthetic shock'.[28] At the same time, this is an absolutely concrete social and everyday contrast:

> There are those who own an estate where at a distance, they can sit out the latest quarantine, and those who have 40 square metres for their whole family while they try to do the same. There are those who can fly about the

world in biologically safe, expensive and comfortable aircraft, and those who will save up for petrol so as once in a few years to make a road trip in a car that for years will have sat in a garage because there is no longer any need to travel anywhere to work. There are those who employ servants, and those who pay the neighbours to look after the children.[29]

The middle classes in relatively prosperous countries have abruptly become conscious of themselves if not as proletarians, then at least as members of a social layer whose rights are infringed, and who sense acutely the scale of the inequality to which they are subject.

An awareness of the scope of the social crisis has become near-universal, affecting experts, politicians and ordinary citizens alike. The main peculiarity of the global pandemic of 2020–21, the Israeli philosopher Yoel Regev wrote in a collection of articles devoted to the social and cultural-psychological effects of Covid, was that 'the entire world was at the same time not just reoriented in a different direction, but was also conscious of this'.[30] In other words, the measures adopted by authorities in the most diverse countries everywhere aroused doubts as to the competence of the ruling class and its ability in principle to react to the challenges of the new period. This was not just because the measures were ineffective (often, they reflected the inability of the elites to suggest anything more effective *in the existing circumstances*), but in the first instance because these measures confirmed and actualised doubts and dissatisfactions that had long been accumulating in society. The principle 'there is no alternative', proclaimed by Margaret Thatcher in the early 1980s, evoked general disagreement precisely at the moment when governments and ruling elites did not, indeed, have any short-term alternative. The reason why they lacked an alternative, however, lay in their earlier decisions that had placed their societies in an inescapable rut of institutional, systemic and economic limitations. After destroying their systems of universally available health care in the course of dismantling the welfare state, the ruling classes of most of the world's countries were faced with a situation in which they were simply incapable, on the organisational level, of resisting the pandemic with anything apart from quarantines, lockdowns, bans and limitations, and on the economic level, with anything except panicked emissions of money. The effort by Sweden to find a special road of non-repressive struggle against Covid became choked up in conditions of enforced isolation. A conspicuous case here was that of Russia, whose government managed to take the situation to the absurd, declaring a lockdown while not assigning serious financial compensation to the population, and then replacing the anti-pandemic measures with political bans and acts of repression.

Consequently, the main problem associated with the pandemic turned out not to be the disease itself, but the state of the health care systems and of the societies themselves, along with the unpreparedness of states to provide support to their own citizens in what were not really emergency situations. 'The Covid crisis once again showed the importance of social services', the earlier-cited Swiss economists note. As a result of the events of 2020–21, they state, the questions of returning these services to the control of local authorities (*Rekommunalisierung*) and of establishing 'local economies oriented towards common well-being' (*lokaler gemeinwohlorientierter Oekonomien*) are on the agenda.[31] But the questions remain: how should all this be done, who is preventing it, and why? The dismantling of the welfare state was not an isolated act, but reflected a changed relationship of forces in developed bourgeois societies, and corresponded to the needs of capital.

The fact that the neoliberal counter-reforms have had deplorable results for most of society, and in any case have not matched the ideological promises used to justify them, is of no significance in this case. Further, the objective social need for particular solutions does not mean they will be implemented if they run counter to the existing structure of dominant interests. The implementing of changes whose time has come does not occur automatically, 'of its own accord' or as a result of 'the natural course of events', but to the contrary, *demands* an active political struggle. Meanwhile, the chances of success in this struggle depend not only on the resolve, heroism or competence of the participants in the events concerned, but also on the objective conditions within which these events unfold.

The crisis of the elites

As always during a serious crisis, a dramatic change in the situation has sharpened and made unmistakeable the contradictions that have accumulated over a lengthy period, and that include contradictions within the ruling class and the apparatus of power itself. This schism within the elites has created the potential for radical social and political changes, but realising this potential will for some time be impossible, since the 'collective subject' of these changes, a new historic bloc, has not yet coalesced. As a result, the elite groups that are confronting one another and fighting among themselves have for some time been left to their own devices, and their conflicts have been decided without the participation of the masses.

The higher echelons of power, after temporarily losing control over the situation in favour of the police structures, regional authorities and the heads of the health and medical apparatus, tried to regain their positions as the virus retreated, but encountered stubborn resistance. In the US and Canada this was expressed in the form of competing claims by the federal government and the states or provinces. In Britain local authorities simply introduced their own regulations, ignoring the government in London (those that took such steps included not only Scottish separatists, but also many completely loyal regions of England). In Russia the presidential administration, after first devolving various powers to the regions, then immediately subjected the regions to strong pressures in an attempt to stop them from using the powers they had just been entrusted with. At the same time, responsibility for the decisions that had been adopted was heaped on the governors.

Even more significant than the conflicts within the apparatus of power was the rapidly spreading mistrust of the official propaganda that dominated the mass media. This mistrust extended to encompass elites in general, whether corporate, political, informational or intellectual. To use the terminology of V.I. Lenin, a global crisis of the elites had broken out.

As is well known, Lenin in his work *The Collapse of the Second International* listed three signs of a revolutionary situation:

1. The impossibility for the ruling classes of retaining their dominance in unchanged form; one or another crisis of the 'elites', a crisis of the politics of the ruling class, creating a rift through which the discontent and anger of the oppressed classes bursts forth. For a revolution to break out, it is not usually enough that 'the lower orders are unwilling' to live in the old way; also required is that 'the elites cannot' live in this fashion.
2. A sharpening, to a higher degree than usual, of the needs and miseries of the oppressed classes.
3. A significant rise, for the reasons indicated, in the activity of the masses, who in a 'peaceful' epoch submit quietly to being robbed, but who in turbulent times are drawn, both by the general circumstances of the crisis *and by the 'elites' themselves*, towards independent historic action.[32]

In this endlessly cited (and by this time almost banal) formulation, it is the last words that are especially important: the ruling groups *themselves* create the new conditions, impelling the lower orders of society to *independent* social and political action. Of course, unlike the military mobilisations of 1914, the quarantine measures prompted by the Covid pandemic did not unite huge masses of the people as one, but to the contrary, divided them. The numerous bans and lockdowns, the introduction of special passes, and the counterposing of vaccinated and unvaccinated citizens all created a sort of new segregation, at the same time as the boundaries between groups and the duration of the bans not only remained unclear, but were also changed arbitrarily by decisions of the bureaucracy. This separation, however, in turn gave rise to a demand for the masses to be able to return to the streets.

Mass protests rolled about most European countries, and then reached their culmination in Canada, where long-distance truck drivers, dissatisfied with the policies of Prime Minister Justin Trudeau, organised a large-scale protest that was joined successively by farmers, road maintenance workers, construction workers, Native Americans, fishers, forestry workers and small-business people. The ties between workers and employers were weakened by the quarantines, while the links to the state, which should have been strengthened thanks to the receipt of compensation payments, turned into competing claims by the people and the bureaucracy. The citizens were complaining at the inadequate levels of assistance, while the bureaucrats were irked by the failure of citizens to observe the regulations – compliance with which had often, and deliberately, been made impossible.

The targeted assistance provided to specific groups not only failed to solve the general problems of social reproduction, but also created new disproportions. Instead of investing money in expanding the health care system, the authorities everywhere implemented one-off measures that did not provide long-term effects. Instead of relying on the potential of the public sector to strengthen social assistance services, or creating new jobs to allow for the flexible replacing of workers who were sick or who needed to be isolated at home, governments preferred to shut down businesses, depriving people of their livelihoods. The obstacle to making rational decisions was not a lack of competence or information, but the interests of the ruling classes and of the elites close to the authorities (oligarchic circles in Russia, and financial elites in the West). The redistribution of funds was conducted in the first instance so as to benefit the strongest interest groups, and to the detriment of weaker but more numerous ones. The result was a general alienation of the mass of the people from the state, at the very moment when in theory, they were in greatest need of one another.

As events continued, the masses were inevitably drawn into politics, but as before, were not ready either to formulate their demands, or to organise themselves into a new political force, or even to find the words that would allow them to adequately express their own needs and hopes.

For the most oppressed layers of society, the developments under way created an acute need for 'restorative justice'. This demand, that took various forms from the justifying by society of mass revolts and pogroms in the United States, to 'freedom convoys' in Canada, New Zealand and Australia, and to a sudden growth in the *conscious* demand for democracy in Russia, Belarus and Kazakhstan, was a general manifestation of a common principle formulated by Lenin: 'The masses are unwilling'.

Conspiracy theories

In conditions where Marxist thought, like the tradition of liberal rationalism, has to a significant degree been discredited by those who have embraced it, protests against elite policies have constantly found expression in a fundamentally inadequate form, centred on conspiracy theories.

The struggle against the coronavirus, accompanied by a major growth of 'police state' methods, has seen a bewildering variety of conspiracy theories spread throughout the world. Since governments in the most diverse countries have without obvious collusion imposed identical bans and control measures on their populations, the feeling has spread that someone is coordinating these measures in centralised fashion, and that the virus was invented especially so as to permit the establishing of a 'digital concentration camp', to allow the installing of a 'new totalitarianism', and to frighten ordinary people.

Ilya Yablokov, who has written a detailed study of the conspiracy theories employed by the Russian elites, states that views of this kind have received their greatest currency in two very different societies, the US and Russia. He does not suggest why this should be the case, but the connection is far from accidental.[33] In both countries mass political culture in the twenty-first century has taken shape under the influence of anti-communism. It is true that the historical conditions for the triumph of anti-communism in the two cases have not simply been different, but directly counterposed: in the US it has been a matter of defending the American way of life from an external threat, while in Russia it concerns the overcoming of the Soviet past. Nevertheless, the consequences of these ideological processes have been surprisingly similar.

The broad spread of conspiratorial interpretations of political and even economic events, and especially, the readiness of people to take them seriously, testify to the weakness or decline of social awareness in society. In real politics, of course, conspiracies, behind-the-scenes intrigues and secret organisations all exist. But they are 'responsible' for only an insignificant share of the processes that occur, and in the main, their effectiveness and success are limited by the objective relationship of forces in society, by existing institutions and by socio-economic conditions. Paradoxically, it is precisely the uniform reaction of the elites to external challenges that shows the spontaneous nature of the process under way – any centralised management would need to be far more varied in its nature, or it would encounter a serious problem with transmitting the same signal in the most diverse environments and bureaucratic systems. To the contrary, the intuitively uniform reaction of the elites of these very different countries, so often hostile to one another, indicates a sort of success for globalisation: the ruling groups throughout the world have become if not homogeneous, then at least of a similar type. And they are ruled by identical political instincts.

Of course, conspiracies exist, just as secret services and secret agencies of all conceivable varieties also exist. The tasks and activity of a conspiracy, however, are always local. A conspiracy may be aimed at the removal or even murder of a particular bureaucrat, at the abduction of an individual or a leak of information, or at preparing a military or political provocation. In this way specific local aims are achieved, always very limited and momentary. By contrast, conspiratorial thinking is completely uninterested in real political or criminal conspiracies, which it finds too dull and petty. Conspiratorial thinking assumes that the most extensive and long-term processes of social development are organised and governed with the help of a 'secret power' that also directs the evolution of political and economic systems. Meanwhile, it is a political purpose (always a malign purpose), and not the logic of the market, the bureaucracy or cultural institutions that determines the course of events. Where sociological analysis sees a social phenomenon or structure, the conspiracy theorist invariably sees some person or group of people consciously directing the process with a view to achieving some nefarious end, the rational explanation for which boils down, at best, to a desire to seize total power over the world or for some unknown reason, to bring someone (us) to ruination.

Indeed, if we take a detached look at many spontaneous processes, while making no attempt to analyse their mechanics, they appear surprisingly coordinated, which can give rise to the illusion that they are completely managed. In reality, the level of coordination results precisely from the fact that these processes operate automatically. There is no need for a fire scene to be under centralised control for all living creatures to try to save themselves from the blaze, and there is no need for someone to rule the market for purchasers to begin seeking cheaper goods. Elemental factors do more than any management to ensure that large numbers of people will act, if not in coordination, then at least simultaneously, and that they will show the same type of behaviour. Of course, by no means all processes are able to proceed spontaneously, and most importantly, constructive and creative activity requires conscious direction, and also a coordination of goals and interests (which, moreover, cannot be achieved secretly when large-scale tasks are performed). This is why people who believe sincerely in a covert power, universal control, a worldwide behind-the-scenes conspiracy and so forth are rarely able to believe in the possibility of democracy – and still more, in socialist planning, constructed on the basis of participation by the people in making decisions.

The growth of conspiratorial moods, proceeding in parallel in the most diverse societies, has also reflected a general decline of humanitarian aware- ness that has occurred as a result of market reforms in the educational field, as well as the commercialisation of science, with research shifting to project- based instead of institutional financing. In sum, even the presence of adequate or even superfluous knowledge of particular problems cannot compensate for a weak understanding of complex socio-economic struc- tures or of the interrelations between different processes in society. In a certain sense, the spread of conspiracy theories is the natural outcome of the ideological triumph of neoliberalism. Marxism and other schools of critical thought have been marginalised politically, and their influence on mass consciousness has been reduced to a minimum.

The ideological basis for the popularity of conspiracy theories is a mass conviction (both among the elites and the lower orders of society) that ordinary citizens, the common people, simple workers and even bureaucrats and members of the middle classes are completely powerless, deprived of their own will, and can act only in the role of objects of management or as the passive victims of manipulation by others. For many years, this belief in the powerlessness of the 'little person' has been instilled into the lower orders of society. But at the same time dissatisfaction, affronts and at times simple material deprivation have driven people onto the streets. This is a completely justified dissatisfaction, aroused by the objective state of affairs, but it has not found an adequate ideological or even lexical expression. The language of the left has been compromised by neoliberal propaganda and not least by members of the left themselves, who have exchanged class rhetoric for the ideology of defending minorities, and who have finished up completely powerless in the face of the problems that agitate the great majority of citizens (including, in their overwhelming number, members of those very minorities, who unexpectedly but with reason have come to identify themselves with the majority in the face of a greater scourge). The crowds coming onto the streets have not been able to articulate clearly what they want. They have demanded one thing and sought another, while having in mind a third. But this has been the indispensable awakening of a society that has not yet succeeded completely in overcoming its long-standing sleep of reason.

8

War, Hunger and Economic Restructuring

At the opening of the New Testament Book of Revelations, the end of the world is heralded by the four horsemen of the apocalypse, symbolising sickness, hunger, war and death. Unfortunately, the twilight of the neoliberal epoch has corresponded in detail to these ancient prophecies. The Covid pandemic has not yet ended, and in Europe a major war has unfolded, between Russia and Ukraine.

Previously, there had been no large-scale wars between states in Europe since 1945. The series of armed conflicts in the Balkans sparked by the disintegration of Yugoslavia had the character of internecine strife, despite being extremely bloody and accompanied by intervention from the West. Developing according to the same logic were the conflicts on the post-Soviet expanse, including the revolt in south-eastern Ukraine in 2014 that led to the separation of Donetsk and Lugansk, and also the annexation of Crimea by Russia. Even the wars that occurred outside Europe did not, for the most part, take the form of clashes between national states. After the drawn-out war between Iran and Iraq, these conflicts either involved efforts by the coalition of the West to deal out punishment to one or another regime in Asia, or amounted to civil wars accompanied by foreign interventions.

The impossible happened

For decades the world lived with the idea that although as in the past wars were possible, such developments occurred exclusively on the periphery of the capitalist system, and did not directly affect its centre. But thanks to the collapse of the Soviet bloc and the formation of new oligarchic regimes on its ruins, peripheral capitalism became firmly implanted in Eastern Europe, in direct geographic proximity to the countries of the system's core.

Nevertheless, the armed conflict between Russia and Ukraine that broke out in 2022 and that rapidly took on the features of a global stand-off, with almost all the world's countries being drawn into it directly or indirectly, did not appear from nowhere and was not the exclusive result of reckless ambitions on the part of Russian president Vladimir Putin. The situation matured over a lengthy period, and not only on the political level.

Analysing the changes that have occurred in the early twenty-first century, the American sociologist William Robinson notes that the dismantling of the welfare state and the cuts to the corresponding items of state spending have been accompanied by a redistribution of funding in favour of the organs of coercion (not only the military, but the police as well). Not only has the structure of budgets changed, but economic processes have been set in train that Robinson describes as 'militarized accumulation and accumulation by repression'. Needless to say, the development of this process has been uneven. The ending of the Cold War was accompanied by dramatic cuts to military spending, something that had considerable significance for the neoliberal project, leading as it did to mass lay-offs of workers in sectors where jobs had earlier been well paid and secure. This enabled a transformation of the labour market, involving the spread of precarious terms of employment and the establishing of a system of 'flexible' labour relations that served the interests of capital. At the same time as purely military spending was being cut, however, various police and security structures grew rapidly. Both state-run and private, these structures required re-equipping and reorganising to take advantage of new technology. In most states the coercive apparatus took on an increasing function of repression and control. Meanwhile, the 1991 Gulf War showed that disarmament was merely a temporary stage in the development of the coercive bloc. The 'War on Terror' (in the West) and the need to suppress separatism (in Russia) provided the ideological basis for new increases in military spending in the early 2000s. Although large-scale production of heavy weapons in many countries had been curtailed, spending on the forces of repression increased or remained extremely high throughout.

The growth of military outlays, Robinson explains, was being covered by borrowing on the international financial markets.

> The money is then spent to finance the circuits of militarized accumulation and paid back to the original lenders with interest. This process that fuses financial and militarized accumulation becomes abundantly clear when we consider that the *interest payments alone* on the debt incurred to prosecute the Iraq and Afghanistan wars is estimated to exceed $7.5 trillion by 2050.[1]

In this respect the processes taking place in Putin's Russia, involving a clear trend to steadily increasing state outlays on the organs of coercion, along with growth in the number of personnel employed by these structures and an expansion of their intervention in various aspects of life, have not been an exception to the general rule. Rather, and as has often been the case in Russian history, they have represented a marked or even extreme manifestation of the general tendency. A no less important trend in the new epoch has been the privatisation of violence, as the state, while formally retaining its monopoly on the use of coercive methods to carry out political tasks, has at the same time subcontracted increasing numbers of technical functions to private business – starting with private prisons and finishing up with private military companies. At first these private military firms, set up with state support, mostly acted in close association with transnational commercial companies on foreign territory (this was the case both with the Russian 'Private Military Company Wagner' and with analogous American, South African, Israeli and even Indian organisations). Following the outbreak of the Ukraine war in 2022, however, units of the Wagner organisation started to be employed alongside the regular army. Wagner head Evgeny Prigozhin was permitted to enter penal colonies and recruit convicted criminals who after military service with the firm would be set free, bypassing the existing legal procedures.

Robinson continues:

> The more state policy is oriented toward war and repression, the more opportunities are opened up for transnational capital accumulation; the more the political and corporate agents of transnational capital seek to influence state policy in this direction, the more political systems and capitalist culture becomes fascistic.[2]

A well-known theatrical saying, attributed to Anton Chekhov, states that if there is a gun hanging on a wall of the set in the first act, it will inevitably be fired in one of the acts that follow. The economic logic of capitalism tends in the same direction, especially since the walls of all the participants in the drama are already hung with weapons. The 'gun' was eventually fired in 2022.

World war on a local territory

The conflict between Ukraine and Russia developed over a lengthy period, and has had nothing to do with the ideological predilections of the elites in these two states. Although what was happening seemed initially like a tragicomic disagreement over how to interpret history, the status of the

Russian language in Ukraine, and how to divide up the flock between the Moscow and Kiev patriarchates of the Orthodox Church, the actual roots of the conflict lay in the area of corporate interests and the economy. The presence of these serious interests was responsible for the acuteness that cultural disagreements time and again assumed, as well as for the absurdity of the ideological rationalisations put forward by the two sides. The struggle to make use of what remained of the Soviet infrastructure acquired by the ruling classes of the two states, the competition on the grain market, and the attempts by Russian and Western capital to seize hold of the most profitable sectors of the Ukrainian economy, which was chronically short of investment, all created a field for numerous clashes and for complicated intrigues. The mutual accusations and constant whipping up of tensions, however, did not prevent the two sides from cooperating with one another. Even after the political crisis that shook the Ukrainian political system in 2014, leading to a violent change of government in Kiev, to a rebellion in the south-east of the country and to the annexation of Crimea by Russia, the conflict did not expand into a genuine war. In supporting the people's republics that were proclaimed in Donetsk and Lugansk, the Kremlin rulers were mainly interested in ensuring that the protests by dissatisfied citizens in south-eastern Ukraine against the new authorities in Kiev did not turn into a social revolution. The radical-minded leaders of the revolt were almost all killed or excluded from the leadership of the movement.

The massive attack on the territory of Ukraine that began on 24 February 2022, and which was termed by Russian president Vladimir Putin a 'special military operation', had been predicted by military experts but nevertheless came as a surprise to Russian society. The conflict between Moscow and Kiev had become a constant background to the relations between the two governments, and the periodic flare-ups had not led to anything. The launching of military operations, however, always comes at a distinct historical moment when at least one of the contending sides considers the situation favourable and military action necessary. The fact that all sides in the conflict would only lose from a war was clear from the outset, causing many analysts to remain certain that armed hostilities could be avoided or kept to a minimum. Nevertheless, events once again confirmed the prophecy of Engels, who explained how control over a situation can come to be lost as a crisis grows more acute: 'It is enough for the first shot to ring out, and the reins fall from the hands of the riders and the horses bolt'.[3]

The outbreak of a large war between European states came as a shock to public opinion throughout the world, and aroused justified indignation at the actions of the Russian leadership. Nevertheless, the widespread idea that the war resulted from the folly of a specific individual – Russian president Vladimir Putin – reflected, at most, only part of the truth.

The reason for the war has to be sought not in bilateral Russian–Ukrainian relations, or even in Russia's relations with the notorious 'collective West'. The actions of the Russian leadership, though completely irrational and criminal, were provoked by a rapidly deepening internal crisis within Russia, a crisis that in turn was linked closely to the crisis of the world-system of neoliberal capitalism into which Russia was tightly integrated. The fact that such mechanisms were not understood even by the politicians who took the decisions, not to speak of ordinary people zombified by propaganda, does not alter their prime importance. This objective logic was crueller and more lethal the less the participants in the events were conscious of it, at least during the initial stage. The scale of the problems was fully revealed only in the second week of the war, when the clash between Russia and the West led to the country being excluded from the logistic chains and economic ties of the world-system. Here it became evident how dependent the Russian economy was, since without interacting with world markets Russia was unable not just to ensure its own reproduction, but also to maintain the fighting capacity of its army.

The aggressiveness of the Kremlin leadership was thus predetermined by its desperate and fruitless attempts to escape from the country's growing internal political crisis. At the same time, it would not be an exaggeration to say that the war that broke out in 2022 was a consequence and one of the manifestations of the global socio-economic crisis that had resulted from the exhaustion of the possibilities of the neoliberal model of capitalism.

It was no accident that the outbreak of the Russian–Ukrainian conflict took place against a background of increased tensions between China and Taiwan, of a popular revolt in Iran and of a whole series of other local conflicts in diverse parts of the world. The stresses in China–Taiwan relations were growing rapidly at the same time as at the other end of Eurasia, Russian and Ukrainian forces were beginning to exchange artillery salvoes. Conceivably, it was the successful resistance by Ukrainian forces to the Russian army that had invaded their territory that convinced Beijing of the undesirability of repeating this experience in an attempt to annex Taiwan.

What began as a mistake then took on the form of a catastrophe. The war that broke out in 2022 revealed the complete unpreparedness of Russia for such a conflict (which, incidentally, also applied to other wars, defeat in which precipitated reforms and revolutions in Russia – as with the Crimean War of 1853–56, the Russo-Japanese War and the First World War). The number of troops once again proved insufficient, the armaments were obsolete, and weapons production depended on electronic components supplied from countries that had adhered to the enemy camp.

The impacts of the unsuccessful military campaign, the plan for which had been based on an underestimate by Russian bureaucrats of the strength of the Ukrainian army and of the readiness of the people to resist, were soon multiplied by the economic sanctions that the West imposed on Russia. The calculation in Moscow that a blitzkrieg would destroy the Ukrainian state and its armed forces in the space of three days proved illusory. The sanctions in turn not only disorganised the Russian economy and brought a sharp fall in output, but also exacerbated the disproportions in the global market. As a result, Putin after seven months of war was forced to declare a mobilisation, trying desperately to supplement the thinned-out armed forces with new recruits. The result, however, was merely to provoke an explosion of discontent and the mass flight from the country of men of call-up age.

The destruction caused to Ukraine by the war, and the economic losses borne by Russia as a result of the sanctions that followed, have reached such dimensions that it is pointless to talk of either of the states involved in the conflict experiencing a recovery on the basis of market methods. The decline in private demand has been so great that the only hope lies in an organised distribution of resources and a planned coordination of work on a national and international scale.

Nevertheless, it is not only the countries directly involved in the fighting that have been affected by these events. At the very beginning of the war the British Marxist Joseph Choonara wrote in the pages of the journal *International Socialism* that the consequences of the Russian invasion went 'far beyond the immediate geopolitical implications for the region'.[4] Western writers have noted mainly the economic problems that bear directly on the European consumer (rising prices, the financial losses of firms operating in Eastern European markets and so forth). Meanwhile, the catastrophe that has resulted from the adventurist actions of the Putin regime in Russia has marked the beginning of far more massive tectonic shifts affecting not just the countries directly involved in the war, but the entire world. In essence, the drama of 2022 repeated on the micro-scale the tragedy of the First World War, demonstrating starkly that in history situations of a similar character, arising from actions of a similar type, are reproduced again and again.

The lessons of the First World War

Explaining to his supporters the significance of the First World War, the British prime minister David Lloyd George spoke in 1915 of 'seismic disturbances in which nations leap forward or fall backward generations in a single bound'.[5] For all their seeming unexpectedness, such cataclysms are in fact the natural results of earlier processes, the sum of accumulated contradictions that for decades no-one sought to resolve nor was able to do so within the framework of the existing order.

Politicians are now beginning to behave as though they had gone out of their minds. In this regard the decision by President Putin to attack Ukraine, while lacking the accumulated resources to cover military needs, the strength that would guarantee overwhelming superiority on the battlefield, and the economic possibility of resisting the inevitable Western sanctions, can stand as a classic example of such madness, even more dramatic than the fit of insanity that seized the politicians and monarchs of the Old World in June 1914. In neither case, however, was the transformation accidental. It should be remembered, meanwhile, that just a few weeks before the catastrophe all these people had the reputation of being completely rational and experienced political actors.

Wars never begin by chance; they are prepared over the long term, and the conflicts that give rise to them mature not only on the political but also on the economic and even social levels. Nevertheless, the states that are drawn into these events have a record of being caught off guard not only by the actions of their adversaries and partners, but even by their own.

Historians of diplomacy, describing the moods in the ruling circles of Austria-Hungary and the German Empire in June 1914 after the murder of the Archduke Ferdinand in Sarajevo, note that at first 'total confusion reigned in Vienna', whereas the government in Berlin demanded harsh actions.[6] After a few weeks, when it had become clear that Britain would not remain neutral, the German government became conscious of the scale of the coming war. 'The picture immediately changed; in Berlin they were close to panic.'[7] The Austrians, however, had issued an ultimatum to Serbia, and could no longer retreat. The Russian government also 'felt uncertain', but could see no alternative to mobilising its forces.[8] German diplomats in their turn reported that the demands of Austria-Hungary had 'caught the Serbian government completely by surprise'.[9] Events, however, were now rolling forward irresistibly. Berlin reacted to the Russian mobilisation by declaring war, impelled by the 'internal political situation', since if military operations were launched 'under the slogan of a war with tsarism' it would be easier to cope with possible opposition from the Social Democrats.[10]

As can be seen, the decisions adopted by all the participants in the process were not consistent stages in the realisation of some earlier-developed strategy or plan. On the one hand, these decisions were the inevitable outcomes of preceding steps by the same governments, while on the other, the rulers themselves did not take full account of where their actions would lead.

What the diplomatic historians fail to discuss is the fact that everything was occurring against the background of a growing economic crisis, of increasingly acute social conflicts and of the obvious failure by the ruling classes to work out any programme for implementing overdue social reforms. Faced with a growing avalanche of problems and amid an unmanageable crisis, conservative governments inevitably begin reacting with panicked aggression, trying to solve internal problems using foreign policy mechanisms, and socio-economic problems through military-political actions. The struggle to expand the territories under their control is not only a means of distracting their populations from the crisis and of achieving national consolidation against foreign foes, but also an attempt to obtain additional resources, to restore socio-economic equilibrium and to export their problems abroad.

During a period of crisis the disproportions of market exchange become especially painful, and the need to concentrate resources, including at the expense of neighbours, particularly acute. Long-smouldering conflicts become more severe, and the behaviour of the various sides grows unexpectedly aggressive. The brief time available for making decisions, together with the stressful situations created by an increasing cascade of problems, multiplies the risk of mistakes at a time when even experienced politicians and state figures are beginning to make gross errors. A sense appears that the members of the elites have suddenly and collectively grown stupid – something that could readily be observed in the events that led up to the First World War. In such circumstances, foreign policy moves not only become mixed up with attempts to solve domestic political issues, but also come to be viewed as the best method for dealing with them.

The American scholars Matthew C. Klein and Michael Pettis argue convincingly that the growing incidence of trade wars and international conflicts, throughout the nineteenth and twentieth centuries and into the twenty-first, has been closely associated with an exacerbation of social contradictions and economic disproportions within the main countries that have been drawn into these clashes. The strengthened exploitation of these countries' own populations, together with the reliance on cheap labour that characterises liberal models of capitalism, forces corporations and governments to seek access to foreign markets, the volume of which is in turn limited. Competition for the remaining markets grows more acute: 'Over the past several decades, demand for goods and services has therefore become the world's scarcest and most valuable resource.'[11] Internal disproportions in the economies of leading countries lead to an overaccumulation of capital and to the clash of imperialist interests described early in the twentieth century by John A. Hobson, Vladimir Lenin and Rosa Luxemburg. As early as 1887 Friedrich Engels predicted that 'a world war of unprecedented scale and intensity' was approaching, a war that over three or four years would bring about economic devastation and the collapse of empires. Crowns, he foresaw, would 'fall by the dozens onto the pavements', and no-one would be found to pick them up.[12] This devastation, even while it drove society backwards and deprived it of a number of social conquests, would nevertheless create the conditions for socialist revolution.

This prediction of Engels was confirmed, even if only in part, during the First World War and the Russian Revolution of 1917 (which in turn was only part of a global revolutionary wave that affected Germany, Hungary, Mexico, and to some degree China and Türkiye. In similar fashion, the combination of an epidemic, a war and a social crisis has now shaken the foundations of states in Eastern Europe. It was not by chance that even before the Russian invasion of Ukraine began, mass protests broke out in Kazakhstan, where the authorities were compelled, albeit not for long, to import troops from allied states. In Canada, Australia and New Zealand public order was disturbed when opponents of the Covid restrictions staged protests, forming 'freedom convoys'. The government of China threatened to attack Taiwan, and soon afterwards, disturbances erupted in Iran. The point was not simply that people refused to be reconciled to the oppressive laws that had been imposed on them, while governments were unwilling to live in peace. Above all, it was that the accustomed order of things, after being in place for thirty or forty years, had broken down irretrievably.

When they heighten conflicts in the hope of solving them through the use of force, however, the ruling classes of warring states or of countries drawn into conflicts merely create new social and economic disparities, even greater than those they were trying to overcome.

It is quite obvious that both in 1914 and in 2022, it was the hope of being able to wage a small victorious war, which would enhance the authority of the government and act as a sort of inoculation against revolution, that prompted the rulers to engage in military adventures. If some of the actions of Russian president Vladimir Putin have seemed completely irrational, it should not be forgotten that even the madness that often afflicts dictators who have stayed in power for many years does not appear of its own accord, but develops as a side effect of the functioning of the system. Different social systems, cultures and political practices give rise to different manias.

'It has long been recognised', Lenin wrote in 1915, 'that wars with all the horrors and miseries that they bring with them perform a more or less important service in that they pitilessly reveal, unmask and destroy a great deal that is rotten, antiquated and moribund in human institutions.'[13] On this level, the Bolshevik leader considered, the war that had begun in Europe had performed an 'undoubted service' by revealing how opportunistic, corrupt and shameless the earlier leaderships of the workers' parties had become.[14] A very similar situation was to be observed in Russia in 2022, where the leaders of the 'opposition' parties in the Duma and even a certain number of left activists succumbed to chauvinist moods, applauding the military efforts of 'their' state in bombarding Kiev and Kharkov.

In 1914 the leading figures in the Russian left took a clear anti-war position. In the State Duma the Bolshevik and Menshevik factions spoke out jointly against the unleashing of armed conflict. Lenin immediately denounced all those who supported the war as social chauvinists whose ideology represented 'a complete betrayal of all socialist convictions'.[15] No less categorical was the leader of the left wing of the Mensheviks, Yuly Martov, who declared: 'The Social Democracy will either be resolutely internationalist in its thinking and politics, or it will depart ignominiously from the historical scene.'[16]

Nevertheless the voices of Lenin, Martov and Rosa Luxemburg, speaking out against the war, were drowned in the chorus of militarist declarations. The opponents of war and aggression everywhere finished up in a minority. They were subjected to persecution and repression, and were denounced as foreign agents. Everywhere, the leaders of the left parties supported their governments, calling on workers to go to the front. The vote by the German social democracy for war credits became a pivotal moment, rendering impossible any serious anti-war mobilisation in society as a whole. The same happened in France: 'When the voting for war credits took place in the Palace of Deputies, not a single socialist deputy spoke out in protest at the war.'[17] Things in Russia were no better. The left-wing Menshevik N.N. Sukhanov wrote later about the first days of the war,

when the patriotic upsurge was, it seemed, universal; when patriotic intoxication or a defencist way of thinking appeared to seize all without exception, when even among socialists one never met people who correctly grasped the significance of the war or tsarist Russia's place within it.[18]

As the historian Mikhail Krom notes, the position of social-democratic politicians who held ministerial posts (for example, Emile Vandervelde in Belgium and Jules Guesde in France) assumed a readiness by the bourgeoisie to make corresponding concessions to ensure class peace and the unity of the nation:

Although the left wing of the international social democracy (including the Bolsheviks headed by Lenin) condemned this step by the leaders of the European socialists, viewing it as 'treachery' and 'opportunism', there was a kind of logic in the leaders' behaviour. Apart from the fact that in the conditions of war hysteria, voicing pacifist and internationalist positions would have placed the party and its chiefs in a dangerous situation (thus, on 31 July 1914, as the war was about to begin, the famous orator, socialist and pacifist Jean Jaurès died from a gunshot fired by a nationalist), reaching an agreement with the government made achieving concrete results in improving the position of workers a completely realistic prospect. Hence immediately after the end of the First World War the earlier-mentioned leader of the Belgian socialists Emile Vandervelde and his comrades managed to win universal manhood suffrage (with limited suffrage for women) and the eight-hour working day.[19]

By contrast, Russian Duma leaders in 2022, while laying claim to the role of a 'left opposition', supported the 'special military operation' against Ukraine, without having obtained concessions or even promises from the authorities.

Opportunist support for the military efforts of a government might be depicted as a wise attempt to orient towards popular moods, but as the events of the First World War showed, these moods are liable not only to change, but to change in the most radical fashion. Once the masses see the light, of course, they do not blame themselves, but the politicians who deceived them. It is precisely the individuals who shouted patriotic slogans the loudest who come to be perceived by the people as bearing guilt for what has occurred.

After the assassination in Sarajevo, it took two years of bloodshed and suffering for mass consciousness to be completely altered, and for the militarist enthusiasm to evaporate. Replacing it was a wave of anger and hatred, directed inward against the governments of the warring countries. In Russia, the revolutionary agitation became more and more convincing amid

military failures combined with the progressive disintegration of the economy.
To a significant degree the Russian events of 2022 displayed the same dynamic,
though now with a quite different tempo. Few had been surprised when the
leaders of the official Duma parties, kept in any case on a short leash by the
Putin administration, spoke out predictably in support of the war, trying to
outshine the pro-government United Russia with their enthusiasm. But even
among the more radical members of the 'left-patriotic opposition', significant
numbers were prepared to support the military operation. When the failures
of the Russian army became obvious, however, anti-war sentiments in
society began growing rapidly, showing the depth of public mistrust of the
government's policies. A crucial point was reached when Vladimir Putin
decided to declare a general mobilisation. Even among the layers of the
population that shortly before had supported the authorities and the
military actions against Ukraine, Putin's move provoked a sharp outburst
of discontent.

The readiness to try to solve problems, both foreign and domestic, through
military action had the same sources as the government's inability to cope
with the pandemic except by resorting to the large-scale use of quarantines,
bans and police measures. As in the early twentieth century, conservative
and self-seeking elites concerned only with accumulating capital had led
humanity to upheavals that threatened the elites' own dominance. Nevertheless, the significance of war as a factor in social change cannot be reduced
to its effect in radicalising the masses, creating crises in government and
feeding moods of protest within society. By destroying the international ties
that allow the capitalist market to function not only on a global but also –
and this is especially important – on a national level, war creates the need for
a new organisation of the economy. This is a need that even the ruling classes
sense and are compelled to recognise.

In all of the major antagonist countries, the First World War gave
rise to the large-scale state intervention that came to be known as 'war
socialism'. For an economy, as M.I. Tugan-Baranovsky observed in 1915,
a large-scale war creates 'completely new conditions, that have nothing
in common with the normal conditions of the capitalist system'. To
ward off collapse, it becomes necessary to 'resort to methods alien to the
capitalist system and which it finds unacceptable under normal economic
conditions. It becomes necessary to use planning methods to distribute
the national product, and to replace the free play of economic forces that is
characteristic of capitalism with subordination of the economic whole to a
single, deliberate regulatory will.'[20]

The ruling circles in Germany had begun to do this as early as the first year of the war, when they established the War Committee for German Industry. After varying periods, the other countries participating in the war also followed the path of government centralisation, planning and regulation. The breaking of economic links, the need to do without imports and the growth of unemployment all required prompt solutions.

The military developments of 2022, from their first weeks, placed the principle of private property in question, forcing all sides in the conflict either to undertake nationalisations and confiscations or to threaten them. The Ukrainian government nationalised companies with ties to Russian capital, including Ukrnafta, Ukrtatnafta, Motor Sich and AvtoKrAz. The gas blockade of Western Europe begun by Russia in 2022 enabled a growth of state intervention in the energy sector. Once the Russian government started demanding that Western countries pay in roubles for supplies of energy carriers, the European states began reducing their purchases, while at the same time trying to optimise their consumption of oil and gas. This needed to be centralised and coordinated at the state level, renouncing the use of market principles in energy matters. The European Commission received the right to make joint purchases of gas and other resources for the entire European Union. Earlier, a similar decision had been taken with relation to vaccines during the pandemic. From centralised purchases, centralised and planned distribution necessarily follows. The way in which events developed thus objectively expedited the introduction of a whole series of measures from the arsenal of socialist planning. At the same time the Russian government, encountering a technological blockade, announced it would cease to observe the norms of intellectual property.

Germany nationalised a number of firms linked to Russian capital, while the property of oligarchs close to Putin was confiscated throughout. In Russia itself, however, the authorities both in 1915–16 and in 2022 showed a reluctance to take similar steps in timely fashion. Dictated above all by a fear of change and by a refusal of the ruling groups to sacrifice their short-term interests, this reluctance exacerbated the process of economic collapse.

'War socialism' and the myth of self-sufficiency

Twice in the twentieth century, world war led to massive disruptions and to the disintegration of economic ties and logistical chains, harming the economies even of countries that had not been drawn directly into the armed conflict. The Russian–Ukrainian war of 2022 set off the same process, despite not being fought on a global scale. The effect concerned, however, became possible precisely because socio-economic development had entered a fateful stage of systemic crisis. Rapid price rises, along with shortages of raw materials and components for industrial products, had emerged on a world scale even before the first shots rang out on the Russian–Ukrainian border. For lack of microprocessors, factories in Russia and many other countries had begun shutting down production or experiencing breaks in the rhythm of their operations as early as the summer of 2021. The military conflict simply completed this process, lending it an irreversible character.

The wave of sanctions that poured onto Russia after full-scale military operations began in Ukraine revived the theoretical concepts of economic self-sufficiency that had characterised the mercantilism of the late seventeenth century. It is curious that these views were often backed up with references to research performed by members of the school of world-system analysis, and especially to Samir Amin's concept of 'de-linking'. Significantly, these ideas were interpreted not in a Marxist but in a mercantilist spirit. While Amin understood by 'de-linking' the ability of a national economy to minimise its export of capital and to ensure development through internal accumulation (ideally, through the nationalisation of large corporations), in Russia's case the term was applied to attempts to secure economic self-sufficiency through autarchy – that is, the breaking of technological, productive and cultural ties to the outside world. This rupture in no way contributed either to the modernisation of the economy, or to freeing it from external dependency. Unlike in the Stalinist period, when the USSR pursued industrialisation by importing technologies and equipment that were advanced for the time, and by using them to create its own machine-building complex, what was now involved was the production of consumer goods corresponding to the standards of forty or fifty years earlier, since producing more advanced models was impossible under conditions where sanctions blockaded the importing of crucial modern components. The well-known economist Branko Milanović described what was occurring as 'technically regressive import substitution', noting that even if successful, this policy would lead to the archaisation of production, the deskilling of labour power, and a strengthening of dependency on the world market at the subsequent stage of development.[21]

To the superficial observer, the events of 2020–2022 may have seemed like a spontaneous and even absurd breakdown of normal life, a collapse of the pillars of the civilised world. Nevertheless, these events had their own logic and consistency. It was simply that this logic lay outside the bounds of conventional ideas of normal life – including the concepts of economists and politicians who championed the ideas and interests of the ruling classes. The underlying basis of the processes concerned was the crisis and gradual disintegration of the system of neoliberal capitalism, a process that had in fact already begun during the Great Recession of 2008–10. On the surface, the situation had been stabilised with the help of emergency financial measures, but these had not only failed to resolve any of the contradictions that were present, but to the contrary, had rendered them still more acute. Covid and war were thrusting the global and national economic systems in one and the same direction, reflecting an identical fundamental problem: the system was simply incapable of maintaining its equilibrium, lacking available resources and suffering breakdowns whenever challenges appeared that were outside the realm of the banal and everyday.

The destruction of logistical chains that had been created under the conditions of the globalised market, and which had been organised to suit transnational companies, began during the period of the Great Recession even before the appearance of Covid. The pandemic and the 2022 war merely accelerated these processes, showing that returning to the starting point even after the health and political circumstances had changed would not be simple. New productive and commercial links had begun forming spontaneously, and these also had a temporary and unstable character, posing the question of the planned reconstruction of networks of economic collaboration. For this work to be performed successfully, however, it was essential to go beyond the bounds of the economic logic that had been formulated on the basis of seeking immediate and short-term profit. In other words, a fundamental break was required both with neoliberalism and with the key economic principles of capitalism.

In essence, the conflict in Ukraine had become a crucially important stimulus for the realisation, in Western countries and on a global scale, of the changes that earlier had been proposed within the framework of implementing a 'Green New Deal', but that in fact were tied up with military necessity.[22] Nevertheless, the inevitable growth of the state presence in the economy does not automatically signify either a transition to socialism, or even that these measures will be comprehensive, effective and in the interests of society. The reconstruction of economic life cannot be successful and consistent in the absence of political and social changes, which in turn require that new people and forces come to power. Consequently, the events of 2022 once again confirmed that the left has a chance of gaining power when the old elites have not only exhausted their potential, but have also brought matters to an obvious breakdown, when the question is no longer one of constructing a new world, but of restoring at least the minimum necessary conditions for social reproduction.

Fascism in the epoch of postmodernism

An ideological peculiarity of the conflict that broke out between Russia and Ukraine in 2022 was that both sides were declaring their opponents to be fascists. Putin and his propaganda cited the activity of the numerous ultra-right nationalist groups in Ukraine, some of which had indeed been integrated into the state apparatus of coercion. The Russian propaganda also referred to the cult in the neighbouring country of the Ukrainian nationalist and Nazi collaborator Stepan Bandera. This was despite the fact that Putin himself regularly named Ivan Ilyin, who held similar pro-fascist views, as his favourite philosopher. Radical-left activists and groups were being subjected to analogous repressions in both states, while nationalist rhetoric featuring a hefty dose of open racism poured through the internet channels of the warring sides. Meanwhile the Ukrainian authorities, in documenting war crimes carried out by the occupation forces, stressed that such treatment of peaceful citizens had been characteristic of the Nazi occupiers during the years from 1941 to 1944.

Appearing repeatedly on the internet was a photo showing how, in the puppet Donetsk People's Republic, a decoration for participating in the de-Nazification of Ukraine had been awarded to the commander of a local militia unit, members of which showed up for the ceremony in uniforms bearing Nazi patches. The nostalgic torchlit processions with portraits of Stepan Bandera and other collaborationists that have been featured on Russian television to prove the need to struggle against 'Ukronazis' have been shown simultaneously with the cheerful depiction of analogous scenes in Russia itself. There, the symbolism of the so-called 'special operation' and the numerous ceremonies have revealed an obvious and conscious reliance on the aesthetics of the Third Reich, while the propaganda texts have been written in the style of the Nazi *Völkischer Beobachter* of 1939–45, using the same arguments and terms.

The spread of nationalist rhetoric in Russia and Ukraine was an important element in the cultural preparation for the slaughter that has shaken both states. Militarised right-wing radical groups in Ukraine have benefitted from sponsorship by the Jewish oligarch Ihor Kolomoiskyi, but this individual also sponsored the victorious presidential campaign of Volodymyr Zelenskyi, on whom hopes were initially pinned for a turn to more democratic development of the state and for the establishing of equality between languages and cultures. These hopes finished up being betrayed, and overcoming the schism within the country will be the work of many more years, despite the consolidation brought about by the resistance to the Russian occupation.

In Ukraine the need to resist the foreign threat has, despite the ideological efforts of the right-wing nationalists, objectively enabled the cohesion of Ukrainian society at least on the everyday level. In Russia the trend observed has been quite the reverse. However much the television shrieks about consolidation, society has experienced a deepening split, caused among other factors by the eclectic attempts of the authorities to combine nostalgia for the Soviet past (including the ideology of friendship between peoples) with misanthropic rhetoric of total annihilation. The mass discontent grew dramatically once Vladimir Putin declared mobilisation. Ordinary citizens, responding with uniform indifference both to the appeals from the authorities to put an end to 'Ukronazism' and to the reports on opposition internet channels on the miseries being experienced by the Ukrainian people, unexpectedly felt that attempts were being made to drag them into a deadly and pointless adventure.

The Kremlin propaganda declares unambiguously that the very existence of Ukrainian statehood and Ukrainian identity represents an existential threat to Russia, and must therefore be done away with. Everything Ukrainian is declared to be fascist by definition, and all those who admit to this identity to be fascists subject to physical extermination. It is clearly stipulated that in the first place, it is only Russians who have the right to decide who precisely is a 'Nazi' (and consequently, should be physically liquidated), while the right to speak in the name of 'Russians' belongs solely to authorised propagandists and state bureaucrats, while the rest of the national population has no voice. If they dare to object in some way they are declared 'traitors', 'foreign agents', 'non-Russians' or 'Nazi collaborators'. It is indicative that in this case the idea of genuine 'Russianness' coincides fully with the concepts of German Aryan identity adopted in the Third Reich.

The paradox is that the fascistisation of public discourse has proceeded under the slogans of anti-fascism. On the level of political culture the Russian authorities stress their adherence to 'traditional values' and even to archaism, trying to revive the age-old traditions of tsarism and Byzantinism, but at the same time the bureaucrats do not avoid making references to the great achievements of the USSR. Waving the red Soviet flag as a symbol of the 'Great Victory of 1945', they have continued demolishing Soviet monuments and purging the education system of any traces of the communist heritage, while simultaneously transforming nostalgia for the territorial unity and might of the fallen Union into a basis for their own claims on the territory of neighbouring post-Soviet states.

This inconsistency does, however, have its own logic. An eclectically aggressive postmodernism has triumphed. Whatever might be said about the Soviet or, for that matter, imperial heritage, Russia's ruling elite has been formed by three decades of neoliberal and globalised capitalism. Its sources of income are tied to the world markets for raw materials, and a complete lack of interest in the social development, science, culture and industry of the country itself serves to explain the catastrophic results that befell the elite's military adventure in the first weeks after the beginning of hostilities. None of this has been remotely like an attempt to construct rational, well-established institutions of totalitarianism; to the contrary, corruption and window-dressing have triumphed, while the state media-propaganda machine has been turned into a profitable sector generating huge wealth for the top figures drawn into it. At the same time any meaningful work, even including the preparation of the army and navy for war, has been pushed onto the sidelines.

David Harvey links the postmodernist thought-games and combining of images with 'the masking of the social effects of the economic politics of privilege'. Even before the epoch of Ronald Reagan this saw the rise of rhetoric that sought to justify 'homelessness, unemployment, increasing impoverishment, disempowerment and the rest by appeals to supposedly traditional values'.[23]

In this sense, the ideological ploys set in motion in Putin's Russia by the deft hand of presidential advisor Vladislav Surikov have in no way reflected a desire to return to the past, either imperial or Soviet, but instead a desire to keep up with the times and to match Western trends. Putin, for all his love of the archaic, has consolidated his power over Russia by being above all a figure of the twenty-first century. That is to say, he is a figure of the epoch of postmodernism, when an integrated worldview is replaced by an unsystematic pastiche of ideas, of fragmentary concepts and of arbitrarily assembled images. Further, he is a pragmatist with no firm principles apart from a conviction of his and the elite's complete lack of responsibility to the people under their control (something which, by the way, was impossible and unacceptable for monarchs in the seventeenth century). Meanwhile, the president himself and the elite circles around him are products of the social and cultural degradation of late Soviet society, together with the degradation of late capitalism. In this sense, too, Russia is not a tragic exception but on the contrary, part of the general current of ideological evolution of modern bourgeois society.

The classical fascism of the period from the 1920s to the 1940s was not simply an ideology, but a complex system within which an eclectic combination of elitist and egalitarian slogans, of anti-communism and of criticism of bourgeois democracy, served the goals of the totalitarian-corporatist reorganisation of capitalism within the framework of the national state. Fascism was closely associated with the anti-crisis restoration of national industry, on the basis of government regulation of the economy and under the auspices of large capital integrated tightly with a well-ordered bureaucracy.

Resting on a Gramscian analysis of the crisis that followed the ending of the First World War, Roger Simon notes that even though the ideological and political hegemony of the capitalist elites was shaken by these events, the workers' movement 'was unable to build an alliance with the different social forces capable of presenting an effective challenge to the ruling groups'.[24] In Italy this ideological and political vacuum was filled by fascism. Far more effectively than the moderate leaders of the social democracy, Benito Mussolini managed to sense the character of the moment, and to present slogans that expressed the rejection of the established institutions. 'In these conditions fascism found a mass basis in the urban and rural petty bourgeoisie who had become much more politically active as a result of the war.'[25] Unlike the left, however, fascism did not offer a socialist and democratic transformation of society, but the preservation and in part, administrative reorganisation of the old economic order in a new ideological packaging – populist and anti-democratic, combining a portion of the dissatisfied masses with part of the ruling class that was now incapable of running the country in the old fashion.

A fascist or Nazi project as comprehensive as this is impossible in the twenty-first century, because the classical industrial system on the basis of which twentieth-century fascism arose no longer exists, while the neoliberal market system has long since become the fundamental mechanism for reproducing the elite, not only in the field of business but also in that of state administration.

The cultural logic of late capitalism does not presume the integration of society, but its fragmentation. This fragmentation, however, is in direct contradiction with the traditions of civil society, of institutionally organised pluralism based on the horizontal solidarity of classes and social groups counterposed to the state and large capital. Precisely for this reason, individual elements of fascist ideology and practice are capable – in complete accordance with the aesthetic of postmodernism, which has its sources in the same social processes – of being employed in the most diverse contexts, though always with reactionary aims.

Elements of fascistisation may be observed even in long-established and still-robust liberal democracies, from Austria to France, where right-wing populism, though not simply a modern form of fascism, makes free use of ideological instruments from the fascist arsenal. This is still more evident in countries such as Ukraine, where a weak state has been combined with a fierce struggle between oligarchic groups capable of fielding their own independent coercive forces, or in Russia, where the raw-materials oligarchy, exercising its authoritarian might, seeks to overcome its crisis through employing totalitarian ideology and practice.

Nevertheless, the very fact that both neoliberalism and postmodernism are logically beginning to take on the characteristic forms of post-fascism indicates that the present epoch is drawing to a close. While making use of totalitarian ideology and rhetoric, the system is not in any state to construct a workable totalitarian machine that corresponds to these principles, either in the sphere of administration, or in that of production and exchange. As a result, the military confrontation that began in 2022 is merely among the symptoms of a crisis from which an escape needs to be sought along the road of recreating the mechanisms of democratic solidarity.

Reconfiguring the structures of capitalism

Among the secrets of wars, which destroy productive capacity and inflict losses on business while at the same time stimulating economic development, is that their causes need to be sought not in the concrete interests of various investors, trying to seize assets or win orders (though both of these take place), but in the general logic of the system. The reasons behind wars, that is, lie not only in the contradictions *between* the different sides in the process, but also in the uneven and contradictory nature of the *very process* of capital accumulation.

The Russian–Ukrainian war of 2022, or more precisely its global economic consequences, should be seen not just as fitting perfectly into the general trend of the structural reconfiguring of capitalism, something that began spontaneously back in 2018–20, but also as a mechanism that in a relatively brief historical time span permits the given tasks to be carried out. This connection was captured very precisely by the ecologist Svetlana

Krakovskaya when she stated: 'Human-caused climate change and the war on Ukraine have common roots – the use of hydrocarbon fuels and our dependence on them.'[26] The point, of course, is not that the dependence of Western Europe on Russian gas created the conditions for launching the war (though the people in Putin's entourage overestimated this dependency and accordingly, underestimated the readiness of the West to support Ukraine). Far more important is the fact that the war created the opportunity to introduce, at an accelerated rate, changes that were already overdue but that were being implemented only with difficulty. The rejection by Western countries of Russian oil and, with some qualifications, gas was not simply a tough and logical (though economically costly) answer to Putin's policies with regard to the neighbouring state, but also quickened the process of structural changes that had already been set in train before the war.

The restructuring of energy supplies would provide the opportunity to install new technologies on a massive scale, unleashing a new cycle of economic growth. What was important in this case was not how 'environmentally sound' these technologies were in themselves, but the fact that they would help overcome a drawn-out stagnation. Whether the results of this process would correspond to the goals and tasks of those who initiated it was a different matter. So too were the questions of whether the transformation would proceed exclusively in the interests of capital, and of whether it would act as the pretext for a new round of social struggles in which the preservation of the bourgeois economic system as such might be at stake.

Unfortunately for the ruling classes, and even for new political forces that might be capable of taking control of the state in a period of historical shocks, armed conflict sets in motion elemental processes that are both destructive and creative, and that in any case cannot be regulated by familiar methods. As Trotsky noted, a war 'cannot be ended at will after it has provided the revolutionary impulse expected of it, like a historical Moor who has done his work'.[27] The whirlpool of the crisis sucks in society and the economy. The relationship of forces in society, in economic management and in the bureaucracy changes, and new interest groups appear that lay claim to influence and power. At times, these are uninterested in solving the problems of which they themselves are by-products. Paradoxically, however, it is precisely the depth of the crisis, the tragic nature of the events and the scale of the destruction (all of which demand correspondingly massive efforts to restore production and normal social life) that have the effect of radicalising the changes, creating the conditions for the ascent to power of forces that shortly before were on the sidelines of the political process or that had no organisational embodiment whatsoever, but that were capable of implementing necessary changes in the most consistent and decisive fashion.

The restructuring that has fallen due within the framework of the world-system can be carried out by various means, at various rates and by different social groups. In essence, a war also poses the question of who will pay for the changes, and who will finish up benefitting from them. Inasmuch as the war gives birth to its own elemental processes, creates new interests and alters the relationship of forces, those who gain from it are by no means always the same people who were present at the sources of the conflict.

War and revolution

The connection between wars and revolutions was already obvious in the nineteenth century, when in France the events of the Franco-Prussian War led to the fall of the Second Empire, and then to the emergence of the Paris Commune. Still more evident was this connection in the cases of the Russian Revolution of 1905, which followed on from the Russo-Japanese War, and of the Revolution of 1917, which unfolded against the background of the defeat of the Russian army in the First World War. Coming soon after was the November 1918 revolution in Germany. In mass consciousness, the idea arose that lost wars inevitably set off revolutionary explosions, or at any rate led to serious reforms (here we may recall the link between the Crimean War and the abolition of serfdom in Russia, and the case of perestroika in the USSR, which began with the situation in which the Soviet army was hopelessly bogged down in Afghanistan). Not everything, however, is as simple as it appears at first glance. Lev Trotsky wrote tellingly of this, noting at one point: 'Defeats disorganise and demoralise the ruling reaction, but at the same time war disorganises the life of all society, and above all of the working class.'[28] It may be said that wars, and especially lost wars, create the need for changes and the possibility of bringing them about. The scale, direction and success of the changes, however, depend on the maturity of the political forces that take part in this process, and not just on their ability to interact with the spontaneous movement of society, but also on the degree to which their efforts conduce to social consolidation and the strengthening of solidarity, while preparing the way for practical solutions under conditions of acute crisis.

Wars shake up society, and impel millions of people to take part actively in events, even if ordinary citizens previously have had neither the urge nor the need to do this. Precisely for this reason, military conflicts often act as catalysts for revolutionary changes. But just as it would be naïve to think that these changes will proceed spontaneously in the direction we need, there is no sense in complaining if a catastrophe that suddenly descends on us has caught us unprepared. *Preparing in advance for such events is impossible in principle.*

The official version of Marxism that held sway in the Soviet Union not only depicted revolution as an instantaneous or very brief historical event, the essence of which would be the seizure of power by a vanguard party, but also presented it as the natural result of lengthy preparatory work conducted by that party on the basis of a conscious plan drawn up in advance. The armed people, flooding into the corridors of the palaces and ministries, would comprise the striking backdrop before which a quite different drama would be played out. The weapons would be celebrated, but it would be politics that steered the course. The dogmatic ideology declared the necessary condition of victory to be the presence of the 'subjective factor', in the form of already accumulated experience, mature leaders, and an organised party headed by them and prepared to immediately take control of the state. In essence, such a view of the transformation of society assumes that all revolutions are made 'from above', even if the initial impulse emerges 'from below' in the form of popular disturbances, uprisings or conspiracies by military officers. If you do not possess such a political instrument, constructed in advance, or if it is insufficiently strong, then it is better not to meddle in events. Instead, the best course is to wait dutifully for the happy moment when everything is just as required by the theory.

The actual history of revolutions, however, has little in common with this schema. The masses of the population who have entered unexpectedly (often, even to their own astonishment) onto the political stage are not in the least inclined to promptly leave it in order to make way for professional revolutionaries armed with a scientific ideology. Meanwhile, the revolutionaries themselves are never prepared in advance for the role they intend to play. Of course, they may at times imagine themselves as leaders who for some reason lack mass support. This support either remains to be won through persistent propaganda for the revolutionaries' ideas, or it will come of its own accord under the influence of experience. The fact that the masses, on acquiring new experience, begin to arrive at their own conclusions is viewed at best as something accidental and destined to be short-lived. The more that socialist and communist parties have sought to act in accordance with plans devised in advance or with ready-made theories, the more they have finished up, once they encounter genuine revolutionary events, in the position of the generals who, as the familiar adage has it, always prepare for the last war.

Genuinely successful revolutionary parties have invariably been the *products* of revolution, taking shape under the impacts of revolution, and to the degree to which a new political culture and practice has been formed.[29] This is why all victorious revolutions have been 'incorrect' from the point of view of theory. The social democrats made this criticism of the Bolsheviks, while the Soviet communists and their followers were unable to understand the Yugoslav, Chinese or Cuban revolutions.

If, however, revolution cannot be imagined or planned in advance, and if a revolutionary party constructed according to ready-made models from the past proves completely useless and even harmful at the moment when the masses begin to act, it does not follow from this that preparations cannot be made for large-scale social upheavals. The point is simply that these preparations must not consist of copying ready-made organisational models or of repeating familiar slogans, but of working within the current social agenda. Mass politics cannot develop in isolation from mass consciousness, and it will not always be the case that millions of people understand, immediately and adequately, the meaning of the tasks before them. The reason for which radical intellectuals and political activists even exist lies in their anticipatory work of understanding the tasks that are *coming due*, and of formulating demands accordingly.

PART IV

The Fallen Banner

9

Who Will Transform Society?

Anger, denial, bargaining, acceptance – in the standard account, these are the stages through which people's emotional state evolves when they encounter a catastrophic but insurmountable reality. The same terms can also be used to describe the successive changes in the state of left ideologues faced with the irresistible advance of neoliberalism.

'Acceptance' occurs in various forms, from open acceptance of the lack of any alternative to neoliberal politics on the part of right-wing social democrats, to the elaboration of all sorts of intricate ideological constructs by intellectuals such as Michael Hardt and Toni Negri.[1] The latter have attempted to justify support for the measures implemented by the ruling classes of the European Union on the basis that the development of capitalism will in itself lead to the system's downfall (while in consequence, the duty of right-thinking leftists is to collaborate with any initiative of the bourgeoisie). The point here is not just that these authors are at pains to pretend that they do not understand the dialectics of class struggle, in which the development of capitalism and the development of resistance to it go hand in hand, but that they also, and consciously, refuse to see the difference between progress and reaction within bourgeois society itself. Replacing analysis of the class structure with a story about a society of completely undefined 'multitudes', and rejecting analysis of concrete economic processes in favour of a narrative about the universality and simultaneous elusiveness of the contradictions of the modern global order, they casually deny the significance of any left-wing political activity. At the same time, they persist in laying claim to a political role within a system where there is no longer any meaningful alternative, but only discourse – radical, or not particularly so. The way in which Hardt and Negri manage to substitute literary images for sociological categories is undoubted testimony to their exceptional talents, but this does not negate the fact that they mistake (or pretend to mistake) the symptoms of the decay of the social structure for the social structure itself.

Meanwhile, the changes that have taken place in bourgeois society since the 1990s deserve serious analysis, and cannot be ruled out of account. Of fundamental importance in this case is the fact that as a result of the globalisation of the labour market, long-established intra-class links and mechanisms of solidarity have been broken. Until recently these played a crucially important role not only in the struggle of workers for their rights, but however paradoxical it might seem, in the effective reproduction and stimulation of the capitalist labour regime as well.

The shattered pyramid

The more integrated – from the point of view of the corporations – the labour market has become on the global level, the more discontinuous, heterogeneous and unstable it has been on the national and regional plane. The traditional pyramid of qualifications that used to exist in every industrial society assumed differences in skill levels and wages (from those of people carrying out the most primitive tasks, requiring no special knowledge or competency, to the members of the 'worker aristocracy' who held a privileged position not just in relation to their class brothers and sisters, but also to the enterprise management). Nevertheless, a direct link was also preserved between all these levels, along with the possibility, if a worker's career developed favourably and they were able to gain improved qualifications and knowledge, of advancement from the lower strata of this pyramid to the middle or even upper levels. Further, a gradual upward movement was encouraged within enterprises, with an employee's work history (including experience of work at the lowest level) becoming transformed into a sort of social capital, strengthening the worker's authority and raising their status. The progress of workers from one stage to the next within the skills pyramid preserved solidarity (the 'upper layers' of the working class, remembering their past and wanting to arrange careers for their children, did not cut themselves off from those lower down), while at the same time it strengthened discipline, maintained a culture of conscientious work within the enterprise, and created prospects that the management could use to stimulate workers. While strengthening the working class, this system also enabled the more efficient use of its labour on behalf of the capitalists.

In the conditions of globalisation, when various fragments of one and the same productive process may be scattered across different regions and countries, big industrial centres that concentrate masses of workers in one place disappear, and the chances diminish of people being able to choose for themselves a workplace that matches their qualifications (the nearest suitable vacancy may turn out to be hundreds of kilometres from a worker's home, if not on the other side of the planet). Within particular countries the organic integrity of the skills pyramid, its elements dispersed now among separate regions, is in turn undermined. Many skilled trades that in the past opened the way to higher status are becoming dead ends. Unbridgeable gaps have opened up between the workers in different sectors, trades and industries.

Andreas Reckwitz describes this as an 'hourglass structure',[2] within which there is almost no transitional space for the workers in the upper and lower levels of the system. Reckwitz links this to the specific features of the creative economy that he has investigated, but in analysing traditional industrial production we obtain a similar picture.

The most dramatic developments have occurred in the old industrial countries, which have experienced mass enterprise closures. Despite all the technological achievements, not a single society in the early twenty-first century has been able to rid itself of the situation in which huge numbers of people perform unskilled labour. In the changed conditions, the numbers of these people are even growing. The simple unskilled labour that earlier might have been just the first (and in its own way, indispensable) step in a lifelong career is now being transformed into a social dead end and a lifelong sentence. Meanwhile, significant numbers of these jobs are being filled by immigrants, or by workers from other parts of the country. While the former may somehow blend gradually into the host society, the latter tend not to develop firm attachments either to their jobs or to their places of residence, becoming in essence an element that is present in the productive process but has fallen out of the social system.

The economist Vyacheslav Inozemtsev, summing up the research devoted to the consequences of the technological revolution of the late twentieth century, states that the growth in the intellectual potential and expansion of the creative activity of one section of the workforce is seeing them increasingly cut off from the other part of the working class that does not have such opportunities, thus giving rise to 'a new type of social conflict'.[3] It is true that Inozemtsev as a convinced liberal does not see any great problem here, honestly believing that within the framework of Western-style democracy the natural processes of development will somehow solve this problem, with everything spontaneously working itself out. In the context of capitalism, he considers, the triumph of 'post-economic society' will come to pass, and thanks to the abundance of material goods the contradictions 'will not be as harsh as those dictated by the material circumstances in economic society'.[4]

Unfortunately, developments in the early twenty-first century have shown how naïve such ideas are. Skilled labour is being torn apart from unskilled labour, and the educated elements of society from the working poor. The atomisation of the workforce, socially and in terms of skills, is blocking the mechanisms of solidarity, while at the same time negatively affecting the general culture of labour, lowering its productivity. The fact that capitalism has consolidated itself on the social and political level is becoming a cause of inefficiency on the productive plane, and this is deepening the crisis phenomena. The contradictions of the system are growing more acute, but this is not leading automatically to popular mobilisation aimed at finding solutions to the growing problems.

Islands of spontaneous solidarity remain in certain trades, where jobs cannot be redistributed between countries and regions, or whose ties to one another cannot be broken down in some other fashion. For example, it was no accident that in 2022 it was actions by long-distance truck drivers that acted as the detonators for major social explosions (earlier, similar protests by drivers had occurred in Russia following the introduction by the authorities of new road taxes). In such cases, however, the solidarity that emerges has a corporate-professional rather than a class character.

The mass of workers, employed in very diverse jobs, only weakly connected with one another, and exploited using different and sometimes extremely sophisticated methods, are more reminiscent of people in the epoch of early capitalism than they are of the industrial working class of the twentieth century. This is why multitudes of angry proletarians are more inclined to come together under populist slogans than beneath the flags of traditional-left parties. It does not, however, follow from this that the familiar agenda of socialism and solidarity has become obsolete. To the contrary, it is becoming even more relevant, since the work of setting the scene for spontaneous working-class solidarity, something that capital itself once achieved for the forces of socialism, is now either not being performed at all, or is being performed very badly. The conclusion thus thrusts itself upon us that these tasks, despite being posed by the economic practice of neoliberalism, must be solved by political methods. If the old labour movement in most Western countries evolved from trade union self-organisation to political self-consciousness, in the twenty-first century this process needs to occur *in reverse fashion* – from populist social mobilisations to socialist and democratic politics, and through these politics, to the creation of class organisation and the restoration of solidarity networks.

The degradation of civil society

Throughout the twentieth century it was customary to think of civil society as a robust counterweight to the degradation of the state, to authoritarianism and to domination by elites or oligarchic groups. Uniting and organising different interest groups, including those on the bottom rungs of the social ladder, civil society in the view of Antonio Gramsci occupies a sort of intermediary space between the state authorities, which remain in the first instance an apparatus of compulsion, and the mass of the people, who through these structures are able not simply to defend their rights, but also to influence the taking of decisions. Gramsci noted that by the beginning of the twentieth century civil society had 'transformed itself into a very complex structure withstanding catastrophic "irruptions" of the direct economic element (crises, depressions and so forth)'.[5] In essence, civil society performs a dual function, restraining the radicalism of mass protests and at the same time creating impediments to arbitrariness on the part of the elites. Gramsci was inclined to attribute the savage nature of events in Russia between 1917 and 1920 to the weakness of civil society and to its inability to soften the form of the class struggle, a situation that in part aided the victory of the revolution. In the West, where democratic practices had a considerable history and were rooted in everyday life, events would develop according to a different scenario, resembling positional warfare, in which socialists would have to advance gradually, winning their own hegemony. Many years later the same point of view would be defended by the ideologue of the German 'new left' Rudi Dutschke, when he called on his supporters to begin a *long road through the institutions.*

Unfortunately, the development of events in the early twenty-first century has proved disappointing not only for admirers of liberal democracy, but also for those parts of the left that have sought conscientiously to implement such strategies. Parliamentary institutions have succeeded in 'digesting' radical politicians who have attempted to penetrate through the medium of these organisations and acquire influence and power. It is enough to recall the leaders of the German 'Greens' party, who began their careers as resolute fighters against bourgeois values and methods, but who later were transformed into ordinary political functionaries who staunchly defended this very system. The degeneration of radical ideologues and politicians, however, has been a minor problem against the background of the accelerating degeneration of civil society itself.

The neoliberal reforms that altered the economy did not leave aside the fundamental structures of society. Market relations, like metastases of cancerous cells, have penetrated civil associations, forcing them to orient themselves towards short-term efficiency and the positions of sponsors. Mass coalitions and movements have yielded beneath the pressure exerted by increasingly professional non-governmental organisations that initially occupied niches as 'representatives' of various interests, but which eventually outgrew this role and forced out the citizens themselves. Over time, the activity of the movements has come to consist essentially of supporting and reproducing these professional structures, made up of technocrats with their origins in civil society. Meanwhile, the grassroots interests have finished up as something of an obstacle to the 'normal' functioning of the NGOs.

The next, natural stage has been the depoliticisation of the population. Evolving in analogous fashion, the ties between citizens and political parties have grown steadily weaker, while the ability of people to organise themselves independently at the local level has diminished substantially even if it has not been completely lost. The place of organisers, propagandists, agitators and even ideologues has been taken over by professional political spin doctors, wonderfully adept at working with the mass media, but with little interest in thoughtful discussion. Worse still, any attempt to impose on society a discussion of essentially any question is now perceived by the system as interference in the normal functioning of the established mechanism of cultural communications, a mechanism that works according to the principles of commercial advantage and of the minimisation of costs and risks (among the last of which are any meaningful degree of unpredictability, and any discourse perceived by the community as undermining its stability).

How much this process has had its sources in a deliberate strategy of the elites, and to what extent it has resulted from a spontaneous process, is now impossible to determine, since both causes have undoubtedly been present. One way or another, the process by the 2020s had taken on a completely finished and to a certain degree irreversible character. The fact that the institutions of liberal democracy have been formally preserved does not ensure that they will function as in the past. Meanwhile society, stripped of its political and civil representation, has been left to itself. People avoid major questions and take refuge in their private lives, which in turn have become less and less free from the economic forces of the market.

Paradoxically, the depoliticisation of society has not, by any means, always served ruling-class interests. It has not negated or mitigated the contradictions of the system, but merely blocked any possibility of the masses understanding these contradictions in a meaningful way. Social conflicts still break through to the surface, but in the form of ideologically formless and unstructured revolts, whose destructive force grows in proportion to the absence or weakness of positive alternatives. This *alienated* form of protest in turn effectively blocks any long-term variety of reformist compromise, since the ruling class, on encountering a sudden threat, finds that *not only is there no-one to negotiate with, but there is nothing to be negotiated.*

At the grassroots level of society a feeling is taking shape, completely justified and reinforced on a daily basis, that the ruling elites and political bosses have lost touch with the people and are not simply indifferent to them, but even hostile. In most cases, intellectuals and opposition politicians are no longer viewed as resisting this state of affairs.

In Russia, the embodiment of the alienation of the elites from society has come to be the image of President Putin, protected by snipers on the rooftops and hiding from his own citizens behind a fence in the Piskarevsky Memorial Cemetery on the anniversary of the lifting of the Leningrad blockade. But in the West too, despite the observance of democratic formalities, the gap is felt no less keenly even if it is not expressed in so grotesque a fashion. Within society there is a firm and well-merited impression that the entire political elite, regardless of its ideological hue (something that for the most part is of interest only to professionals), represents a united, exclusive club that is off limits to outsiders.

By the late 2010s the divorce between the population and the political elite had not just become obvious, but was manifesting itself in mass revolts that shook countries of the most diverse character. The sudden vote by the British masses to take their country out of the European Union, the protests by the 'yellow vests' in France, and the urban uprisings and street clashes in American cities were all signs of impending disaster. The situation was aggravated by the Covid pandemic, which *irreversibly* undermined the familiar way of life. The huge and in essence revolutionary uprisings that seized such dissimilar countries as Kazakhstan, Canada and Iran in January 2022 were impressive symptoms of a systemic crisis, and at the same time an obvious manifestation of a catastrophic ideological weakness not just of the left, but of society as a whole.

The uprising of the forgotten

In late January 2022 Canadians in the most diverse parts of their country witnessed one and the same gripping spectacle. Thousands of trucks, decorated with national flags, slogans and sometimes also with the flags of particular provinces moved along the roads in the direction of the capital, Ottawa. This was a protest against compulsory vaccination, and received the name Freedom Convoy 2022.

Serving as the cause of the demonstrations were new obligatory norms adopted by Canada and the US at the beginning of the year. Fearing a new wave of the coronavirus epidemic, the Canadian and US governments adopted a complex of measures that as envisaged by the officials, would prevent the number of infections from rising. These measures included compulsory vaccinations, the presenting of test results, and quarantines. In Canada the new rules came into force on 15 January, and in the US a week later.

The long-distance drivers, who usually travelled alone in their cabs, were astonished and angered by the requirement for compulsory vaccinations. Although of course they moved between provinces, there was no way they could be considered active carriers of the disease. It was much easier to catch the virus on public transport than on the open road. The truckers considered compulsory vaccinations a violation of their rights. The slogan of the protest became the maxim: 'My rights don't end where your fear begins.'

It is not hard to guess that this whole story was no more than a pretext for a protest movement that had long been brewing. The scale of the movement, the massive support it received in the space of a few days, and the huge resonance it acquired throughout the world showed that more was involved than a specific labour conflict. Indeed, the protesters did not conceal the fact that their actions had far more serious goals that simply forcing the revocation of the decision taken by the federal authorities. The truckers stated that they had risen up in order to restore to people the freedom that had been stolen from them. But what was the freedom they were talking about?

The mass protests of the 2010s and 2020s, which began even before the coronavirus pandemic, have had two general and consistent sources. The drawn-out economic crisis, the stagnation and the loss of social rights, along with the blocking of vertical mobility that has robbed people in the lower strata of the social pyramid of any particular chance of rising higher, have provoked widespread discontent with the existing system. The protests have had a diffuse and unspecific character, but concealed behind their indirect and very modest demands has been a profound anger. Although the claims of the protesters have been exceedingly moderate (rescinding fuel price rises in Kazakhstan, and ending compulsory vaccination in Canada), the authorities have not only refused to make concessions but also to engage in dialogue, instead employing harsh repressive measures. In both cases *the authorities have understood the essence and causes of the protests better than the demonstrators themselves.* The majority of the protesters have been too poorly educated and too confused by propaganda to clearly formulate the reasons for their grievances, but they have felt clearly that something is wrong with the system.

In both Kazakhstan and Canada those who have risen up have been from the bottom rung of society, toilers who for many years have borne the burden of a disintegrating economy, and for whom talk of the successes of 'genius entrepreneurs' has seemed like just another admission of corruption. If we look at the people who took part in the Freedom Convoy, if we listen to their songs, delve into their complaints and evaluate their claims on the authorities, then we are reminded irresistibly of similar campaigns at the height of the Great Depression of the 1930s. The only difference lies in the power of the trucks – technology has not stood still over ninety years. These were the same working people, 'rednecks' performing hard work in the outdoors, of whom John Steinbeck wrote in his famous novel *The Grapes of Wrath*. In the mid-twentieth century such a movement would have been seen (and would have seen itself) as unquestionably left-wing. In the case of the recent Canadian protests, however, the tone among the ranks was set by right-wing populists, whom liberal intellectuals in the capital cities immediately christened extremists, racists and even fascists. The protesters were accused of 'western Canadian separatism', although the truckers themselves proudly waved Canadian flags and stressed that the movement united people from all ends of the country. Unfortunately, most members of the left intellectual and political elite also remained silent or uncritically repeated the discourse of the state propaganda. It is striking that no attempt was made on the left to analyse the situation independently, investigating its social and economic character.

The reasons for this outcome should not be sought in the supposed stupidity, ignorance and lack of culture of the 'rednecks' (though there were more than enough wild and uneducated people among them), but in the snobbery and opportunism of the leftists themselves, who preferred to socialise with refined members of the capital-city bourgeois establishment rather than to work with tough, harsh drivers, timber-cutters, steelworkers or farmers.

While the workers struck, organised demonstrations and imposed blockades, the deputies of the left-centrist New Democratic Party in the Canadian parliament sat quietly in their seats, trying not to remind anyone of their existence, though sometimes, it is true, calling for the police repression to be more severe. In university faculties, numerous left intellectuals made a point of discussing anything except the events unfolding outside their windows. By contrast, conservative deputies who earlier had not been noted for their sympathies with workers styled themselves as defenders of ordinary people, scoring political points in the process. The conservatives, at least, understood the scale and significance of what was occurring.

Of course, if the movement had been inspired by calls to struggle against the oppression of minorities – racial, religious, sexual or even gastronomic – the attitude to it would have been different. In such cases, however, the *economic* interests of the people who made up the minorities concerned would have aroused no interest among the intellectuals. The presence among the demonstrating truck drivers of Native Americans and even Afro-Americans would have altered nothing. After all, any attempt to appeal to class solidarity in order to resolve shared social problems is viewed as outdated and deserving of moral censure.

Culture wars

The intelligentsia has been drawn into endless 'culture wars' that began in the US, but that have spread gradually throughout the world. Issues such as the clash between 'traditional' and 'contemporary' values, questions of identity, and discussions of race and gender as the basic factors dividing people have now taken the place of earlier topics such as unemployment, social inequality and the contradictions between labour and capital.

Analysing totalitarian political systems in his *Prison Notebooks*, Gramsci remarked that these systems gave birth to situations in which political questions took on cultural forms, and as such, became insoluble.[6] The experience of the twenty-first century has shown, however, that the same tendencies can also be observed in formally democratic societies living according to the rules of neoliberalism. Confronted with growing crises, the ruling classes have a stake in diverting the protest energies of the people into the sphere of 'culture wars' that do not affect the economic foundations of society, and in provoking various groups of workers to struggle against one another.[7]

In culture wars the problems typically are not analysed, much less resolved (in principle, they cannot and should not be resolved on this level), but instead are labelled or at best, described. Otherwise, it would be necessary to admit that most of the questions concerned result from quite different factors, lying outside the bounds of culture or individual behaviour in the proper sense. The factors involved here are in the areas of economic and social relations, and a change of social relations means in turn that the questions under debate become irrelevant, or at least, need to be reformulated.

Cultural differences and contradictions, of course, exist and will continue to exist. Indeed, they are in principle unavoidable, though in the course of history they have altered their forms repeatedly, and will continue doing so. Particularly important, however, is the fact that the logic of culture wars is aimed at *transforming secondary personal differences into major political questions*. Since the late 1960s the ideology of various radical-left currents has been aimed at expanding the realm of the political to the maximum possible degree, including through transforming the personal into the political. Counterposed to the complete dominance of bourgeois normative culture has been multiculturalism. This has not, however, been presented as a choice between proletarian and bourgeois cultures (as in the works of Lenin and of the more radical members of the Russian avant-garde), but as a sum of the cultural practices characteristic of oppressed minorities, for the most part ethnic. The objective, while avoiding major struggles around questions of real weight, has been to give radicals the chance to enter politics, so to speak, through the back door, by prompting the main social forces to react to discussions on which, very often, they simply have no thought-out positions. Or else these positions, formed within the framework of traditional values and customs, have been exposed as weak within the context of modern public controversy.

This tactic (in part deliberate, and in part arising spontaneously due to the failure of struggles waged along different lines) has been stunningly successful. The main reason for this success, however, has been the benevolence of the ruling classes themselves and of large media corporations, which have viewed dialogue of this kind as a means of safely integrating former radicals into the establishment, and of reviving public life after the shocks of the 1960s. Neoliberalism has seized delightedly on the idea of expanding the sphere of the political, as advanced by a section of the left, since the more this sphere is broadened, the greater the degree to which politics becomes diluted and loses its sole genuine content as the struggle of different classes to win power or exert influence on it. The fragmentation of interest groups, their formation on a chance basis, and the institutional strengthening of these casual alliances through a system of well-organised and consistently financed non-governmental organisations led to a corresponding fragmentation of public discussion and to the disappearance (so far as mass consciousness was concerned) of 'grand narratives' – that is, of discussion of strategies for the development of society and of conversations about the fundamental *common* values on which this strategy might be constructed.

Needless to say, the end of 'grand narratives' did not by any means signify the disappearance of major social problems. Now, however, these problems were *not interpreted as such*, and were viewed as a mass of individual instances, with these individual cases able to acquire a thoroughly global scale (as, for example, with the case of the absolutely real – but far from unique, even on the environmental level – problem of greenhouse gas emissions). At the same time, there was one 'grand narrative' that remained completely untouched, and which in the absence of any alternatives became totally dominant. That was the tale of the universal and limitless possibilities of the private market.

The diversity affirmed by the logic of multiculturalism appears, of course, to be a development and confirmation of the principles of democracy. Simultaneously, however, it reveals contradictions of democracy that are especially important precisely in the context of bourgeois society. In the 1920s the conservative theoretician Carl Schmitt, analysing the constitution of Weimar Germany, noted that 'excluded from the purview of democracy are certain protected entities, individuals or groups of people that are free of obligations, and that as a result, are in a privileged position relative to the majority – as more or less exclusive, special communities'.[8] In Schmitt's view, this did not mean that such minorities had no need of certain guarantees: 'In reality, this need for protection may be very significant.'[9] The problem, however, is that the objects of this protection acquire a sort of exclusive status, being 'safeguarded from the majority because of their special innate value and probably, even due to their sacred character', while with regard to the majority, the effect is to express 'an undemocratic, even anti-democratic mistrust'.[10]

Here Schmitt, who personally always viewed democracy with scepticism, laid bare the obvious contradiction of democracy, a contradiction that has reached its apogee in the early twenty-first century. Defence of the rights of minorities is of course an indissoluble part of the modern democratic order, but what is involved here is the right of these minorities *along with the major-ity* to be free from persecution and discrimination. It is not an entitlement to special rights and privileges, which grant these minorities particular advan-tages. In this sense, the positive discrimination on which a section of the left insists is not just in contradiction to democracy, but like other neoliberal reforms, is an instrument serving to destroy it. This is not to speak of the fact that such policies *deliberately and consistently* drive the socially and culturally oppressed majority into the camp of reaction, creating what are at best false alternatives in the spirit of culture wars. These alternatives must inevitably come to replace the discussion of objectively important questions of social development strategy. Hence in the early twenty-first century it is proving necessary not only to defend minorities against democracy, but also to defend democracy against the dictatorship of minorities, or more accurately, against the dictatorship of neoliberal elites who hide behind an ideology of defending minority rights, and who call on members of the left to serve as their allies.

In this case, the fundamental problem is not the minorities themselves (as a rule these minorities have their own elites who have achieved their inclusion into the system, as well as their own majorities, who receive nothing or almost nothing from this 'defence'). The real problem is the neoliberal policies that consistently fragment society, turning the mass of citizens into an endlessly growing number of minorities that compete with one another for attention and privileges, just as buyers and sellers compete with one another in a marketplace. All the groups in this process are isolated from one another (at best, they are given the chance to forge coalitions among themselves), while their number multiplies as a result of the entirely conscious construction of identities, a task pursued by a growing army of intellectuals and professional media specialists. *The result is that the majority disappears, to be replaced by a mass of minorities who need to be protected, no longer from the majority but from one another* (feminists from conservative women, gays from Muslims, Muslims from Jews, Jews from antisemites and so forth).

The insistent public affirmation of group identities not only helps to divide people and to bring about an endlessly increasing fragmentation of civil society, but also to destroy civic identity as such. As Eric Hobsbawm observed in the 1990s,

> Human beings cannot be described, even for bureaucratic purposes, except by a combination of many characteristics. But identity politics assumes that one among the many identities we all have is the one that determines, or at least dominates our politics: being a woman, if you are a feminist, being a Protestant if you are an Antrim Unionist, being a Catalan, if you are a Catalan nationalist, being homosexual if you are in the gay movement. And, of course, that you have to get rid of the others, because they are incompatible with the 'real' you.[11]

According to Hobsbawm it is the presence and the combination of a multitude of identities that provides the basis for general politics, as opposed to the politics of identity. Left-liberal ideologues, of course, have taken punctilious account of this question, trying as always to resolve it mechanically and on a verbal level. They proclaim the principle of *intersectionality* – in other words, of combining a number of agendas dictated by different identities. The trouble is not just that the sum of these variegated parts fails to add up to an organic whole, but also the fact that a real unification is achieved in politics, and in life as a whole, through concentrating attention precisely on the *general*, thus allowing the differences to be overcome. Combining specific agendas constructed on the basis of identity politics may allow the building of coalitions, but not of a movement with a long-term programme for the comprehensive transformation of society. Further, this is not the goal of intersectionality, which does not propose altering social relations, but ensuring a more comfortable existence for a series of specific groups (or more precisely, for their elites) within the framework of the existing system.

This process, in whose development the left has played a considerable role, is leading not just to an undermining of class solidarity between workers, but to the total destruction of all social bonds apart from those that are inevitably fostered by the capitalist market economy – the ties between workers and employers, between superiors and their subordinates, between providers and clients, and between purchasers and sellers. As the French sociologist Christian Laval has noted, a 'dissolution of social bonds' is under way.[12]

The eventual political outcome of the spread of multiculturalist ideas among the members of the Western left has been a decisive breach between the intellectual representatives of so-called *cultural Marxism*[13] and the traditional worker masses. The stigmatising of 'white males', which has become a key element in the culture wars, has not simply divided America but has also undermined the fundamental cultural bases of class solidarity. A completely logical outcome of bourgeois hegemony, it has given rise in the postmodern epoch to a sort of *reverse racism* that has nothing in common with the real interests of ethnic minorities. This ideology, which conservative commentators identify as a manifestation of the 'Black racism' that they link to the emergence of the Black Lives Matter (BLM) movement, in fact has quite different roots. This is indicated by the evolution of the BLM movement itself, which arose as an attempt to solve the completely specific problem of police violence against Black Americans. Also significant is the fact that this movement arose after Barack Obama had spent eight years in the White House. The promises made by the progressive intelligentsia, whose members had convinced themselves and society that the colour of a president's skin would be of decisive importance in public life, and would help to radically improve the position of the socially deprived, turned out to be worthless. As noted by the political scientist and left activist Chris Cutrone, BLM arose 'from disappointment with a black president'.[14] In the context of American left-liberal politics, however, this protest quickly changed its vector and was transformed into a media symbol of struggle against 'the violence of white males', which was not what Afro-Americans were waging at all.[15] In reality, what is involved here is a new version of the same *white racism*, but now turned *inward* and reproducing in a negative sense the same idea of *white exclusivity*, but in the spirit of Freud, replacing pride with shame and with the demand to recognise a collective responsibility of ordinary workers for actions committed not just by other people in a different epoch, but also (and this is especially important) by members of a quite different class that is hostile to them.

In the late 1990s, when multiculturalism and identity politics were merely beginning to come into fashion, Slavoj Žižek warned that concealed behind the progressive façade of these ideas was a new racism that represented an 'ideal form of ideology' for the new global capitalism, a cultural project for a sort of new colonialism, directed not only outward from the West but also inward, and for which the colonisers no longer had any need of a 'Nation-State metropole'.[16] Meanwhile, the people of the former metropoles were themselves being transformed into objects of colonisation, without ceasing to be part of the capitalist core. If the classical imperialism had used the exploitation of the colonial and semi-colonial countries of the periphery to lessen the sharpness of the social contradictions in the states of the centre, neoliberalism was using the same method of global expansion in order, through harsher competition, to do away with many of the concessions that had been made to workers in the wealthy countries. At the same time, it was cultivating a sense of guilt among the populations of these countries, undermining their self-respect and in their societies, inspiring a sort of cult of victimhood. People were finding it more advantageous to declare themselves victims, in need of being defended, than to *overcome their differences* and to join in struggle for their common rights. This was, of course, still the old maxim of 'divide and conquer', but in a far more cynical and hypocritical form than under the earlier empires.

It is significant that the spontaneous popular protests in Canada in 2021 and 2022 provided an unexpected deconstruction of the system of slogans and discursive arguments that underpinned the logic of political correctness. Thus, for example, the slogan 'My body – my choice', used previously by feminists demanding the right to abortion, was now proclaimed by opponents of vaccination, while the liberal Canadian premier Justin Trudeau told the protesters that he would not take their rights into account since they were a minority. Earlier, Trudeau had stressed that defending minorities was his policy priority.

Fortunately, the gap between the left and the worker masses was not everywhere final and irreversible. In France, for example, the demonstrations by the 'yellow vests', like those of the 'convoy of freedom', found determined support from the 'France Insoumise' movement of Jean-Luc Mélenchon.

France Insoumise became the largest force on the French left, while after zealously repeating modish ideas in the spirit of identity politics and participating actively in the culture wars, the old left organisations, the Socialist and Communist parties, went into rapid decline. Against a background of consistent failure by other movements, organisations and projects, Mélenchon's unique success testifies to the acuteness of the problem and to the need for a rethinking.

The left against the workers

In the early 2000s the American sociologist Thomas Frank published a book entitled *What's the Matter with Kansas?* showing how this state, which had been considered a stronghold of the progressive movement, had become conservative. Since the beginning of the 2000s workers in the US, to the horror of the liberal left, have preferred to vote for conservative republicans. 'The backlash seems so improbable and so self-contradictory that liberal observers often have trouble believing it is actually happening', Frank remarked.[17] The same trend has also begun spreading gradually in Europe, where despite the customary ties between the worker masses and left parties, an analogous shift has been occurring in the direction of right-wing populism. Meanwhile the left liberals, who have abandoned the workers to the whims of fate, not only refuse categorically to admit that they bear responsibility for what is occurring, but also refuse categorically to do anything to put the situation right. In these circles the conviction has gradually taken shape that the task of politics is to defend enlightened and progressive people, who naturally belong to the top layers of the middle class and to the bourgeoisie, against the barbarous mass of the uneducated who make up the lower orders of society. In the view of Tom Frank, the trend in the US Democratic Party towards rejecting efforts to retain the votes of workers amounts to 'a criminally stupid strategy'.[18] Even more stupid and irresponsible, however, has been the position of those members of the left who have found nothing better to do than to line up behind this strategy, trying to lend a more radical meaning to politics that remain unchanged.

Early in the twentieth century Werner Sombart wrote:

The United States of America is a promised land, a Canaan, for capitalism. Here for the first time all the conditions indispensable for the full and clear development of its essence have come into being. Like nowhere else, the country and its people are suited to the development of capitalism in its highest forms.[19]

In the US there were no institutions inherited from feudalism, resources were present in abundance, and dominating business life was 'an *economic rationalism* of a purity unknown to any European society'.[20] American workers linked their prospects to two official parties that, while of course expressing the interests of the ruling class, at the same time also created significant career possibilities for people from the lower orders of society. Meanwhile, the wages of working people were rising far more rapidly than in other countries. Nevertheless, the German sociologist at the end of his research on America drew this conclusion:

> All the factors that until now have held back the development of socialism in the United States must soon disappear or turn into their opposites, and all the signs are that among the next generation of Americans socialism will, as a result, develop with exceptional force.[21]

Sombart's text was written at the very beginning of the twentieth century, and we know from history that during the century and more that followed his forecast has not been confirmed, despite the shocks of the Great Depression, the protests of the 'new lefts' in the 1960s and 1970s and the rapid development of academic Marxism in American universities. The reason for this state of affairs should be sought above all in the place occupied by the US in the capitalist world-system; by the beginning of the twentieth century it had become the world's leading economy, and would soon be the global hegemon. But more than a century after Sombart made his forecast, there are very good reasons to recall his prophecy. As American global hegemony grows weaker, all of the internal contradictions that for many years have been implicitly undermining the social order in the world's leading power have become more acute. At the same time, the ideological hegemony that allowed the ruling classes to subject American workers to the prevailing agenda has vanished into the past. In the history of Britain, the gradual but relentless decline of the empire was accompanied in exactly the same way by a parallel growth of socialist moods and by the emergence of the workers' movement from beneath the tutelage of progressive liberals. In the US the ideas of socialism have begun rapidly winning popularity, and the various successes scored by the presidential campaign of Senator Bernie Sanders, who put forward openly left-wing slogans, were merely symptomatic of far more profound changes. Unlike Britain in the early twentieth century, however, the ideological crisis of the old order in the US has not been combined with the appearance of a clear ideological and moral alternative, since the consciousness of leftists themselves has been littered with the ideas of radical liberalism and of 'cultural Marxism', ideas that for many years have been a sort of password for participation by intellectuals in the politics and apparatus intrigues of the US Democratic Party.

In 1977 the Spanish Marxist Professor José Bermudo remarked that the Western left was characterised by 'a definite sense of powerlessness, a lack of faith in the revolutionary character of the labouring classes'.[22] It was these sentiments that became the basis for strategic decisions. Over a lengthy historical period the socialist movement became degraded, losing its class character and basing itself instead on ideology. Then from being ideological this basis became cultural, and ultimately, the movement was transformed into a heterogeneous sum of subcultural groups. The result was that a crucial gap opened up between the movement's working-class supporters and the left intellectuals, a gap that was widened further by the aggressively dogmatic culture and scandalous condescension of the left elites.

No-one on the left, of course, has ever accepted the blame for what has been happening. Worse, no-one has ever called for the reasons behind the situation to be analysed. At first glance, the response required is obvious: if the left does not like the way the workers see things, then it should try to change their views. But any attempt to do this will require the left to undertake a radical self-criticism.

If the mood of the masses is to be changed, the need is not to orient to their views, but to their interests. The tragedy is not that workers in the US voted in 2016 for Donald Trump, or that they did so in even greater numbers in 2020. The real tragedy is that in doing so, they were correct after their own fashion, since the Democrats had done nothing to prove to them that the reverse was true. If the preceding Democratic administrations had been clearly and perceptibly better for workers than the rule of Trump, then people would have discovered their error and reoriented themselves towards the political force that better corresponded to their interests. This has failed to occur, not least because the left wing of the Democrats has capitulated again and again before the right. This fact is no secret to anyone, but it is still necessary to ask why it should have been the case. The answers need to be sought not in the weakness of the members and leadership of the left, but in the very nature of their politics, which is oriented exclusively towards their current values. These values, meanwhile, align them precisely with bourgeois liberals, with whom they find it easier to discover a common language on the level of discourse.

Analysing this situation, Andreas Reckwitz notes that to the extent that the values of the creative middle class triumph within society, the people at the bottom of the social heap become the objects of 'negative culturalisation, of devaluation'.[23] Their problems are seen less as the consequences of economic and class relations than as the results of their own cultural backwardness, of their inability to accept and assimilate new values, and of their reluctance to alter their way of life. Rejected by the progressive liberal establishment, members of the lower classes in their turn seek support from right-wing populists. And they find it.

The result is that the majority of workers in the US – and not only there – view the left as a handful of dissolute elite intellectuals, not just alien to the cares and problems of the masses, but also deeply hostile to most of the population. The saddest thing is that for the most part, this idea of the left corresponds completely to reality.

It is necessary to recognise something that was obvious to socialists during the nineteenth and most of the twentieth centuries, but which politically correct members of the left in the early twenty-first century refuse to take into account: workers have their own interests that are completely objective, and the left is obliged to express these interests and defend them. If the left is unwilling to do this, then the workers will defend these interests anyway (at least in economic terms). *The workers will do this without the left, and if necessary, in opposition to it.*

A hatred for the working class, undeclared but persistent and almost instinctive, has now become a fundamental part of the new 'left' culture that from the US has penetrated into Western Europe, and which by the early 2010s had reached Russia as well. The uneducated toilers are perceived as a malign and threatening mass, belonging in effect to another biological species, who, naturally, cannot have sovereign rights, or legitimate interests, or thoughts and especially values that deserve to be taken into account. This has led intellectuals, in logical fashion, to approve of virtually any measures restricting the civil rights of those who are not included in the agenda of the liberal establishment, not to speak of the fact that any propaganda lie spread by the liberal mass media is not just accepted as truth, but is deliberately spared from critical examination. This has all became strikingly reminiscent of the depiction of the future in the novella *The Time Machine* by H.G. Wells, in which society has finished up divided into two incompatible species, the refined Eloi and the fearsome Morlocks who toil on their behalf.

Meanwhile, the trucks travelling towards Ottawa have provided a powerful signal – not only for the establishment, the politicians and the financial magnates, but also for the multitude of intellectuals who consider themselves critics of the system: the grapes of wrath are in fact ripening. Regardless of whether we like the form that the protest movement is assuming, it is becoming a legitimate product of the crisis.

Describing the protest moods of the precariat, Guy Standing notes that the dissatisfied masses lack any clear ideology or programme, and moreover, perceive their own interests only very dimly:

> They are prone to listen to ugly voices, and to use their votes and money to give those voices a political platform of increasing influence. The very success of the 'neo-liberal' agenda, embraced to a greater or lesser extent by governments of all complexions, has created an incipient political monster.[24]

As Standing observes,

> the ageing trade unionists who normally orchestrated May Day events could only be bemused by this new parading mass, whose demands for free migration and a universal basic income had little to do with traditional unionism. The unions saw the answer to precarious labour in a return to the 'labourist' model they had been so instrumental in cementing in the mid-twentieth century – more stable jobs with long-term employment security and the benefit trappings that went with that. But many of the young demonstrators had seen their parents' generation conform to the Fordist pattern of drab full-time jobs and subordination to industrial management and the dictates of capital. Though lacking a cohesive alternative agenda, they showed no desire to resurrect labourism.[25]

In reality, the precariat described by Standing is in no sense a class. Further, the inability of this mass of people to formulate their own programme, or to construct organisations that even after a fashion speak in their name and defend their interests, is more than significant. In the few cases in which the economic goals of the precariat have in some manner been realised, this has been achieved by the traditional left, organising these workers as if *from outside*, relying on the traditional structures and resources of the trade union movement (as, for example, in the case of the successful strikes in Russia in 2020 and 2021 by delivery workers, organised by the Kuryer union). Nevertheless, it does not by any means follow from the social weakness and contradictory consciousness of this oppressed and disempowered mass that these people lack their own interests. The problem is simply that in the first place these interests, even those that are purely economic and immediate-term, cannot be realised or defended except within the framework of more comprehensive social reforms, implemented on the basis of a socialist programme. Second, the scheme that was characteristic of the old workers' movement, and in which trade union mobilisation and the defence of economic rights preceded political struggle, does not work. In this case everything occurs in the opposite fashion. Political mobilisation is becoming the most important condition for social consolidation.

Of course, if we look at the history of the workers' movement in the classical industrial period, it too was far from developing in a linear fashion. The activity of thousands of trade union activists and socialist agitators bore a direct relation not only to the formation of the organisational structures and ideology of the labour movement, but also to the emergence of the working class itself (or at least as a 'class for itself', capable of recognising its interests and defending them). Under the conditions of the crisis of neoliberal capitalism, however, this work in many cases has not only to be performed afresh, but also has inevitably to be carried out in a *more radical* form, since as has already been seen, purely economic struggle is now becoming insufficient, and at times impossible. In exactly the same fashion, it is also impossible to try to rebuild the structures of the welfare state that capital has destroyed. To restore the social cohesion of society under the new conditions, a far more decisive assault on capital is required.

Classes and interests

In the historical perspective, György Lukács wrote, class interest 'does not coincide either with the totality of the individuals who belong to a class, or with the actual, immediate interests of the class as a collective unit'.[26] But who, in such a case, formulates and expresses this most general interest? Who takes care to see that this interest is realised through fundamental social transformations, often at the cost of these same immediate interests of the class, and especially of its individual members? From the point of view of the classical Bolshevik ideology of the 1920s, to which Lukács himself adhered, the bearer of this consciousness becomes the proletarian party, armed with Marxist theory. Hence also the belief of many old Bolsheviks, repeated even in the heat of the Stalinist repressions to which they themselves fell victim, that the party could not be mistaken. In the twenty-first century, unfortunately, we can no longer recognise such formulations as correct, not only because of what happened in the Soviet Union (and not just in the 1930s), but also because modern politics and society simply do not permit the construction of a united, ideologically motivated vanguard party able to formulate and put into practice the collective will of the entire movement. The pluralism of the left forces, whose reflections also include the heterogeneity of the class interests of working people, is now not just a political but a sociological fact. This, however, in no sense does away with the problem that Lukács identified.

It would appear that the objective class interest is formulated and realised only *in the process of history*, as the incompleteness or even failure of each of the various attempts at revolution merely brings us closer to understanding the objective tasks and possibilities of the movement. The task both of theoreticians and politicians, however, is nevertheless to try to comprehend this interest (which has a social as well as class character) as well as can possibly be managed, to formulate it and to act on its basis. It is necessary to do this while having no possibility of compelling others to accept one's understanding of the truth, but while acting nevertheless on a firm and soundly based conviction that knowledge of the truth gives us the *chance* of historical success. Here once again we confront a fundamental problem of social thought: theory cannot remain abstract, since it cannot have any prospect for being developed outside of practice. Consequently, a socialist theoretician who is unwilling and unprepared to engage simultaneously in politics is a bad theoretician.

The logic of neoliberalism exacerbates the fragmentation and atomisation of society, on the social, cultural and even technological levels. In itself, however, this problem is far from new to capitalism. As Roger Simon has written,

> The very notion of bourgeois society is self-contradictory because the class power of the bourgeoisie is rooted in the *anti-social* individualist logic of the market. Liberalism, the bourgeoisie's classical and essential legitimizing ideology, emerged from the atomized relations of buyers and sellers on the market.[27]

The sociologist Charles Thorpe, analysing how neoliberalism shapes the system of rules and values of the *post-normal* society of the 2020s, voices similar thoughts: 'The contradictory anti-social competitive sociality of the market, whereby what brings people together is what holds them apart, is reflected in the contradictions of liberalism and of liberal sociology.'[28]

> Consequently, the mosaic-like social structure of late capitalism is not only incapable of fulfilling the completely traditional tasks of struggling for the consolidation and defence of social interests, but to the contrary,

it demands of members of the left a consistent loyalty to their fundamental mission, which defines their role not only as a force acting to overcome capitalism, but also as a factor stabilising and strengthening society within the framework of capitalism.

It is significant, however, that the extremely mosaic-like nature of the *social fabric* of late capitalist society in many ways replicates the similar heterogeneity and illogic of the social relations of the late feudal epoch, when numerous social ranks and caste rules inherited from the Middle Ages were superimposed on the new social relations that had been created by market forces and by the dynamics of the emerging period. This resemblance not only bears witness to the fact that capitalism, like feudalism in earlier times, has outlived itself, but also testifies to the onset of a revolutionary epoch that will demand of society a *radical simplification*.

Unfortunately, the fact that there is a crisis and that social contradictions are growing increasingly acute does not by any means guarantee that these problems will be solved. Gathering different social forces, classes and groups beneath a common flag is like transforming a mosaic-like scattering of elements into a coherent picture that nevertheless consists of innumerable discrete fragments. Attempts to draw up all the participants in the process into a single column, subject to strict discipline or centralised direction, will not yield the expected result. Such attempts worked badly in the twentieth century, and certainly will not work now.

Nevertheless, the endless rivalries and conflict within the left do nothing to strengthen the movement, and are also demoralising to society. Describing the crisis of left-wing political structures, Johen Steinhilder, who analyses global political questions for the German social-democratic Friedrich Ebert Foundation, observed that the differences between radical currents and groups reflect the objective diversity of society and of the working class (something already noted in the 1970s by Soviet researchers studying the Latin American left). Hence the obvious conclusion that it is necessary to 'work positively with these differences'. At the same time, it is essential to recognise that 'today this is not so easy, since there is a great deal that divides us (and that needs to be clarified)'.[29]

The answer, however, lies not just in the left searching for compromises and for positions that allow unity, but also in its coming to understand the concrete social interests on which this unity must rest in the long term. In other words, the need is for the reconstruction of the working class (as a 'class for itself') through practical activity and political struggle *for its most general interests*.

Referring to the Gramscian concept of hegemony, Roger Simon notes that the formation of a new historic bloc capable of taking power and transforming society

> requires a transformation in the political consciousness of the working class and also of the members of other classes and groups whose support is needed for the broad alliance. Ideology acts as the cement or cohesive force which brings together a bloc of diverse classes and social forces. The cementing ideology cannot therefore be a pure class ideology expressing only the class interests of the capitalist or the working class.[30]

The role of intellectuals and politicians is not, of course, to invent ideologies but to find historically significant points of convergence between different social forces, while directing their energies into serving the common cause. To achieve this, the intellectuals and politicians need an understanding of these matters and of their social significance, along with an understanding of their own mission. Here again one can only recall the precept of Max Weber: if you want something, you need to orient towards the essential elements involved, and to take responsibility for the *consequences* of your actions.[31]

Victories that have turned into defeats

As Weber wrote, 'all historical experience confirms that the possible could not be achieved if people in the world did not reach out again and again for the impossible.'[32] Anyone who wants to change the world 'has to be a leader, and moreover, has to be – in the simplest sense of the word – a hero. Even those who are neither one nor the other need to arm themselves with a firmness of spirit that will not be broken even by the collapse of all hopes; and they need to arm themselves with it right now, since otherwise they will not be able to achieve even what is possible at present.'[33]

Unfortunately, after surviving a series of failures and defeats the members of the left have painstakingly reduced their proposals to a 'realistic minimum' that reflects not the overall interests of working people, but the thinking of particular politicians on the changes that are acceptable to the ruling elites. Again and again, the left has proven incapable of implementing even this modest programme because of the irreconcilable opposition of the bourgeoisie. At the same time as studiously demonstrating their moderation on questions of substance, left-wing politicians have not been sparing in their use of radical rhetoric that contrasts catastrophically with their minimal demands and still more modest achievements. Reduced to a contest of rhetorics, the political struggle has turned into a meaningless waste of breath, at the same time as the rhetorical inflaming of social moods has resulted in mass frustration, the only beneficiaries of which have been the ultra-right.

The experience of the past few decades in Latin America has shown that the left is capable of winning votes and taking power. On the electoral level, left populism has proven extremely successful.[34] Each of these victories, however, has invariably been followed by a defeat. In some cases the regime established by the left has undergone a degradation, becoming transformed into a corrupt bureaucratic dictatorship, which unlike the post-revolutionary regimes of the twentieth century in the USSR and Cuba has not even tried to do anything serious to alter the social structure of society, not to speak of advancing towards socialism. This is what has happened in Nicaragua, where after a lengthy interval the Sandinista movement returned to power but turned out to have lost its revolutionary potential. It has also occurred in Venezuela since the death of Hugo Chávez. In most cases, however, the left governments after carrying out a number of successful but limited reforms have become bogged down, have lost their perspectives, and at the next elections have yielded power to the right. This is what happened in Brazil with the Workers' Party, and so it was too in Argentina and Uruguay. As Max Weber would have said, 'the curse of seeing their creature turn into nothingness hangs over the most seemingly powerful political successes'.[35]

In itself, to be defeated in an election is nothing calamitous. This is the normal succession of parties in office under the conditions of democracy. The trouble is that again and again, such defeats have led to the dismantling of all the progressive changes achieved as a result of the preceding victories of the socialist parties and coalitions. While in the period after the Second World War the reforms introduced by social-democratic governments (often with the support and participation of communists) were consolidated, remaining as the foundations for further development, in the epoch of neoliberalism the opposite has happened. Following the defeat of the Labour Party in Great Britain in 1951, the Conservative cabinet of Winston Churchill did not do away with any of the reforms enacted by the cabinet of Clement Attlee. But after the defeat of the Workers' Party in Brazil the right-wing government of Jair Bolsonaro began steadily abolishing the social programmes, including the extremely popular Bolsa Familia programme of assistance to the poor, that had helped millions of people climb out of destitution.

The political failures of left-wing governments around the turn of the twenty-first century are easiest to explain on the basis of the simplistic maxim that power corrupts everyone without exception, and that politics is a dirty business from which no good can ever come. This ideology, penetrating into mass consciousness, becomes a crucially important factor for reducing citizens to passivity, and acts ultimately to liquidate democracy, in essence if not in form. Fortunately, political history shows that everything happens quite differently, and that in each instance the corruption of state figures has completely specific causes that must be sought in the particular circumstances of their rule and in their modes of operation. As the distinguished culturologist Leonid Batkin wrote when analysing the works of Machiavelli,

> in the course of political struggle, honest people will in all circumstances remain honest people. But first, they will have to accept responsibility before their consciences not only for their own actions, but also for the actions of the other people with whom they act in concert, and not only for the immediate results of these actions, but also for the indirect and remote historical consequences. Nor, to take a well-known example, is it excluded that if, say, they encounter the need to resist the merciless and hypocritical violence of a totalitarian regime, such people will be forced to decide afresh what, properly speaking, it means for them to remain honest. Morality is born at the moment when they make their choice – on their own responsibility, and not as the result of imposing some ready-made paradigm. In politics and in history, the defining by the individual of the limits of this responsibility becomes in turn a crucial moral question.[36]

Employing Machiavelli's categories, we can say that the reasons for the degeneration of left-wing governments should be sought in the way in which the 'mode of action' (*il modo del procedere*) of these governments is related to the existing 'order of things' (*l'ordine delle cose*).[37] The fact that events have developed again and again in this fashion cannot be explained solely on the basis of the miscalculations or venality of particular politicians. The problem is systemic. The rhetoric of left parties, a rhetoric demanded by the masses, allows these parties to triumph. Nevertheless, the party leaders and even the radical elements of the movements concerned lack both the strategies for reform and the unambiguous priorities that would allow them to follow a consistent political course. In this, they differ radically not only from the revolutionaries but also from the reformists of the past, people who had a clear concept of where they were headed, and of the route they intended to pursue.

Early in the twentieth century, Max Weber pointed correctly to the difference between social reforms and the calls for 'justice' that 'charismatic leaders' were constantly urging should be put into practice, while laying claim to dictatorial powers or trying to retain an authority that was slipping away from them. This ideology of *public redistribution* has nothing in common with socialism, which as Weber very aptly remarked, poses its task not as a 'just' redistribution of goods, but as 'the rational organisation of their *production*'.[38]

As a rule, the programmes of left-wing victors in political contests amount to a range of diverse and not especially well-integrated proposals aimed at solving a number of specific problems inherited from the preceding authorities, along with pledges to raise the incomes of the deprived layers of the population. This politics of redistribution generally makes it possible to improve the situation of the lower orders of the population in the short term, and may also ensure support for the left in subsequent elections. But the new order has almost never been consolidated through structural reforms in the sphere of production.

The politics of redistribution resembles the behaviour of someone who regularly grabs meat from a tiger's feed-bowl, confident that the tiger will treat them with understanding provided the pieces taken are not too big. Finding themselves in continuous conflict with their country's oligarchy, the socialists have lacked the resolve to undertake measures that would undermine the economic basis of the oligarchy's power. While hoping to avoid a harsh confrontation, the socialists have nevertheless been powerless to reconcile the ruling class to the new political order.

The effect of the contradiction between the initial radical rhetoric and the more-than-modest reforms is to demoralise the masses. The longer a left-wing government remains in office after choosing this mode of activity, the weaker its support from the lower orders of society becomes. As the government's constitutional term in office continues, disappointment mounts, and the confidence of the masses in their own strengths and possibilities melts away. Promising more serious, large-scale changes at some point in the future, the politicians sacrifice the trust they enjoy in the present. Here once again we should recall Max Weber: 'Time is by no means a secondary factor where the historical process is concerned; mixing up the present with the future is far more dangerous in politics than it is in grammar.'[39] By postponing systemic reforms, the politicians of the centre-left rob themselves of the dynamic that is essential to consolidating even the few results already achieved. Their understanding of the questions that are key to the development of the current situation becomes diluted, while the major (and most dangerous) developments finish up being obscured by a multitude of day-to-day trifles that have to be attended to. The reform of society is replaced by the current tasks of management and administration. In their capacity as administrators, however, the members of the left fail to match the conservatives. Losing their initial impulse, no longer thinking of themselves in terms of their historical mission, and living by the rules of the system they once rejected, these politicians find they lack the moral will to resist the numerous temptations that accompany power. They become corrupt, in some cases, even more rapidly than the functionaries of the traditional right-wing parties. The less acute the confrontation between the left-wing government and the oligarchs, the more easily the oligarchs ultimately achieve their revenge.

It is a sort of consolation that the return to power of the right (unlike the situation in Europe in the mid-twentieth century) continues the pattern of instability. This return is accompanied by a further wave of antisocial measures, stirring new protests and opening a road to power for a new group of left-wing politicians (and sometimes providing a second chance to members of earlier administrations, as occurred in 2021 and 2022 in Argentina, Bolivia and Brazil).

Although the succession of parties in power is an unquestionable achievement of democracy, the whole point for the left of political struggle is not simply to form another government, somewhat less bourgeois and a little more progressive than its predecessor. Unless the question is posed of ownership of the resources that are vitally important for society, and if not even an attempt is made to increase the role of the public sector in the economy, everything will be reduced to the mere providing of state benevolence. And if workers do not gain access to decision-making power, the term in office of the left will end in another defeat.

In 2021 and 2022 the forces of the left again won a number of significant victories. The presidential elections in Peru ended in the triumph of the former schoolteacher Pedro Castillo, while in Chile the candidate of the left Gabriel Boric became head of state, borne into office by the energy of the mass protests that not long before had swept across the country. The main sensation on the South American continent, however, was the success in the elections in Colombia of Gustavo Petro, a former guerrilla fighter from the insurgent group M-19. It is noteworthy that all these victories were achieved against the background of sharp social polarisations, with the left-wing candidates confronting candidates of the extreme right. Meanwhile the success of Gustavo Petro, like the earlier victory of Pedro Castillo in Peru, was secured by only an insignificant majority of the votes. Even in Chile, where Boric gained 55.87 per cent of the votes in the second round, his edge was not especially impressive. In Brazil in October 2022 Luiz Inácio 'Lula' da Silva, the candidate of the Workers' Party who had already been elected twice as president, defeated Jair Bolsonaro and returned to office. Again, Lula gained victory only with great difficulty, winning an insignificant majority of votes of less than 1 per cent. Nor did the left win a majority of seats in the organs of the Brazilian legislature.

The results of these apparently successful campaigns were indicative. Faced with a choice between a candidate of the left and a representative of the extreme right, the people again and again chose the left. But the narrowness of the majorities with which these victories were gained was no accident. The centrist electorate 'sagged', while at the same time a growing apathy could be observed on the part of the population. Analysing the changes that were taking place in Latin American countries, the Russian scholar Lyudmila Dyakova wrote that what was involved was 'the beginning of a process of marginalisation of centrism as an ideological current, with a substantial sector of society growing "tired" of it and seeking a clear political identity on the right or the left'.[40] The successes of the left were thus a by-product of the institutional crisis that had arisen as a result of neoliberal policies. The old parties, both centrist and moderate, were losing influence. The vacuum was being filled in part by more radical forces, and in part was not being filled at all; the yawning gap in the centre of the political spectrum testified to the inability of any political force to mobilise the ordinary voters, who were confused and disoriented. Politics was being reduced to a contest of radical minorities, leaving a substantial mass of citizens indifferent.

The successes of the left thus offered no more than a chance of effecting changes, while at the same time giving rise to new dangers. Amid the conditions of institutional crisis, it was not an alternative that was winning out, but uncertainty. This was the case to a significant degree not only in Colombia but also in France, where parliamentary elections took place almost simultaneously with the presidential elections in Colombia, but did not see any party win a majority.[41] In Chile the Boric government was unable to win the adoption of a new constitution that had been drawn up with the mass participation of citizens. This democratic experiment ended in complete failure when at a referendum the overwhelming majority of Chileans voted against the changes. The reason for this turn of events was not any shortcomings of the new Basic Law, but the ineffectiveness and lack of resolve, noticeable to all, of the Boric government during its first months in office. In Peru the administration of Pedro Castillo proved completely dysfunctional. In the space of a few months the country saw four prime ministers replaced, with the resignation of each of them followed by a change of government position on a whole range of questions. As the Russian scholar Aleksandr Shinkarenko noted, 'from the moment he came to power the president enjoyed great popularity among the establishment, while the regular crises his administration encountered were associated with the work of his team'.[42] After a little more than a year in office, Castillo was removed by the Congress of the republic following an attempt to repeat the 'coup from above' carried out in 1992 by the right-wing president Alberto Fujimori. It is noteworthy that those who voted to remove the president from office even included many representatives of his own party.

The main question at issue has not been how well or badly left parties have coped with the tasks of government. The very tasks and problems confronting government authorities have changed radically. This is true not only of Latin America and Western Europe, but still more so of Russia and the countries of Asia. The beginning of the 2020s represented a historic milestone, after which the old political world everywhere vanished into the past. It is significant that the year 2022, if it did not break records for political instability, nevertheless proved exceptionally volatile. The massive popular outpourings that accompanied the beginnings of democratic reforms in Kazakhstan; the war in Ukraine; the parliamentary crisis in France; the victory of the left in Colombia; the mass disturbances in Sri Lanka; the revolutionary uprising in Iran; and the increasingly severe political repression seen against a background of mass discontent in Russia were all merely symptoms of a far more dramatic and large-scale crisis looming over the global system.

The difficulties for the left in Latin America have merely revealed the general problems of left-wing political movements, placing them in especially sharp focus precisely because in that part of the world the left has fared better than elsewhere. While losing faith in revolution, the members of the left have not become consistent, conscientious reformists, since the serious and resolute implementation of reforms demands no less persistence, strategic concentration and boldness than revolutionary struggle. Taking the place of strategy and resolve in pursuing a concrete and systematic programme of change has been empty radical rhetoric.

When the forces of the left fill a political vacuum, they receive only the *possibility* of initiating socially important changes. In the late twentieth and early twenty-first centuries, this possibility has constantly turned into ineffectual attempts at administering the system. Of course, any systematic work necessarily consists of a multitude of partial and specific decisions, but the success of these moves depends in no small degree on the extent to which they are united by a shared concept, orientation and strategy. Meanwhile, the ability to formulate a strategy and to mobilise diverse social forces towards a common end, while correcting mistakes and not losing sight of the goals being pursued, is not easily or quickly developed. Overcoming neoliberalism cannot be solely the task of a few wise intellectuals and of politicians seated in government offices. Victory is not just the sum of a fortunate conjunction of circumstances that improves the electoral chances of gifted populist orators. In order for systemic changes to become a reality, left-wing organisations themselves have to undergo radical transformations, not only discarding much of the old baggage, but also throwing overboard the political trash accumulated during thirty years of continuous retreat.

10

The Problem of Control

Summing up the ideas of Rosa Luxemburg, Michael Brie wrote that the key problem the political activity of the left needed to resolve was 'the contradiction between the real possibility of socialism and its realisation'. There was no way this contradiction would resolve itself through a process of gradual evolution, so in order to realise the possibilities that arose out of and were required by the objective course of development, the left needed to work out 'a strategy of struggling for political power within the state', since the latter constituted 'the main obstacle on the path to the socialist overturn'.[1]

Meanwhile, one of the main political achievements of neoliberalism has been to block not only any practical efforts to bring about change, but even any serious discussion of such a possibility. On this level, Francis Fukuyama's declaration of 'the end of history' has in its own fashion proven correct. Not, of course, in the sense that the historical processes driving human civilisation forward have ceased to operate, and that a future involving changes of epochs, systems and social relations has been replaced by an endless repetition of the present, but that discussion of possible variants of a transition of society from one state to another has become completely impossible. The crisis of the left movement has exacerbated this situation. Although the members of the left have uniformly condemned attempts to construct a picture of the world that rules out alternatives, their own discourse has tended to promote exactly this outcome. Practical alternatives for development have been replaced by pointless utopian dreams of 'another world', while at the same time the possibility is proclaimed of 'an endless range of alternatives', ruling out even the idea of formulating general strategic priorities and of mobilising forces around them.[2]

The trap of electoralism

The processes unfolding in the late twentieth and early twenty-first centuries may be described as the flight of the bourgeoisie from democracy. Contrary to accepted thinking, the key principle of democracy is not securing the freedom of the individual, but the limiting of the freedom of the elites by the collective will of society. The significance of political freedoms consists above all in the fact that they constitute a tool with which the collective will can potentially be formed, expressed and consolidated. Strictly speaking, the bourgeoisie has never had any need of democracy; its social interests consist in the formation of a law-governed state with independent judges, reliable information, guarantees that contracts will be observed, clear legislation, a disciplined and predictable bureaucracy, and secure property rights. To a degree, these rules can also be observed within the frameworks of authoritarian regimes, as demonstrated by the examples of China, Taiwan and Singapore in the late twentieth century. For the same reason, the bourgeoisie in nineteenth-century Europe stubbornly resisted the expansion of electoral rights, imposing all sorts of qualifications and trying to link full citizenship to the ownership of a particular amount of property. Nevertheless, the existence of a certain level of democratic freedoms is a natural accompaniment to the law-governed state, and for the lower orders of society inevitably opens up the prospect of waging a struggle, if not for power, then at least for participation in decision-making.

The dilemma faced by the bourgeoisie in the late twentieth century was centred on the need to minimise social controls over business, controls regarded as 'excessive' in scope and extremely 'expensive', while maintaining democratic institutions and universal voting rights as such. A solution was found through eliminating one category of economic questions from the sphere of democratic discussion via 'freeing up markets', and through transforming another category into a topic exclusively for expert discussion, supposedly incomprehensible to the broad public. Finally, a massive transfer of production took place to countries of the periphery, which were attractive to capital not only for the cheapness of their labour power, but also for their effective authoritarianism.

Paradoxically, the late twentieth century in many parts of the world not only saw an unprecedented spread of formal democratic institutions, including multiple parties, elections and smooth transfers of power, but also a widespread emasculation of these procedures, with the banishing of an ever-greater number of social questions from the field of public discussion. It is not surprising that the first years of the present century everywhere became an epoch of unprecedented alienation of society from the state, leading on the one hand to mass disturbances, protests and conflicts in countries that laid claim to the role of model democracies, while on the other hand, and not just in Russia but also in many other countries, a revival of authoritarianism could be observed. The processes of partial democratisation that had begun in Asian states finished up being slowed and curtailed, while the defence of political freedoms from the simultaneous pressures of markets and bureaucracies became less and less reliable.

The parties of the left, regardless of the radicalism of their slogans, were transformed into electoral machines interested solely in winning votes. What should be done with these votes was a question that no-one could answer precisely, since no particular thought had been devoted to such matters. After all, it was on the election results that the very existence of the organisations depended. Extra-parliamentary groups meanwhile basked in sectarian self-satisfaction, condemning participation in elections as such, since this would not bring about a rapid socialist overturn (they had trouble, however, explaining just what would accomplish this end in the current circumstances).

Historically, campaigning in elections had served a dual purpose for the left. It had been a means of forming and consolidating a majority grouping of the population around a strategy of change (here the question of whether this involved reform or revolution was secondary). At the same time, winning the support of a majority and achieving victory in elections would represent a necessary stage in the struggle to conquer power – but precisely to win power, not merely to secure parliamentary mandates or ministerial armchairs. By the late twentieth century, however, both of the above goals had been forgotten by the socialist and communist politicians. The struggle for votes had been transformed into a self-sufficient and self-justifying process.

During periods of peace and prosperity all political parties shift towards the centre, trying to win the support of apolitical voters, but this reflects negatively on the left, since in demonstrating caution and moderation they are recruited into the very bourgeois system that they were founded in order to change. The slogans inscribed on the party banners play little role here, serving not so much as a guide to action and an indication of the goals of the struggle as a justification for the lowest forms of opportunism. As Herbert Marcuse noted, following such rules amounts to attempting to 'reduce the opposition to the discussion and promotion of alternative policies within the status quo'.[3] This occurs regardless of the degree of democracy in one or another state. The trouble is that a stability that is based on the prosperity of a consumer society, as described by Marcuse in the 1960s, cannot be eternal. As the fruit not only of technological progress, but also of social compromise, this prosperity will be undermined at the very moment when the ruling class considers itself to be free of obligations and concessions agreed to earlier. In this case, these were the obligations and concessions that during the twentieth century had been snatched from the ruling class under the threat of revolution.

Living by the rules of the system, the left has feared most of all that it will finish up marginalised, or that it will appear so. In the event, it has been more or less successful in solving this problem. At the same time, its organisations have become degraded ideologically, morally and often structurally as well. Meanwhile, the price of this gradual degradation has been an inability on the part of left parties that have promised to transform society and life to react to social changes when these have in fact occurred.

While in peaceful times the centrist electorate gradually expands, to the point where it includes an overwhelming part of society, in a period of crisis it rapidly shrinks, forcing the socialist politicians and apparatchiks who are still living by the accustomed schemas to move further and further to the right, in search of 'moderate voters' who no longer exist in their previous form. The socialist politicians suffer abrupt and crushing defeats, not just electoral in nature, and the place of these individuals is taken over by radicals of a different type. This is the point when new people and parties (or ones that shortly before were considered marginal) come onto the scene. If the political vacuum is not filled by the left, then it will inevitably be occupied by the extreme right.

The way that political events have developed in the early twenty-first century clearly confirms that political parties whose legitimacy rests on the habitual loyalty of voters, or on the niches that these parties occupy in the established system, are not only growing weaker but are beginning to fall apart. This crisis is a moment of truth that is unleashing a *mechanism of political reconfiguration*. Journalists and political scientists who reduce their analysis to describing observed processes are inclined to draw the conclusion that the very concept of the political party has become fundamentally obsolete. Even if this is partly correct, it is equally true that the epoch of late capitalism has been unable to suggest any other robust form of political organisation, and that the final disappearance of party politics will only become possible when the question is one of the disappearance of politics in general.

In reality, it is not that the party form of politics is disappearing, but that specific political organisations have outlived their time. These are organisations that have maintained their place in the system not so much due to their real influence, as because of administrative and technical capacities accumulated over many years. This is not the first time that history has witnessed such things. 'At a certain stage in their historical journey', Gramsci observed, 'social groups break with their traditional parties.'[4] Of course, the bureaucratic machinery that maintains the viability of political structures is notable for its extraordinary durability, and is able to function for extended periods as if independently, regardless of what is happening in society or even to the members of the organisation. Nevertheless, the effect of such a break is that during a period of acute crisis the party will 'lose its social content, and come to resemble an empty shell'.[5] The problem is that the collapse of old parties and the loss of their connections with society occurs far more quickly than the formation of new political forces. An uncertain and dangerous situation appears, in which chance individuals can come to the forefront, while coercion becomes more attractive the worse familiar political mechanisms operate.

Even in the late nineteenth century many people were warning that the institutions of liberal democracy were becoming a historical trap for socialists. The problem, however, is that occurring alongside the degradation of the left alternative is the degradation of liberal democracy, which is falling victim to bureaucratic procedures (from within) and populist pressures (from without). Mass mobilisations to save democracy are thus becoming at once a challenge to the decrepit institutions of parliamentarism, and the sole radical means through which the democratic content originally contained in these institutions can be returned to them.

The privatisation of control

Authoritarian populism, strongman politics and an expansion of bureaucratic powers have traditionally been considered the main threats to the democratic process, and none of these dangers have disappeared in the early twenty-first century. Indeed, they are proliferating. Contrary to the historical optimism that characterised the thinkers of the Age of Enlightenment, neither social progress nor freedom of the individual are irreversible. Attacks on them occur not only from the state and from authoritarian political movements, but also from corporations.

The American scholar Shoshana Zuboff writes of the onset of an 'epoch of surveillance capitalism', which she describes as 'a new economic order that claims human experience as free raw material for hidden commercial practices of extraction, prediction, and sales'.[6]

Zuboff also insists that surveillance capitalism is characterised by a 'parasitic economic logic',[7] since this system, which organises control over people's behaviour through the use of electronic detection and manipulation technologies, transforms the consumer into a subordinate element of production. Commodities are not sold to people who want to buy them, but on the contrary, future buyers are included in technological plans and are 'designated' by corporations for consumption of their goods. The electronic surveillance imposed by capital thus differs substantially from the traditional practices of control over people's behaviour implemented primarily by the state and described by Michel Foucault. While the classical mechanisms of control and discipline have had the goal in the first instance of preventing unruly, dangerous or otherwise undesirable conduct,[8] surveillance capitalism goes further, seeking to control, direct and subordinate to its ends people's positive conduct, their desires, needs and strategies of behaviour.

Historically, of course, there is nothing here that is fundamentally new. Even in the mid-twentieth century, sociologists studying advertising and the mass media noted that with the help of these mechanisms people were being subjected to systematic manipulation aimed at imposing on them particular ideologies, values and choices of goods. What is new in the twenty-first century is the use of new, more powerful electronic and digital technologies for performing these tasks, and the fact that the collecting of information about people and the manipulating of their conduct are now combined within the framework of the same technological systems. We all supply information about ourselves when we use mobile telephones, social networks and technical equipment, the latter often completely inoffensive, such as 'smart' vacuum cleaners.

One of the outcomes (and in a way of speaking, 'achievements') of neoliberalism has been an unprecedented depoliticisation of society under the conditions of information openness and even information abundance. During the Cold War the illusion existed, not only in the Soviet bloc but also in the West, that free access by citizens to information was itself among the key conditions for the existence of democracy. Twenty-first-century reality, however, has shown how much more complex everything in fact is. In the early twentieth century Max Weber wrote that large-scale publishing enterprises owned by huge capitalist corporations were 'typical mentors of political indifferentism'.[9] Later, Guy Debord was to show convincingly that the managing and manipulating of information flows had become an important part of bourgeois politics in the 'society of the spectacle'. As Debord explains, what is involved here is not just the outward appearance created by propaganda and the mass media, but also the fact that the spectacle organised by the ruling class penetrates all areas of life, constructing or altering our entire everyday existence:

> In all its particular forms, whether information or propaganda, advertising or the direct consumption of entertainment, the spectacle is the readily available model that is dominant in the way of life of our society. The spectacle represents the universal affirmation of the choice that has already been made in production, and is its subsequent application. By analogy with this, the form and content of the spectacle serve as the total justification of the conditions and goals of the existing system.[10]

The multitude of new channels for receiving information, whether commercial or domestic, political or cultural, create in the public a sense of almost limitless freedom, and this sense cannot be called illusory. But the reverse side of this situation is control by private corporations over the information platforms that we use, and which we support through our participation. While generally accessible and for the most part free, these platforms are not completely open and public, and nor can they be considered neutral, as shown by the numerous cases of corporate censorship of social networks (this censorship varies from the blocking of specific political content, such as the Twitter account of former US president Donald Trump, to the marginalising of particular utterances or the banning of specific topics, expressions and words that do not correspond to ideas of political correctness or that are viewed as unacceptable).[11] Liberal ideology, which condemns all forms of state censorship and limitation of rights, shirks the challenge of the corporate censorship that embodies the principles of the free market and private property. This is especially remarkable since the contradiction between 'totalitarian' government censorship and the multifarious (and thus seemingly less dangerous) private corporate censorship is only apparent (or more precisely, exists solely in the heads of ideologues), since in practice they comprise a single system, comprehensive and mutually reinforcing.

In essence, the information sector not only reproduces, but raises to an unprecedented level of acuteness the contradiction noted by Marx between the social nature of production and the private nature of appropriation. It is obvious that information is in the first place a social value, since any reports about me that enter the system are of significance first and foremost to *other people*. Further, these reports are transformed from concrete facts into information precisely and exclusively after they are appropriated and are communicated to these others. While artefacts of one kind or another are transformed into commodities only when placed on the market for sale, information is quite unable to exist outside of social communication. The communications media are inherently social, of their very nature. Meanwhile, the management of the communications process, the automation of information gathering, and the synthesising of this information all have a private-corporate character, and are subject to little in the way of public control (though this in no way excludes attempts at control on the part of authoritarian states). As a user, of course, everyone who is included in the system has the opportunity to extract their small advantage from participating in it. Nevertheless, the *entire mass* of the information that enters the system is automatically appropriated by the owners of the platform. Does this not mean that we are approaching the point where the question of the *economic* socialisation of these platforms is becoming a central question of *political* democracy?

Digitalised capitalism

Analysing the corporations that operate in the information field, the Canadian sociologist Nick Srnicek notes that despite the ideological hype, the cultural innovations and the unnerving prospects of total control, the new technological companies represent 'economic actors within a capitalist mode of production'.[12] These companies are also obliged to chase after profits, to compete among themselves, and most importantly, ultimately to confront the same problem of the limited size of the market, like the capitalist economy as a whole.

Against a background of discussions on the digital economy, on ideal (in the philosophical sense) productive forces and on non-material values that influence the trends of economic development, a serious discussion has unfolded among members of the left on the applicability to this situation of the principles of classical political economy. The concept of 'ideal productive forces' had begun to be used back in Soviet times by the historians Marat Cheshkov and Vladimir Krylov, basing their work on Marx's prophecy that science itself would become a productive force. Reflecting on the future of the economy in an epoch when scientific output would become a critically important factor of production, they formulated a thesis on ideal productive forces.[13]

Of course, it is impossible for any knowledge or technology to exist without a material bearer. The information society rests on the production of electrical energy and sharply increases the demand for it, as well as for other digital technology produced by industry. Capitalism uses information as a resource, regarding it in a certain sense as unlimited and self-reproducing. If this is true, however, it is only in a technical sense. There are social and cultural limits to the use of information flows in society. These flows depend only in part on technological capacity, since information needs not only to be accumulated and processed, but also to be employed effectively. When an excessive amount of information has been obtained, the efficiency of its use inevitably declines, even if the most modern methods of processing and sorting it are applied. Superfluous information turns into *noise*. The possibility of extracting further profit from it diminishes, *just like the rate of profit in any other sector, to the degree that the market becomes saturated.* The same applies to control over politics and behaviour. Information gathered through technical means can be very important, but it will never be enough *in itself* to gain an understanding of people's behaviour or to make accurate predictions. To know everything is impossible in principle, and to know the *main* things, it can sometimes be necessary to avoid being distracted by the partial and secondary. Excess information flows drown what is important and informative in a mass of trifles. Of course, the method of total control can be satisfactory for managing technical processes set up artificially according to parameters defined in advance, but it is completely unsuited to the successful management of people.

Like the 'network corporations' described by Manuel Castells,[14] information companies for all their progressive technological nature are not locomotives able to draw the rest of the economy behind them. In part, this is related to the same problem of the limited nature of the market. Under the conditions of neoliberalism, technological innovations come up against the same boundaries of private demand as all the other participants in the economic process. These limits are rendered still more narrow by factors that include neoliberal reforms aimed at reducing wages and extracting money from households compelled to pay for 'social services'. The digital companies in turn create relatively small numbers of jobs, often serve to replace qualified labour with unqualified, and most importantly, do not give rise to as much demand as other sectors. The Covid pandemic of 2020–2022 of course enabled the digital companies to grow strongly, but it also showed the limits of this growth.

As Srnicek notes, the new technology sector in the US during the 2010s accounted for only 2.5 per cent of the workforce, while industrial production, despite widespread deindustrialisation, employed four times as many. In Great Britain as well, almost three times as many people worked in industry as in the technology sector.[15] The same picture could be observed in other

THE PROBLEM OF CONTROL • 181

countries. There are no reasons to speak either of a sizeable change in the structure of employment, or of the activity of the new platform companies enabling the growth or transformation of other sectors. Rather, the technology firms are playing the role of a counterweight to the general crisis trends that are accumulating in the 'traditional economy', for a time supporting an overall 'macroeconomic stability', softening the crisis of overaccumulation and so forth. The process, however, is being accompanied by growing disproportions and unresolved contradictions, preparing the way for a new and more acute crisis whose victims will include the 'platform corporations'. Meanwhile, today's information and communications technologies can also act as an important catalyst for the development of direct democracy and self-management, including in the field of production. This, however, will require changing not the digital platforms, but social relations.

The fate of the little person

The offensive by corporate capital against the rights and freedoms of the individual appears unstoppable, especially since it is no longer only labour power, as in the time of Marx, that is becoming the object of exploitation, but the individual themselves, both as consumer and worker. In reality, however, things are somewhat more complex. Just as in classical industrial society, the new technological conditions are also giving rise to new opportunities for resistance, and are creating new problems and contradictions that limit the possibilities of capital.

In this context it makes sense to revisit the polemic that took place in the late 1970s and early 1980s between Michel Foucault and Michel de Certeau. Foucault's works draw a picture of total control and manipulation, carried out by the authorities (in the broad sense) with the aim of 'disciplining' society. As bourgeois rationalism, capitalist industry and the modern bureaucracy develop, a system of surveillance practices is being devised that is capable of organising social life down to the level of petty details, and whose significance we cannot even grasp. Industrial production and prisons, hospitals and schools, mass quarantine measures and military mobilisations – everything is being drawn up according to one and the same principle:

We are required to record whether we are present or absent; it is necessary to know where one or another individual is and how to find them. We have to determine which of our ties are useful, and to break off all others. There is a demand to be able to exercise minute-to-minute surveillance over everyone's behaviour, to be in a position to assess them, to subject them to punishment, and to measure their qualities and services. What is involved, in short, is a methodology aimed at cognition, possession and exploitation.[16]

It can be seen that in 'surveillance capitalism' the disciplinary process described by Foucault is not simply reproduced, but takes on new dimensions, making control and management truly absolute. But is this control really effective?

Replying to Foucault, his compatriot de Certeau notes that the methods through which the ruling elite subjects society to itself come into conflict with a rich social reality that, moreover, is still constantly changing and that eludes the attention of the observer. 'The question remains of how to regard other, equally petty procedures that history has not granted "privileged" status, but that nevertheless act in innumerable ways between the links of established technologies.'[17] In de Certeau's view, the 'little person' resists the *strategies* of state and corporate power using their own *tactics*, including the mechanisms of sabotage, hackwork and 'counter' manipulation. These tactics of resistance were worked out by peasant societies in the remote past, and have been continually developed and refined in later epochs:

> The present order of things is that 'popular' tactics are put to use without any illusions that the situation will change in the near future. The ruling authorities take advantage of this order of things, and the ideological discourse may simply deny it, but here it is *outsmarted* with the help of a variety of artful ruses. Hence a certain style of social exchanges penetrates into the official institutions, a style involving technical inventiveness and moral resistance, that is, an economy of the *gift* (of generosity, answered by others with generosity), an aesthetic of *tricks* (the devices of artists), and an ethic of *stubbornness* (of finding numerous ways to refuse to recognise the status of the law as the established order, or to see it as reason and fate).[18]

Twelve years after the publication of his book *The Society of the Spectacle*, Guy Debord also stated that the ruling circles on the one hand were constantly strengthening 'technical and police control over people and the forces of nature', but that this was a control within which failures were multiplying to the degree to which the technical means were refined.[19]

The Good Soldier Švejk, who in the classic novel by the Czech writer Jaroslav Hašek does his best to evade being sent to the front, is a sort of 'ideal type' of the little individual who in reality devotes great efforts to sabotaging the process set in train by the state and the ruling classes. Švejk, however, is not motivated by any particular ideas, but remains merely an ordinary person and even at heart a conformist. Nevertheless, he succeeds intuitively in finding solutions that allow him again and again to dupe the system in his own interests. As de Certeau notes, the mechanism of control, constructed according to rational principles and reflecting the rational goals of its creators, often simply *fails to see* these popular practices, and if it suppresses them, does not recognise the degree of their vitality or their ability to reproduce themselves again and again in new forms:

> Nevertheless, these practices have a chance of surviving this mechanism too. In any case, they also represent a part of the collective life of society, and moreover, a resilient one, that is flexible and adaptable to constant changes. When we examine this elusive but unchanging reality intently, the impression arises that we are examining the 'night-time' side of the life of societies, a night that is longer than their days, a dark shroud where there are institutions successively replacing one another, the immensity of a sea in which socio-economic and political structures arise like ephemeral islands.[20]

The tactics of the 'weak' also allow them to block the strategy of the 'strong' because these tactics are spontaneous and unconscious, often irrational, and even, from the point of view of the larger political scene, foolish. Of course, they do not of themselves make it possible to change society, but they impede attempts to transform it from above in ways that do violence to people's needs. These tactics

> benefit from 'chance developments' and depend upon them, while lacking any basis for accumulating advantages, for strengthening positions and for planning forays. They do not retain what they conquer. This non-position, undoubtedly, lends them mobility, but in trying to seize momentary opportunities, they are dependent on accidents of time. While constantly remaining watchful, they are compelled to make use of the weaknesses that particular circumstances open up in the surveillance by authorities who have their own positions. There, they engage in poaching, and create unanticipated situations. They are able to appear where they are not expected. They are devious.[21]

The limits of surveillance capitalism became particularly obvious during the pandemic crisis of 2021–2022, when spontaneous mass resistance in one country after another led to the failure of campaigns attempting to enforce compulsory vaccination or other forms of medical control over the population. In the strict medical sense this protest, taking the form of sabotage, direct resistance or evasion, appeared completely irrational, since the policy being implemented was viewed by the authorities and was announced to society as a means of protecting the health of citizens against the pandemic. From the US and Canada to Russia and Kazakhstan, the authorities were everywhere acting in strict accordance with Foucault's concepts of discipline. But for all the irrationality of their motives, the delusional nature of their arguments and the illogic of their methods, the masses of people who evaded the campaigns (and few of whom can have read either Foucault or de Certeau) finished up being more effective, and in their own fashion acted reasonably. They did not so much understand as *sense* intuitively that the essence of the matter had nothing to do with concern for their health (even if this was present as a *secondary* motive of the governments), but lay in the control itself. They further understood that once the space concerned had been yielded to the authorities on the pretext of medical care, it would be very difficult to win it back once the situation changed. Having to choose between the real risk of infection and the obvious prospect of losing their personal freedom, people preferred the former.

The spontaneous resistance to the mobilisation in Russia in the autumn of 2022, during the war with Ukraine, provides a no less significant example. At least initially, the extremely low level of solidarity and trust in society prevented the mounting of any collective actions against the decision by the Kremlin to order a mass call-up of men to the front. People resisted individually, concealing themselves from the mobilisation, hiding in forests, leaving the country in their hundreds of thousands, and sometimes also setting fire at night to military enlistment offices so as to destroy the documentation held in them. But despite the lack of organisation, the net effect of this spontaneous draft avoidance was no less significant than if a powerful protest movement had developed within the country.

Another typical popular practice has been mass sabotage by consumers, though its effects as a rule are less noticeable. Despite the expensive research and huge advertising campaigns that are conducted in order to manipulate them, potential customers are suddenly becoming 'invisible'. Adapting themselves to a changing situation, 'ordinary people' are constantly proving to be more flexible than large organisations using artificial intelligence and employing whole teams of analysts.

Becoming an even greater problem than resistance by citizens or consumers, however, is the objective resistance of the economic, technological, social and natural environment, which for its steady reproduction requires quite different decisions than those the proprietors of large companies take in their own distinct interests.

The might of capital, however impressive it might be, again and again proves insufficient to impose the desired control over people and social processes, not to speak of the processes of nature. Nevertheless, the spontaneous resistance of the environment as it constantly blocks the plans of powerful ruling groups and even reduces their effects to zero cannot solve the main problem, since it does not create the new institutions that are essential if human society is to enter a new spiral of development.

11

Between Reform and Revolution

The standard answer of socialists to the multiplying problems of capitalism has been to cite the potential of revolution to resolve the system's accumulated contradictions. The truth is that revolution not only solves the problems innate to capitalism, but also creates its own problems, arising from the uneven dynamic of change; from the lack of preparedness of the masses (and often of the movement's leaders) for the tasks that are immediately heaped onto the victors; from the inertia of radicalism; and simply from the woes inherited from the previous regime (since political and social systems do not leave the scene 'just like that', but give way to the new social relations through a process of crises and shocks). It is thus perfectly understandable that from the moment the communist and socialist movements appeared, the hope was present in their ranks for milder scenarios, for gradual (even if very far-reaching) reforms that would make it possible to avoid the convulsions of revolution. The experience of the twentieth century showed that this hope was far from unwarranted. Of course, the reforms were also won with great difficulty, against resistance from the ruling classes, and were the objects of extensive struggles. Nevertheless, during most of the twentieth century these reforms moved forward, at least in democratic countries. Such successes transformed even young, ideologically motivated revolutionaries into pragmatic reformists, ready to make concessions not only in order to mitigate conflicts with the ruling elites, but also in order to retain the support of the masses, who also preferred gradual changes to social cataclysms.

Unfortunately, the last decades of the century showed that a substantial amount of what had been achieved was reversible.

The lessons of Rosa Luxemburg

The twentieth century ended not only with a series of political defeats for the left, but also with the successive dismantling of the social reforms enacted earlier. In the space of fifteen or twenty years the countries in which one-party communist regimes had been ousted managed not just to lose almost all the social conquests of the preceding period, but also to transform themselves into a periphery of the bourgeois world-system, reproducing all the worst features of early capitalism. In various parts of the world, the question of revolution and of its relation to reforms thus came to be posed afresh. In a certain sense the process of change had to begin again, though not, of course, in an empty space. Further, since the dismantling of social rights that was everywhere under way also served to undermine the bases of modern democracy, it was necessary to begin again the conquest or defence of democratic freedoms that at least in the countries of the West, had seemed in the mid-twentieth century to have been secured irreversibly.

Examining the interrelationship between democracy and social reforms, Rosa Luxemburg showed that it was precisely civil liberties that provided the basis for hopes of transforming the state into an instrument for asserting the will of the majority. Thanks to democracy, the state and society were drawing closer together, and it was even possible to speak of 'the development of the state within society', something that 'served as a stage in progress towards the socialist overturn'.[1] Democracy, however, was turning the contradictions of the state inward, so that the state machine itself was being transformed into an arena of struggle between various class forces. The old ruling classes could prevail in this struggle only by limiting, overturning or emasculating popular participation in politics. This is why the period that saw the turn to neoliberalism and the dismantling of the welfare state also witnessed a retreat by democracy even in the freest and most advanced countries. This process took on especially catastrophic forms in the states that had arisen on the ruins of the USSR and that had proclaimed the goal of constructing democracy. The newly acquired freedoms were consistently abolished or restricted in the name of national interests, for the sake of which social rights had to be sacrificed as well.

The embracing of the goal of a market economy and the limiting of social rights in no way reduced the importance of the state or brought cuts to the bureaucracy, any more than these moves led governments to reject attempts to influence economic processes. Despite the policies of 'de-statisation' that were enacted almost universally, the 'big state' that had arisen in the twentieth century did not depart from the scene in the twenty-first. The key question involved was not the 'dimensions' of the state, but its functions. In Luxemburg's view, the expansion of state functions that occurred in the natural course of events was in no sense a negative factor.

The question was how society would make use of the situation that had arisen:

> Of course, capitalist development itself alters the nature of the state significantly, constantly expanding the sphere of its influence and assigning it new functions, especially in the field of economic life. As a result, it makes state intervention and control increasingly essential. In this way the future merger of the state with society – the reverse transfer of state functions to society, so to speak – is gradually being prepared.[2]

Unlike liberals who strive to limit the role of the state, the left thus poses for itself a far more ambitious task: altering the nature of the state itself, bringing about its radical transformation. There is no reason, however, to hope that this will happen spontaneously, as a natural progression. To the contrary, every time the state strengthens its intervention in the economy, it also strengthens its own internal contradictions.

> If the state in the interests of social development assumes various functions in the common interest, this occurs only because and to the degree to which these interests and the social development coincide on the whole with the interests of the ruling class. Hence, for example, the capitalists as a class have just as direct an interest in occupational safety as does society as a whole. This harmony, however, persists only to a certain point in capitalist development. As soon as development has reached a certain level, the interests of the bourgeoisie as a class and the interests of economic progress even in the capitalist sense begin to diverge.[3]

At the point where making a choice becomes indispensable, the state 'acts in a fashion *contrary* to social development, thus increasingly losing its character as the representative of all of society', and again becoming 'a class state'.[4] The final period of the twentieth century showed this dialectic clearly. It was precisely the gains that had been achieved in the course of political and social reforms that became the most important premise of neoliberal reaction. 'The productive relations of capitalist society are coming increasingly to resemble those of socialism, but the political and juridical relations are erecting an ever-higher wall between capitalist and socialist society'.[5] Politics must break down this wall, through a social overturn that is simultaneously a victory for democracy.

As can be seen, the problem with the relationship between reforms and revolution is not that reforms make revolution unnecessary, but that to the contrary, it is successful reforms that create the conditions for a radical clash of interests, though on a new level. Meanwhile, experience shows that a ruling class that senses a threat to its positions will not watch passively as developments unfold. Its answer to the successes of reforms will, to use an expression of Herbert Marcuse, be *preventive counter-revolution*,[6] which can take a variety of forms – from a violent coup as in Chile in 1973, to a gradual erosion of public life as in Western Europe during the late twentieth century. In Russia the same process has variously taken the forms of the state 'coup from above' in 1993 and the bureaucratic 'self-coup' in 2020 that saw the 'correction' of the constitution. In both cases, the authorities themselves annulled their own basic law and radically altered the rules of political life.

In its turn, the need to defend democracy also places on the agenda the preservation (or restoration) of its social basis. In the twenty-first century, in other words, any programme that reduces the struggle for freedom solely to an assertion of the formal procedures and rights proposed by the theoreticians of liberalism is doomed, since these freedoms are already inadequate *even to ensure their own reproduction*. Social revolution and democratic revolution are becoming indivisible.

'Premature' socialism

Conventionally, the revolution in Russia is considered to have occurred despite Marx's views and even, in a certain sense, to have refuted his prognoses. Indeed, the author of *Capital* associated the triumph of socialism with the changes that were occurring in the most developed countries. This does not, however, in any way signify that Marx expected the revolutionary impulse that would unleash global changes to come from precisely that source. The growing interest in Russian populism that he showed towards the end of his life was no accident, and nor was his readiness to entertain the possibility that Russia would avoid the need to repeat all the stages of bourgeois development (something that Russian Marxists themselves considered inevitable and obligatory). In 1882, not long before his death, Marx wrote that Russia represented 'the advance detachment of the revolutionary movement in Europe'.[7] Developing this idea later, Grigory Vodolazov noted that the chances of reform and revolution needed to be evaluated 'proceeding not only from the productive relations in a given country, and not only from its internal contradictions, but *from the totality of world productive relations*'.[8]

Ultimately, a backward country can catch up with or even overtake its leading rivals, as Soviet communists strove to ensure happened. Whether socialism was possible in the Russia of the early twentieth century depended not only on the level of its economic, social and cultural development, but also on the global level of development of humanity as a whole. Implicit in this, however, was also the key question reflected in the fate not only of the Russian Revolution, but also of the socialist movement as a whole: whether Marx and Engels, along with other socialists of the late nineteenth and early twentieth centuries, were correct when they argued that capitalism had already ripened sufficiently for the transition to socialism to be carried through. The historical experience of the twentieth century shows that the resources of development of bourgeois society and its economy were far from exhausted. This same historical experience, however, allows the above question to be posed differently: could capitalism throughout these hundred-odd years have developed without an infusion of socialism?

In the strict theoretical sense the socialism of the twentieth century, in the shape both of social-democratic reforms and in that of Soviet 'actually existing socialism', was not socialism at all, but merely a satellite of capitalism, a factor in its transformation and humanisation, irrespective of how the communists and socialists regarded themselves. This does not signify in any way that they were working unconsciously for the bourgeoisie, and in carrying out the work of developing society, they were bringing nearer the triumph of qualitatively new social relations. Needless to say, this process turned out to be far more complex and tortuous than they had thought, while the progress they achieved was inconsistent, reversible and attained at horrifying cost. As Marx wrote:

Just as one cannot judge individual people on the basis of what they think of themselves, such an epoch of upheaval cannot be judged by its consciousness. To the contrary, this consciousness must be explained on the basis of the contradictions of material life, of the existing conflict between the social productive forces and the productive relations. No social formation perishes before all the productive forces for which it provides sufficient scope have developed, and new and higher productive relations never appear until the material conditions for its existence have ripened in the depths of the old society. Humanity thus always poses for itself only the tasks that it is capable of carrying out, since on closer examination it always turns out that the task itself only arises when the material conditions for its fulfilment are present, or at least are in the process of formation.[9]

How long, however, will this process take, and what will its form be? What will be the political content of the epoch of transition that corresponds to it? Like any general formula, Marx's idea of course demands very serious refinement when we make the transition to concrete-historical or sociopolitical analysis. There is no question that all models of social development have their natural limitations. We are able to criticise or approve them, to struggle against them or defend them, and to reform them, in the process extending or abbreviating the epoch in which they are dominant. In any case, attempts to ignore or block objective economic, social and cultural processes cannot lead to anything good – social processes that in other circumstances might go ahead more or less smoothly take on a character that is both revolutionary and catastrophic.

The exhaustion of capitalism's potential for development, as described by Marx, is not in the least a steady or linear process that allows us to place a sort of full stop in the line of historical chronology, and to declare that a level has been reached at which a particular system has definitively used up all its possibilities. The non-uniform character of social, economic, technological, political and cultural changes that are further superimposed on the complex geographical hierarchy of the modern world-system means that while exhausting its potential in one sphere, capitalism is able to preserve its viability and even show dynamism elsewhere. This to a significant degree also creates situations in which socialist revolutions have occurred and have solved certain problems that are *already* insoluble under capitalism, but in which these revolutions have stumbled when confronting other problems for which socialist solutions have not *yet* existed.

The defeats and victories along this path, the reforms and revolutions, have to an equal degree though in different forms and on different scales been stages of one and the same global historical process. If the social reforms enacted in developed, democratic countries during the twentieth century were simply a means of stabilising capitalism and adapting it to changing conditions, then what explains the ferocious stubbornness with which the neoliberal counter-reformers have struggled against all this? Why did active work to dismantle the social conquests of working people begin immediately, as soon as the political challenges facing the bourgeoisie weakened (whether as a result of the ending of competition with the Soviet bloc or of a slackening of pressure from the organised labour movement and its parties)?

Unquestionably, the social reforms softened the contradictions of capitalism, but they achieved this through implanting socialist relations. The accumulation of such elements within the system, while solving its technical, organisational and cultural problems, simultaneously undermined its integrity, creating *institutional enclaves of socialism* within capitalism. During the twentieth century the ruling classes were forced to stabilise the economy by weaking their hegemony, not simply through concessions, but also by a sort of institutional compromise with the workers in which the relations essential to the new society matured gradually within the old, creating the possibility of a qualitative shift. Precisely for this reason capital was forced, in order to defend its class interests, to pursue a path of systematic reaction even at the risk of destabilising the system (as emerged in the crisis that engulfed the world following the Great Recession, of the years from 2008 to 2020). In the twenty-first century the social character of production has reached such a scale that capital cannot realise its interests economically without taking into account the mass of social interests that restrict its freedom. Meanwhile, as the ruling circles try to escape these limitations, they create new dangers for themselves, dangers with their sources in the mismatch between the capitalists' own class institutions and the new reality. Thus in the early twentieth century the political and ideological victory of capital has destabilised the economic conditions for its rule.

What is preventing revolutions?

The essence of socialism, as understood by Marx, lies in society 'openly and without resorting to any devious pathways taking possession of the forces of production, which will have outgrown every other means of administering them apart from social means'.[10] The natural course of events, along with the crises that recur periodically against a background of growing technical possibilities, show *the incompatibility of social production with capitalist appropriation*.[11] In other words, socialism is growing out of capitalism, and elements of it are already present in capitalist society, though in the absence of a revolutionary change of system these elements will not become dominant, will not be able to operate at full strength, and most importantly, will not allow a historic resolution of the accumulated contradictions, which are simply growing more complex and confused.

A specific feature of neoliberal (late) capitalism, as described by Fredric Jameson, David Harvey and other writers, lies in the total spread and dominance of commodity relations, which subordinate to themselves various spheres that earlier lay outside the direct influence of the market. This all-permeating *commodification* in turn reflects a sort of exhaustion of the dynamic of bourgeois development, since due to the lack of new fields and opportunities for expansion, capital has begun to absorb and refashion those areas of life that in the interests of its own stability, it earlier allowed to remain 'protected' (something that Schumpeter described exquisitely). But having for the first time in its history become total, capitalism is not only unleashing mechanisms of its own self-destruction, but paradoxically, is also undermining any possibility of a critical interpretation of what is occurring within the framework of the dominant culture and social consciousness.

From the point of view of political economy the market and the movement of capital represent a definite structure of reproductive and evolutionary relations, but for the participant in the process, what is happening has the appearance of a relatively chaotic mosaic of events, a chain of specific deals and transactions whose systematic nature becomes evident only if everything that is occurring is examined 'from outside', from the position of science or culture.[12] Unfortunately, under the conditions of total commodification this 'external' position disappears, since culture, science and even personal emotions are absorbed by the market, becoming part of it. Intellectuals themselves, from being critics and observers, find themselves in the position of being *ordinary participants* in market exchange, and unlike workers, enter into this exchange in relatively weak positions. While protected to a certain degree by their status, they are at the same time completely deprived of the mechanisms of solidarity; the intellectual and cultural communities, which rest on the tradition of mutual recognition of personal achievements, have been absorbed by the capitalist market too quickly, and thus have not managed to develop the minimum necessary mechanisms for mutual assistance.

Due to the changes that have occurred, the position of the observer, critic and analyst, capable of seeing the development of the system 'from outside', is simply vanishing. The observer now is located inside the very kaleidoscope of events and private processes, incapable of assembling this mosaic into a more or less intelligible whole. As a result, the critical-minded intellectual ceases to identify social classes, which instead are transformed for them into chaotic 'multitudes', no longer perceives the 'grand narratives' of history, replacing them with brief sketches of an endless number of individual cases, and ceases to understand the economic meaning of *exploitation*, replacing it with numerous types of *oppression*. Meanwhile, the crisis of the old forms of party-political organisation, or the inability of left intellectuals to unite in advancing political projects, is interpreted as the impossibility of political action as such, or as a lack of prospects for social transformation.

The combination of the accustomed intellectual self-assurance with a newly acquired sense of intellectual helplessness is giving rise to new concepts that appear self-evident despite their clear logical and sociological absurdity, and failure to accord with empirical facts. Hence the change in the social composition of districts on the outskirts of Paris, where the place of native French factory workers has been taken by immigrants with unstable conditions of employment, is perceived by intellectuals as 'the disappearance of the proletariat'. In reality the working class has not gone anywhere, but has merely changed its structure and sometimes its 'residence registration', migrating from the outskirts of Paris to those of Shanghai. Although millions of workers in the old industrial countries that have lost part of their productive base are being subjected to exploitation through a multitude of *new* means, this has either not become a topic of sociological reflection at all, or else the reflection goes no further than a statement of the facts (for example, the rise in the West of a mass precariat, living by approximately the same rules as those long endured by the overwhelming mass of workers in the countries of the periphery).

The problem is that maintaining the specific position of the intellectual within the market requires the constant production of ever-new theories, to be put on sale as powerful innovative commodities needing to compete with other, similar commodities. The collective search for truth and the development of the social sciences through common efforts are replaced by the reproduction and constant refining of discursive practices, which comprise the material and the nutrient medium employed by intellectuals to reproduce themselves in the market of ideas. It is also understandable that these ideas are not required to be complex and profound, and that like other mass-produced modern commodities, they are not meant to have a long life or extended use. Words do not explain things or even denote them; instead, words themselves become virtual things subject to sale and exchange, just as all conceivable types of status, including academic status, are subject to sale and exchange.

Past intellectual and creative services, transformed into *social capital*, are of course taken into account, and for this reason former members of the left who long ago ceased to be such cannot allow themselves to cross over publicly to the positions of the bourgeoisie and become conservatives, in the manner of their more honest forebears in the nineteenth and the first half of the twentieth centuries. Such transformations now risk the sacrifice of accumulated social capital, along with a loss of status and most importantly, of the competitive advantage accruing to the position of a critical thinker who criticises nothing.[13] Meanwhile, this degradation of social thought is in turn becoming a problem for the capitalist system; in bringing the intellectuals to heel, the ruling elite loses its capacity for critical reflection and for evaluating its own practice. The result is that while stepping onto a minefield of irreconcilable conflicts, fraught with the danger of large-scale social explosions, the elite does not stop and look about itself, since there is no longer anyone to warn it of the inevitable consequences of its own decisions.

Neither critical thinking as such, nor the social sciences in the familiar sense have vanished from the scene. But they have finished up ever more marginal not only in relation to the dominant system, but also in relation to the milieu that earlier supported, defended and cultivated them. It is now necessary to defend not simply the right to dissidence, but also the right to systematic sociological reasoning. Both now require a readiness not just to swim against the current of 'bourgeois thought', but also to defy the majority of left intellectuals.

PART V

The Return of Hope

12

Where to Begin?

Over two centuries, numerous agitators have presented workers with images of a wonderful future, while often stumbling over the question of which specific steps should be implemented first. On the other hand, programmes of specific measures advanced by politicians have constantly been criticised for a lack of perspectives, being perceived as reformist and excessively moderate. But whatever the case any programme of social change, even if utopian and especially if actually realisable, consists of partial steps and measures. At times this list is not as important as the consistency of the social changes enacted, and the interconnections between them.

Michel de Certeau has defined strategy as 'the ability to transform histori-cal uncertainties into calculated spaces'.[1] Examining a situation, we see it not simply as a set of chance circumstances and as the sum of problems each of which needs to be solved on its own, but also as a totality of the possibilities opening up before us. They 'open themselves up', however, only if we our-selves clearly understand what exactly we want and can achieve.

For Antonio Gramsci the task of politics and the point of political activity was to form a historic bloc combining related (but far from identical) interests into the channel of a general cause:

To direct one's will towards the creation of a new equilibrium of actually existing and operating forces, resting on a particular force that is con-sidered progressive and creating the conditions for its victory – all this means, of course, to function on the soil of an actual reality, but to act in such a way as to be able to exert hegemony over it and to transcend it (or to collaborate in this).[2]

Politics does not begin where we give ourselves over to dreams of a better world, but only where these dreams begin to be embodied in real actions that connect our strivings, interests and possibilities into one. Politics, unquestionably, requires rhetoric, models and shared terms, without which not only propaganda, but also a simple recognition of what is 'ours' and what properly belongs to 'others' is impossible. The essence of political action, however, is determined not by slogans but by practical tasks, which the slogans mobilise us to fulfil.

It is in this, categorically, that left activists, ideologues and artists have been lacking during the epoch of the triumph of neoliberalism.

A transitional programme

In the practical programme of *The Communist Manifesto*, Schumpeter noted 'the absence of any plank that we should recognize as typically or exclusively socialist if we met it in another entourage'.[3] To substantiate this judgement, he referred to the fact that these demands could also be encountered *in isolation* in the works of radical bourgeois authors. Meanwhile, it is true that one could just as successfully argue that a whole series of bourgeois reformers, intent on saving or rectifying their system, have employed initiatives from the arsenal of socialists. It may be added that almost all the measures for which Marx and Engels fought in 1848 were not just destined to be realised in practice, but to be realised within the framework of capitalism. What Schumpeter is unwilling to recognise is that it was pressure *from the left* and the political successes of the workers' movement that led to the implementation of such reforms. Meanwhile, we run up here against the fundamental question that not only liberal thinkers such as Schumpeter, but also numerous members of the left have sought to evade. What is it that makes one or another *technical* measure *socialist* in its essence?

It is significant that the authors of *The Communist Manifesto* spoke of the need to enact 'measures that in economic terms appear inadequate and inconsistent, but that as the movement proceeds will outgrow themselves, and that are indispensable as means for bringing about an overturn in the whole mode of production'.[4] In other words, it was quite apparent to Marx and Engels that none of the suggested reforms could *in and of itself* create a new society. The system would be radically changed only when new institutions and laws began to operate, creating *in their totality* a new logic of development.

In the view of Marx and Engels, the measures implemented by revolutionary governments would be 'different in different countries'. Nevertheless, they drew up a short list of reforms including the expropriation of landed property and the turning over of land rents to cover state spending; a high progressive income tax; abolition of the right of inheritance; and the centralisation of credit in the hands of the state through a national bank with state capital and an exclusive monopoly. They also called for the centralisation of all transport in the hands of the state; for an increase in the number of state factories and other instruments of production; for bringing about a gradual end to the difference between city and countryside; for confiscation of the property of all emigrants and rebels; for ending the employment of children in factories; and so forth.[5] It is perfectly understandable that the specific initiatives proposed by the authors of the *Manifesto* were meant to be applied in the socio-economic and political conditions of the mid-nineteenth century. But far more important for the modern reader is to understand the general logic and direction of their initiatives.

It was no accident that Marx and Engels formulated precisely this complex of measures. Most striking is the fact that their demands do not propose either a complete end to market relations, or the abolition of money, or a ban on private entrepreneurship. Nevertheless, these measures were extremely radical for their time, and to some degree, remain so in our time as well. In essence, what was involved was the formation of a new core of the economic system through creating a strong public sector in the sphere of finance, industry, transport and agriculture. These new economic institutions would change the general logic of social reproduction and the relations between people, leading in natural fashion to further changes that Marx and Engels refused on principle to predict, since they were a *question of natural democratic development*. The revolution that abolished the hegemony of the bourgeoisie would create, above all, the *possibility* of socialist relations. This possibility, however, would never open up unless certain historically timely steps were taken, unless a mechanism was set in motion for drawing society into the administration of its own affairs – not only political, but also economic, social and cultural.

Explaining his concept of a 'transitional programme' some ninety years later, Lev Trotsky in 1938 wrote that under conditions of systemic crisis 'every serious demand of the proletariat and even every progressive demand of the petty bourgeoisie will inevitably lead beyond the bounds of capitalist property and the bourgeois state'.[6] Of course, Trotsky was wrong in his forecast concerning the looming crash of the capitalist system, something that he considered inevitable in the very near future. The life of the old regime, in his view, was being prolonged only by 'the opportunist character of the proletarian leadership', while the objective conditions for the triumph of socialism had matured to such a degree that any attempts to express doubt about this conclusion represented 'the product of ignorance or conscious deception'.[7] The crisis of which he spoke, however, was on a truly massive scale. The Great Depression and the Second World War indeed shook the bourgeois world, which survived only through profound reforms in the countries that made up the core of its world-system. Meanwhile, communists were coming to power in a large number of European and Asian countries, from Albania and Poland to China and Vietnam. Trotsky's analysis of the current crisis was thus completely correct, even if the conclusions he drew turned out to be prematurely optimistic.

The greater the scale of the problems that capitalism encountered, the more 'subversive' many reformist demands that had seemed at first glance to be relatively moderate turned out to be. On the one hand, the system was simply unable to satisfy them without running the risk of shattering the dominant social relations and a relationship of forces that it found to its advantage. On the other hand, these demands not only failed to prefigure a prompt end for capitalism, but were also dictated by capitalism's own current position. In economic terms their time had come, and they were indispensable, but politically they were impossible to fulfil:

> If capitalism is incapable of satisfying the demands that flow inexorably from the miseries to which it has itself given rise, then let it perish. In this case, 'feasibility' or 'unfeasibility' is a question of the relationship of forces, and this can be decided only through struggle. On the basis of this struggle, whatever might be its direct practical successes, the workers will best of all come to understand the necessity to do away with capitalist slavery.[8]

The disorganisation of the world economy and of the processes of social reproduction, a situation that began with the Great Recession of 2008–2010, has shown that in the twenty-first century capitalism is encountering the same problems and contradictions as a hundred years ago, but on a new level. In exactly the same way, the debates that accompanied the period of revolutionary and military shocks in the first half of the twentieth century have become relevant once again. In the context of the crisis phenomena that have not ceased to afflict the world economy during the second decade since 2008, the contours of new transitional demands are already emerging clearly.

Above all there is the necessity to exert direct social control over the sectors that satisfy collective needs, and that carry out the tasks of social reproduction. In essence, Marx and Engels were talking of this in *The Communist Manifesto*, and subsequent experience has shown that attempts to satisfy collective needs through market competition between firms and individuals, which are compelled to try to cope with a *common task* through using the sum of private decisions with no connections among themselves, in the best case will give rise to monstrous inefficiency and unnecessary expenditure of resources.

Within capitalism itself, the needs of its own development lead to a rapid and continuing growth of the state sector of the economy. This occurs long before the demands for nationalisation raised by socialists come to dominate the political agenda. The state, Engels noted in the late nineteenth century, 'is forced to assume the leadership of production. This necessity for state ownership arises above all in the case of large-scale means of communication: posts, the telegraph and the railways.'[9]

Collective needs and collective demand also presume collective property. Transport, water supply, energy, and providing the economy with the basic resources essential for its existence, not to speak of science, health care and education, are among the categories in this sphere. There is no need for collective ownership in these areas to involve centralised state control. A great many tasks are best carried out on the local level, through democratic organs of power set up on a regional or municipal basis. The forms of socialisation can be diverse, as can the associated methods of administration, but whatever the case there cannot be a serious left alternative, even a reformist one, unless such questions are posed. In the mid-twentieth century, under the pressure of objective necessity, most industrially developed countries took steps in this direction, but almost everywhere neoliberalism brought a massive wave of privatisations. It is quite obvious that the privatisation process has now to be turned back, not so much in order for left ideology to triumph, as simply for good sense to prevail. The expansion of the state sector is thus an urgent task, in the first instance in the raw materials industries, in science-intensive production, and in the transport and communications systems that operate directly to ensure public benefits. Also of prime importance is the return to state control of strategic enterprises and of the social services taken from the state sector in the course of privatisation.

What should be done?

The capitalist financialisation that developed rapidly in the late twentieth century transformed the banking sector, which had simply been one of the branches of the economy, into a force controlling the development of other economic areas, as well as into a factor of mass employment and of the organising of people's everyday lives. Indeed, during the twenty-first century the financial infrastructure has become part of the life support system of the urban population in the majority of countries. Inevitably, the need has arisen for the socialisation of finances, a process that in essence began to occur during the crisis of 2008–10. However, the measures to reorganise banks and grant them state support that were implemented by governments in the West as well as in Russia and Latin America were carried out at the cost of society and in the interests of capital. These measures have shown that neither the owners of the banks nor the top managers, who are oriented towards maximising profits, are coping with the spontaneous processes and forces that they themselves have unleashed. Nationalisation of the banks that are recognised as essential to the reproduction of the system – that is, as being 'too big to fail' – is the order of the day. A necessary consequence of this policy will be the democratisation of credit and the transformation of the financial infrastructure into part of a properly organised system of generally accessible services for citizens and enterprises.

A growing public sector is indispensable not just in order to optimise the processes of the collective use of resources. Its most important task is to give citizens genuine control over economic and social processes. Trotsky in his time wrote that the essence of socialism lay in creating, on the basis of advanced technologies, an economic order in which labour had no need of compulsion, and did not require 'any other control than that exerted by education, custom and public opinion'. Bluntly speaking, he continued, it would require 'an unusual degree of stupidity to regard this ultimately modest perspective as "utopian"'.[10] In the twenty-first century, the requirements of the time include the democratisation of decision-making in the public sector, openness and transparency in all procedures, and the adoption of general laws regulating the work of state enterprises.

For the same reason, the socialisation of the economy does not necessarily take the form of state ownership. Since the time of *The Communist Manifesto*, Marxists have seen the nationalisation of private property as the decisive instrument for bringing about socialist changes. Nevertheless, Marx and Engels warned unambiguously that property was no more than a juridical form behind which were concealed definite productive and social *relationships*. The social significance of revolution lay precisely in altering these relationships: 'State ownership of the forces of production does not resolve the conflict, but it contains within itself the formal means and possibility of resolving it.'[11]

Realising this possibility, like any other, depends on people's activity and on their ability to form new institutions that correspond to their needs. The nationalisation of industrial enterprises, financial institutions, private estates and cultural assets inevitably places before society not just the question of how to manage all this effectively, but another question as well: *how, and in whose interests, will the decisions be taken?*

'In order to become social,' Trotsky wrote, 'private property must necessarily pass through a stage of state property, just as a caterpillar, in order to become a butterfly, has to pass through the stage of being a pupa. But a pupa is not a butterfly. Countless pupae die without ever managing to become butterflies.'[12] Over the twentieth century a rich experience was accumulated of developing municipal enterprises, working in close cooperation with social self-management. We can now, of course, see the limited nature of the concepts of *workers' control* that were typical of the early twentieth century, when self-management was reduced to periodic meetings of enterprise workers. At times the workers involved themselves in technical questions that needed to be entrusted to specialists, and in other cases declined to take part in deciding questions of development, reducing their role to that of choosing the management. Even in the industrial epoch self-management by worker collectives was by no means a utopia, encountering obvious problems with the workers' limited competence. Karl Kautsky stressed that the socialisation of production had to be carried out 'on the basis of the rule of democracy within the enterprise as well, that is, on the basis of democratic management of the enterprise with the participation of the workers on the one hand, and of consumers on the other'.[13] Nevertheless, social democracy never posed the question of productive self-management as a practical issue, even when companies were nationalised under social-democratic governments. At best, the questions addressed were those of trade union rights, and of guaranteed working conditions and employment in the public sector.

In exile, Lev Trotsky actively supported the idea of economic democracy: 'Under the conditions of a nationalised economy, quality presupposes democracy of the producers and consumers, freedom of criticism and initiative, that is, conditions incompatible with a totalitarian regime of fear, lies and flattery.'[14] During the years when he had been part of the government, dealing with matters that included economic questions, Trotsky however had insisted on extremely tight discipline and centrali-sation, at times even militarisation in the management of industry. This was far from accidental. The tasks arising from the need to mobilise indus-trial production under wartime conditions, when neither market stimuli, nor conventional management methods, nor democratic mechanisms were going to work, had to be performed by administrative and command methods.

Nevertheless, during the Spanish Revolution of 1936–1939, in the Mondragon cooperatives, or in Yugoslavia under Josip Broz Tito, enterprises managed by elected organs proved perfectly able to organise production effectively. To argue that all attempts at workers' self-management have ended in failure is thus incorrect. The limited nature of self-managed socialism, however, lies in the fact that it not only fails to take account of the interests of consumers and of whole social groups that do not participate directly in the process of production, but also fails to create mechanisms for the formulation and realisation of a strategy for the long-term development of the economy. This problem was already noted by Max Weber when he analysed the revolutionary events in Europe between 1917 and 1920, and showed that the socialism of workers' councils was in sum a 'socialism of distribution' based on the interests of workers.[15]

In practice, the contradictions that arose were resolved through the spontaneous or conscious use of market stimuli, in essence returning the work of enterprises to the conditions that existed during the epoch of early bourgeois society. Paradoxically, self-managed socialism in practice finished up far closer than corporate capitalism to the models of the 'classical' market. The experience of the twentieth century thus shows that in the first place, productive self-management can and will work in the interests of society when it is integrated into a broad system of democratic institutions, including economic and social planning that is subordinated to representative organs. Second, it can work when it ceases to be exclusively 'productive'. In such a case, those who participate in decision-making include professional, scientific and local communities that work out their own priorities and formulate their proposals. Does such a system mean the abolition of the market? This is by no means obligatory. But the participation of workers in management necessarily creates different stimuli and priorities, which not only make up for the failures of the market that Schumpeter showed are inevitable, but which also extend far beyond the market's limitations.

Aleksandr Shubin, describing the experience of workers' self-management acquired in the course of the revolutionary waves occurring between 1917 and 1923 (not only in Russia, but also in Italy, Austria and other countries), emphasises that the spontaneous self-organisation of workers has everywhere ended in defeat:

> The left in Austria and Hungary tried to do what the Bolsheviks had not been able to achieve – to balance the different levels of management and self-management in socialised (non-capitalist) industrial production.

But the structures they established were intended not to encourage initiatives from below, but to restrain these initiatives through various counterweights of a bureaucratic nature.[16]

Nevertheless, Shubin comes to the conclusion that the main problem lay in the worker masses themselves, who culturally and psychologically were not ready to take control over social and productive processes into their hands on a long-term basis. Considered historically, however, this situation is destined to change, since the classical machine production of the early twentieth century is being replaced by new technologies, and together with them, a new type of worker is being created, someone who will be more successful in advancing the cause initiated a century before. 'The mission of the left socialists, which they did not usually recognise, consisted of creating reserves for the future that would be more than adequate for the coming tasks, and that would be able to open the way to completing modernisation.'[17]

Managing production cannot be entrusted exclusively to those engaged directly in it, since there are large numbers of questions that affect consumers and subcontractors, or that bear on the environment or on the interests of the region where production is carried out. Further, and especially in the twenty-first century, the economy can never be reduced to industrial enterprises. Nevertheless, the technological and information revolutions that since the 1980s have transformed the nature of economic life are at the same time opening up a multitude of new opportunities for participation by workers in management, through creating the corresponding organisational *platforms*.

The development of technology, proceeding in parallel with the exhaustion of demand and the deepening of the systemic crisis, is creating a demand for *the transformation of commercial platforms into generally accessible tools of development, and for the replacing of private corporations with public-sector institutions*. The use of public infrastructure by independent participants, including those operating by the rules of the market, is becoming a reality even now. The successful development of the opportunities opened up by this new reality, however, depends on social changes and on the ability of society to control the new information platforms, making them open, transparent and free. Fulfilling this task requires not only political will, but a determination to struggle against obsolete bourgeois relations and the corresponding corporate interests.

Those who take the decisions may not only be labour collectives of the classical industrial type, but also *professional associations* (and not just traditional trade unions), organised as part of civil society. Unlike the authoritarian corporations that are formed under capitalism on a vertical principle, such associations are constructed from below, often spontaneously on a basis of self-organisation, and at times in the course of conflict with the state and business.

On the basis of the self-organisation of professional associations, socialist transformations may be carried through in the fields of science, health care and education. The welfare state for which we struggle must be free from the dictates of bureaucracy, just as the political institutions are free of the dictatorship of the elite.

Democratic planning

There is a well-known statement by J.M. Keynes on the socialisation of investment as a critically important and, in a certain sense, adequate means for overcoming the anarchy of the market. A rejection of neoliberalism cannot occur without a radical re-examination of the socio-economic structure. In the concluding section of his *General Theory of Employment, Interest and Money*, the British economist stressed that a 'somewhat comprehensive socialisation of investment will prove the only means of securing an approximation to full employment, though this need not exclude all manner of compromises and devices by which public authority will co-operate with private initiative.'[18]

Thinking on analogous lines was the eminent Polish economist Oskar Lange, who insisted that the socialisation of investment would not only allow an increase in its effectiveness, but would also make it possible to pay all members of society a social dividend from part of the profits received by the state sector. The amount of this payment would depend directly on the successes achieved by the economy, and also on the collectively formulated priorities, which would be set by a representative council.[19]

The ideas of Keynes and Lange are still more relevant in the twenty-first century, when questions of environmental and social planning are coming to the forefront, and most importantly, when it is impossible to ensure in any other fashion that the democratic process has meaningful content. The choice is obvious: either planning becomes the main task of the representative institutions of the state (and of institutions of international cooperation founded on *this* basis), or else democracy will die away and be transformed into an outdated façade that barely conceals a new corporate totalitarianism.

Although the growing demand for the strategic planning of development is forcing a return to the thinking of Keynes on the socialisation of investment, this question cannot be reduced to appeals to restore the principles of Soviet planning, supplemented with the recent achievements of digital technology. The Soviet Gosplan, which sought to plan everything from the building of atomic power stations to the production of teaspoons, was a tool of accelerated industrialisation, essential for concentrating the extremely limited resources of the first half of the twentieth century. While fulfilling this role, it also demonstrated the limitations and drawbacks of such an approach, with the effectiveness of management declining in proportion to the successes that were gained. A diverse, science-based economy requires flexibility, freedom not only for the people who are making decisions, but also for those directly engaged in the practical fulfilment of the tasks that are set. This, however, does not in any way negate the need for coordination in planning and for the joint working out of strategic perspectives. To the contrary, this need is growing rapidly, as indicated not only by the crisis of the environment, but also by the disproportions between demand and supply, social and economic development, the growing wealth of society and the simultaneously growing inequality of its distribution.

The Covid pandemic, military developments, financial crises and the need for a global shift to new energy technologies (irrespective of whether in order to save the planet or to lend dynamism to technological development) all united in the early 2020s to prompt the introduction of new elements of state planning and regulation. The main struggle, however, has not concerned the degree to which planning decisions will help to transform the market, but the questions of who will perform the planning, how, and in whose interests. The initial relations between people, arising in the process of production, are forming and modifying the social structure that is appearing on this basis. In turn, society on this basis is creating new interests, opportunities and needs, which are exerting a direct influence on the economy. Hence the conflicts of all types that arise in the course of the distribution of goods do not exist in isolation from economic practice, preventing or complicating the 'smooth' operation of the process (as market economists are inclined to think), but are a natural and indispensable part of economic life, without which it simply cannot develop.

Of course, taking account of social interests, environmental limitations, cultural needs, and democratic rights and procedures inevitably reduces company profits. But the maximisation of profits in the market is not a guarantee of efficient operation by each individual enterprise, quite apart from the effects on society as a whole. Hence Max Weber, referring to research by Jean Charles de Sismondi and Werner Sombart, showed that high profitability 'often has nothing in common with optimal organisation of the economy from the point of view of use of the available means of production'.[20] The overall degree of efficiency of social reproduction is achieved through the interaction of different sectors, branches and companies, and is not to be reduced to the level of efficiency with which each individual enterprise operates. At the same time, the maximisation of profits in one link of the chain may sharply reduce the efficiency of operation of all the remaining links.

Socialist politics cannot be reduced to a call to make all economic development subject to planning. We fight for organs of planning to be under the control of society and of its democratic representatives. Where state finances are concerned, the task that arises is to mobilise funds not simply for the purpose of financing government expenditure, but in order to support public investment in production, in regional development, in science and education, and in raising people's quality of life. Here, the goal is to improve people's existence not just through raising their levels of consumption, but also through upgrading the environment they inhabit.

Corporate planning has long been a fact, and without it the capitalist economy of the twenty-first century would be fundamentally impossible. Complex logistic chains, the optimisation of spending and the distribution of work have long since become crucial elements in managerial practice, and this practice is no longer oriented towards the market and clients so much as towards raising the internal efficiency of the organisation. The struggle for efficiency, however, not only ignores social interests, the needs of workers, the environment, and cultural and organisational questions related to the regions and communities within which the subdivisions of the corporation are located. This search for efficiency is in fact mounted in order to ensure that all these interests are sacrificed to the drive for maximum profits.

Planning is being developed within capitalism, but is aimed at serving private interests. Meanwhile, institutions of planning were also established during the twentieth century within the framework of the welfare state. The transition from regulated capitalism to neoliberalism, however, has led to institutions of planning being privatised.[21] A typical example of this is the transformation of central banks into institutions independent of the state, under the direct control of the financial oligarchy and issuing dictates to sovereign governments. The primary purpose of introducing a common European currency was the same. Stripping governments of control over monetary emission, financial capital has transformed countries with relatively weak economies into its hostages, compelling them to borrow at usurious interest rates the money they need and which they would otherwise simply be able to create. The tragic consequences could be observed in Greece during the crisis of 2010. Socialist planning can and should make use of the accumulated organisational and technical experience of modern corporate planning, but should subordinate the process to the new tasks and to the new, democratic interests of the masses, making the reconciling of these diverse interests an organic part of the decision-making process.

Summarising the demands and proposals emerging 'from below' is not the simplest of tasks, and it is by no means always the case that these demands correspond to the available resources. Also, the demands at times contradict each other. Precisely for this reason, it is essential to create institutions and procedures that allow the initiatives from below to organise themselves, to direct their activities into constructive channels, and to lay the foundations for a new democracy of participation.

As a matter of principle, such questions cannot be settled in advance, and still less can they be described on the basis of theoretical constructs alone. These are questions primarily of a practical nature, while the task of theory in this case lies in the critical generalising of practical experience. Fortunately, the necessary experience has already in part been accumulated, even within the framework of the capitalist system. An instructive example of such practice has been the participatory budgets worked out in many cities since the last years of the twentieth century.

The participatory budget introduced by the Workers' Party in the Brazilian city of Porto Alegre, and later throughout the surrounding state of Rio Grande do Sul, can be seen as one of the mechanisms of democratic planning. In Russia the five-year plan for the development of Irkutsk Province, implemented between 2015 and 2019 when Sergey Levchenko was governor, was worked out on the basis of similar principles. It is noteworthy that the drawing up of the plan began with collecting proposals and suggestions on the municipal level. The regional administration held consultations with city mayors, deputies and private citizens. By no means all the suggestions and aspirations were fulfilled. In total, '1741 suggestions were received from residents of 36 municipal entities of Irkutsk Province (85.7 per cent of all the municipal entities) on more than 30 topics.'[22] As a result of implementing the 'Levchenko five-year plan', the province sharply improved its economic performance indicators, and increased its wage levels. The growth of industrial and agricultural production finished up clearly exceeding the figures for Russia as a whole. Particularly impressive were the financial results, as the province freed itself almost entirely from debt. The political consequences of these successes were paradoxical, but predictable: the federal authorities forced the resignation ahead of time of the 'red governor', who with his achievements had discredited the activity of the federal government and of his fellow governors, who were unable to show comparable results. This once again confirms a well-known truth – that without a struggle for power, it is impossible to achieve serious social changes even on a local level.

Since distributing public funds in the form of investments is a crucially important question of socialist planning, democratic organs face the question of the criteria and priorities behind this allotting of resources. Without question, one of the criteria remains profitability. Along with this, however, the social effects of projects, their environmental consequences and so forth play important roles. Investments in environmental, social, scientific or educational programmes can become critical factors in economic growth, according far better with the interests of humanity than putting money into military production, the simplest means under capitalism for the state to create new jobs.

A further example of an enlightened approach to investment can now be seen in the work of the Sitra corporation in Finland. Set up within the framework of the state sector, this venture investment fund aided substantially during the 1990s and later in reviving the economy, which had been in severe depression. It also assisted in the country's technological modernisation, and made it possible to fulfil a range of social tasks that included overcoming or mitigating gender inequality and economic inequalities between regions. The fund acts under the control of parliament, and its decisions are made by a supervisory council representing different social interests.[23]

The transformation of corporate into socialist planning also presupposes information openness on the part of all enterprises of the social sector with relation to one another, their employees and society. Open and free access to information and to computer software and technologies is not just a tribute to the principles of democracy. This principle increases the overall efficiency of the socialist sector of the economy. On this basis, cooperation is organised between collectives and organisations, and various *platforms* (including self-organised platforms) become available for democratic coordination.

'Green New Deal'

In the early 2010s, when the Great Recession had clearly confirmed the fears expressed by critics of the neoliberal economy, experts, journalists and later politicians as well began speaking of new guidelines for development. It was not only members of the left who engaged in these discussions, and in this way, the idea of the Green New Deal made its appearance. Its supporters were inspired by the precedent of the New Deal enacted by US president Franklin D. Roosevelt, whose reforms helped the US overcome the consequences of the Great Depression. The public works such as road construction that were organised by the state, along with arms production during the Second World War, created millions of new jobs for Americans and laid the foundations for a growth of prosperity that was to last for three decades.

The idea of the Green New Deal proposed the use of the same methods, but advanced somewhat different priorities of development. The stimulus for economic growth was to become investments in preserving and restoring the natural environment, replacing relatively 'dirty' (ecologically speaking) technologies and consumption practices with others that were 'cleaner'. The latter initiatives would include the development of public transport infrastructure that would reduce people's demand for personal cars. Other aspects of the programme would include the development of education, science, health care and social services. The state, according to the Green New Deal concept, should act as the main investor, a sort of locomotive drawing the private sector out of the crisis wagon by wagon.

The Green New Deal ideology united moderate leftists, environmental movements and even substantial elements of business that saw in it the prospect of economic growth. Senator Bernie Sanders employed Green New Deal slogans during his presidential campaigns in 2016 and 2020, while the less radical wing of the US Democratic Party was also prepared to make use of ideas from this source. The topic of a Green New Deal also began to be actively discussed in other Western countries. Nevertheless, practical enactment of the reforms was postponed indefinitely, while the crisis of the neoliberal economic order developed far more rapidly than the political discussion moved ahead.

The Russian–Ukrainian war induced Western governments to place numerous arms orders with industrial enterprises, spontaneously reinstituting more traditional forms of Keynesianism in which jobs were created through weapons production. It is true that the sharp reduction in Russian fuel shipments to Western Europe stimulated discussion on alternative sources of energy, but predictably, preference was given to short-term solutions.

Nevertheless, the question of the need for environmental priorities of development remains on the agenda. Calls for planting forests in order to remove excess greenhouse gases from the atmosphere, or to develop public transport in order to save cities from air pollution and traffic congestion, are perfectly rational. Such moves make it possible to create a multitude of genuinely useful jobs, to stimulate scientific research and to strengthen local communities. The only problem is that a politics that is oriented solely towards environmental priorities and that ignores other contradictions of modern-day capitalism simply will not work.

The very fact that we are forced once again to speak of a 'right to education' or 'right to health', and even of a 'right to clean air', is a testimony not to social progress but to a serious degradation of society that has transformed things that once were generally available into privileges. Baudrillard in his time noted that the talk of a 'right to clean air' in fact signifies 'the loss of clean air as a natural good, its transition to the status of a commodity and its unequal social redistribution'.[24] The climate crisis, along with growing social inequality and resource shortages (resulting less from the objective exhaustion of resources than from their specific mode of use under late capitalism), is becoming a key stimulus for transforming planning from a phenomenon found within corporations into a whole-of-state and ultimately, global practice.

At least in theory, left parties have always called for strict laws blocking the possibility of the urban environment suffering destruction under the guise of 'development'. But these laws, intended to restrain the predatory actions of capital, have acted exclusively as a limiting factor transforming numerous members of the radical left into opponents of economic growth as such, and even into aggressive technophobes. This position represents a dead end, since it conflicts with the objective needs of society, needs that do not require restrictions on people's economic activity, but the redirection of this activity into tasks that extend beyond the bounds of capitalist interests. The strategic perspective is not to block economic growth (though this growth is not an end in itself), but to create positive stimuli and to form new conditions for economic progress. The development of the public sector, placed under the control of local communities, creates favourable conditions for restoring and preserving not only the natural environment, but the urban, cultural environment as well.

It is quite clear that practical work on this scale cannot stop at the national level. But in their turn, decisions that affect global processes can only be reached and implemented if they rest on corresponding institutions that exist on the national, regional and local levels. To paraphrase the well-known remark of Georges Clemenceau that war is too serious a business to be left to generals, it may be said that the environment is too serious a matter to be entrusted to environmentalists, and that the economy is too important to our lives to be entrusted to government technocrats, even if these technocrats are honest and convinced socialists.

The politics of socialism are complex, aimed at restoring the *social* quality of government, a quality undermined by the logic of the market competition that has acquired a more radical form under the conditions of neoliberalism. Overcoming the consequences of fragmentation, however, is no longer a question of affirming the ideological principles of the left, but is becoming one of meeting the social requirements felt in different fashion by people who hold diverse views and who even belong to different social groups and classes. The problem is one of uniting these people for shared constructive work, without dividing them either on the basis of identity, or of ideology, or of class in the narrow sense. This is especially true since as the process of transformation goes ahead the class structure of society and its culture inevitably change, and attempts to preserve them in their initial forms, to fix or freeze them bureaucratically, become a factor of social conservatism, even if these efforts are accompanied by revolutionary slogans. Society cannot be integrated successfully through an enforced common ideology, but only through participation in the building of a new economy and through joint decision-making on different levels.[25]

The main paradox of the modern socialist project is that there is no need to devise anything fundamentally new. There is no point whatever in inventing a new round of utopias. Not only have a great number of ideas made their appearance over the 200 years of the development of socialist movements, but a vast practical experience has been accumulated, even if this experience has not always been of success. Ultimately, the failure of previous socialist experiments has also enriched us with a vast amount of theoretical and practical knowledge. Critically assimilated and generalised, this experience is becoming a completely adequate basis for a new economic and political practice. All we need to do is fit the puzzle together. This, however, also requires political will, along with a movement capable of developing this will and of directing it collectively towards the solving of practical problems.

13

Plan and Market

In summarising the history of the attempts made during the during the twentieth century to implement socialist projects, it is impossible to ignore the discussions on the topic of plan and market.

The fall of the Soviet Union was presented by many as definitive proof of the impossibility of effective planning, seen as doomed to lose out to market exchange for ensuring the rapid and optimal distribution of resources. Unfortunately for supporters of the free market, the subsequent crises have provided a serious basis for doubting the correctness of these conclusions. Meanwhile, the information-processing technologies that became widespread in the first decades of the twenty-first century have inspired hopes that centralised planning may be able to rid itself of bureaucratic hindrances and become more dynamic. The British *Financial Times* at one point prophesied: 'The Big Data revolution can revive the planned economy.'[1]

It would appear that there is every reason to return to the well-known 'calculation debate' on plan data that was once conducted by liberal critics of socialism, whose positions now appear to be far weaker.[2] In reality, the question of planning cannot be reduced to the problems of how to make an optimal calculation of resources and of how to process information promptly. Far more important is to recognise that planning is a means of organising social reproduction in the interests of all of society and under society's control. The attitude of socialists to both plan and market must be determined by the degree to which the *means* employed correspond to the given goals.

The history of the question

However paradoxical it may seem, the question of the existence of market relations under socialism did not immediately become a topic of intense discussion among revolutionaries. The question that took priority was the transformation of property relations. Marx and Engels stressed that these changes were not dictated by ideological or moral demands, but by the natural logic of capitalist production itself:

> By more and more transforming the great majority of the population into proletarians, the capitalist mode of production creates a force that under the threat of its demise is forced to carry out this overturn. As it increasingly forces the transformation of large socialised means of production into state property, the capitalist mode of production itself points the way to the completion of this upheaval. *The proletariat takes state power and transforms the means of production primarily into state property.*[3]

On the topic of how this property was to be organised and employed, only general hints are to be found in the works of the founders of Marxism. The fundamental projection was that from that point onward, the economy would be organised and resources applied *directly* in the interests of the majority of society.

It is true that in his writings Engels several times voiced the idea that once private property had been overcome the need for commodity production would also disappear, since the economy would be aimed at the direct satisfaction of the needs of society. Although the programme of measures set out in *The Communist Manifesto* does not propose abolition of commodity relations and the market, Marx and Engels in reflecting on the character of the future socialist economy foresaw no connection between its development and market relations. Engels expressed his views on this topic quite explicitly: 'Once society takes the means of production into its possession, commodity production will be done away with, and along with it, the domination of the product over the producers.'[4]

Meanwhile, the socialist movement since it first came into existence had displayed an ambivalent attitude to the market. Socialists had sharply criticised the dominance of market relations and their penetration into all areas of life, but in the late nineteenth and early twentieth centuries it was clear to the members of the movement that abolishing market relations by decree would not work, and that most importantly, there was nothing that would force the victorious proletariat to act in this fashion. This ambivalence reflected an objective contradiction of economic history itself, since market relations were in no way a product of the bourgeois order; they had become established long before the bourgeois order arose, and consequently could also survive capitalism. Nevertheless, it had been precisely within the framework of the bourgeois order that the market had achieved its greatest development, becoming the main regulator not only of economic activity but of human activity in general. Everything was being bought and sold, everything was becoming a commodity, and the hold of the market was becoming total.

Nevertheless, in the late nineteenth century, as the concentration of capital had grown stronger and as monopolies had taken shape and come to dominate economic life, grounds had emerged for maintaining that despite the formal support that capitalism gave to market principles, it was itself tending to negate them. Engels stated:

> Free competition is being transformed into monopoly, and within cap-italist society unplanned production is capitulating before the planned production of the coming socialist society. True, this is at first only for the benefit of and to the advantage of the capitalists.[5]

As joint-stock companies and monopolies developed, capital not only overcame its private character (becoming transformed into a collective exploiter), but its 'absence of planning' also vanished into the past.[6] This, however, did not put an end to the contradiction, since the planning was carried out not in the interests of society, but in those of the elite.

On the whole, the events of the early twentieth century confirmed Engels's prediction. The First World War and the opening phase of the Russian Revolution showed that even under capitalism situations arise in which market methods have to be rejected, and that this has nothing in common either with the ideological positions of socialists, or with the collective will of the proletariat, or with the individual convictions of revolutionary leaders. Amid the global shocks of the First World War the market collapsed of its own accord. Centralised planning measures and the non-market distribution of foodstuffs began to be introduced by the warring governments at the various ends of Europe even before the Bolsheviks came to power in Russia.

During the First World War 'military socialism' in Germany, like 'military communism' during the Civil War in Russia, arose out of the collapse of the system of monetary circulation and from the need to make use of natural exchange, about which Max Weber wrote quite openly. In conditions where the market is operating free from the challenge of emergencies, the illusion appears that all economic calculations can be reduced to financial accounting, ignoring the objects and commodities that are subject to distribution. To the contrary, any large-scale crisis poses the question of the 'rationalisation of natural accounting', and requires the corresponding methods of economic organisation to be worked out. 'The current war, like any war in history, is once again and with enormous force making them critical in light of the difficulties of the wartime and post-war economy.[7]

Meanwhile, the wartime economy in solving some problems inevitably encountered others. Weber commented on these as well: 'The calculations here are only *technically* correct, and in economic terms (with regard to materials that are not threatened with imminent exhaustion, and to labour power) are very approximate.' The calculations did not take into account the 'competing goals' that exist within a complex society, and hence could not 'ensure the long-term rationality of the distribution of labour and of the means of production' that had been adopted.[8] The same problems, however, also arise within a corporate capitalist economy, since with such a great concentration of resources in a few hands 'they calculate precisely where and when they are *forced* to do this'.[9]

By the 1920s the experience of 'war socialism' in Europe had shown that an economy could survive and develop without the market. Whether it was worth striving for this, however, was another question.

Discussing the possibilities and limits of the socialisation of the economy, Weber referred to the theoretical and practical activity of his teacher Otto Neurath, and came to the conclusion that with the complete collectivisation of all economic activity money could in fact become unnecessary, and that the relations of exchange could be regulated using natural accounting. But is such a solution possible and desirable in practice, at least in the real world we are concerned with? It makes more sense to divide economic life into the spheres that objectively require and do not require socialisation, with the boundary between them 'determined in form and extent by effective prices'.[10]

The need to guarantee supplies to the cities and ensure the operation of industrial enterprises despite the devaluation of money and dramatic changes in all the familiar relationships between demand for different groups of commodities forced governments of different ideological hues to resort to compulsory food requisitioning in the countryside, to issue ration cards, and to impose norms on the distribution of resources. Trying to assess the efficiency of such an economy using market criteria made no sense, since the task of administration was not to secure an increase of production, or of the income or well-being of citizens, but merely to permit their survival and the preservation of urban society. 'War communism' coped successfully with this task. But to the degree to which the various decisions and measures assumed the shape of a more or less logical system, a corresponding ideology, later to become an organic part of the communist tradition, arose as well.

Even at the height of 'war communism', Lenin in 1918 understood perfectly that the total collectivisation of property and accordingly, a complete rejection of market relations was impossible and undesirable. Large-scale capital had to be subject to merciless expropriation, but as the Bolshevik leader insisted, there were 'no decrees able to turn small-scale production into large', instead of which it was 'necessary to convince people gradually, through the course of events, of the necessity for socialism'.[11]

To a degree, the New Economic Policy introduced by Lenin and the Bolsheviks in the early 1920s shook the ideology that had come to prevail in the Civil War years. It should, however, be remembered that even at that time many communists perceived what was occurring as a retreat. What the return to market methods of running the economy contradicted was not so much the principles of communism as ideas of how these principles should be implemented in practice.

Nevertheless, the experience of 'war communism' and the NEP together convinced all the participants in Soviet economic discussions of the need to combine plan and market principles in the new economy. Trotsky, a convinced critic of 'retreat' during the NEP years, understood perfectly that abolishing the market (at least during an epoch of transition) was impossible:

> For the regulation and adaptation of plans, two levers are needed: a political lever, in the form of real participation in leadership by the motivated masses, something that is inconceivable without soviet democracy; and a financial lever, in the form of a real verification of *a priori* accounts using a general equivalent, which is unthinkable without a stable monetary system.[12]

Meanwhile, he adhered to the concept, extremely conservative even for his epoch, that 'the only genuine money is that which is based on gold'.[13]

The commodity economy in the USSR

The theoretical discussions of the 1920s and 1930s were interrupted by the political repression that struck at supporters of virtually all points of view. During the period of collectivisation and forced-draft industrialisation in the USSR, increased shortages of foodstuffs and numerous other goods again led to the introduction of rationing. As noted by the historian Vadim Rogovin, 'this was treated by the Stalinist propaganda not as a forced, temporary measure, but as a step on the way to the complete abolition of market relations, to the direct non-monetary distribution of products'.[14] Before long, however, the policy changed once more. As supply came to be normalised, elements of the market returned to the Soviet economy. Although on the ideological level the Soviet planning that was established during the years of the first five-year plans reinforced the ideological attitudes that had appeared as early as the 'war communism' period, the economic model that took shape in the USSR could not be termed *non-commodity*. The workers were paid wages, and manufactured items were sold for money, though at fixed prices, and in the collective-farm markets the sellers were able to set their prices independently. The market criteria employed by the Soviet planning organs and enterprises received the name *khozraschet* (collective accounting). Speaking at the Eighteenth Congress of the party, Stalin emphasised:

> For the country's economic life to go full steam ahead, and for industry and agriculture to be stimulated to further increase their production, it is necessary to meet a further condition – developed commodity exchange between city and countryside, between the country's regions and provinces, and between different economic sectors. It is essential for the country to be covered by a rich network of trading bases, stores and shops. It is essential that by way of the channels between these bases, stores and shops, goods should flow incessantly from the places of production to the consumer. It is essential that the state trading network, local industry, the collective farms and individual peasants should be drawn into this activity.[15]

The policy implemented from the mid-1930s is characterised by Rogovin as 'the Stalinist neo-NEP'. Adding to the slogans of struggle were calls to citizens to bring about a 'prosperous life', associated in turn with an abundance of goods.[16] Market factors came to be taken into account in the process of drawing up plans:

> Following the abolition of rationing, workers and salaried employees began to spend their earnings in the collective-farm markets, where prices were unregulated, and in the state shops where a certain degree of consumer choice was available at fixed prices. In this way, a broader consumer market arose in the country. With freedom to choose where they would apply their labour, urban residents were now guided to a greater degree by wages and other consumer stimuli. A market for labour power also came to exist in the country, inducing enterprises to compete to attract workers.[17]

In Stalin's view, this situation was associated with the existence in the USSR of two forms of property, state and collective-farm cooperative:

This is bringing about a situation in which the state is able to dispose only of the production of state enterprises, since the production of the collective farms, as their own property, is disposed of only by the farms themselves. The collective farms, however, are reluctant to dispose of their products except in the form of commodities, in exchange for which they want to obtain the goods they need. At present the collective farms are unwilling to accept any but commodity ties to the cities, that is, any relations apart from those of sale and purchase. Hence commodity production and commodity circulation are now just as much a necessity for us as they were, let us say, thirty years ago, when Lenin spoke of the need to develop commodity trade to the utmost.[18]

Of course, Stalin's reference to the collective farms being 'unwilling' to surrender their production except for money was no more than an ideological subterfuge. Real control over the taking of key decisions remained in the hands of the party and economic bureaucracy. The existence of commodity relations was associated on the one hand with the need for economic accounting and control, without which planning would have been impossible, and on the other, as Ota Šik later showed, with the fact that different interests existed within society. On the economic level, a spontaneous harmonisation of these interests occurred in the process of market exchange, and even the centralised planning was obliged to take account of this.[19]

Meanwhile, the Soviet bureaucracy by the mid-1950s was no longer coping with the increased complexity of the tasks before the economy, whose declining effectiveness eventually provoked a major new discussion.[20] Also taking part in the debates during the 1950s and 1960s on the prospects for economic reform were experts from other countries of the Soviet bloc. The outcome of these controversies was the theory of 'market socialism'.

Market socialism

Initially, it thus emerges, the interest in the market did not stem from ideology but was linked to the need to increase the efficiency of economic management in Soviet-type states, and to overcome the limitations of bureaucratic centralism.[21] Before long, however, the same began to occur with 'market socialism' as had happened with 'war communism': it became an ideology. Logically enough, this train of thought was to lead a whole series of the economists who had originally embraced it into the liberal camp. This occurred not only in the case of Kornai, but also, towards the end of his life, even in that of the distinguished Polish Marxist Włodzimierz Brus.[22] This ideology, despite the substantially altered economic and technological conditions, continues to shape the ideas of socialist reform embraced by the majority of moderate-left authors in the early twenty-first century. Thus, Axel Honneth sees the task of the left as being, through an orientation towards ethical values, to bring about a transformation of market institutions:

> Today, one of the most vital tasks of socialism is once again to cleanse the concept of the market of all the admixtures of properties, specific to capitalism, that have been inserted into it retroactively, in order thus to acquire the possibility of testing its resistance to moral stresses.[23]

The problem is that in calling for the market to be 'cleansed' of capitalism, Honneth cannot define what distinguishes a socialist from a bourgeois economy, apart of course from ethical values, which unfortunately change beneath the influence of social development.

In the late 1980s, when perestroika was already portending the twilight of the socialist system, the British *New Left Review* carried a remarkable discussion between the Belgian Trotskyist and ideologue of the 'Fourth International' Ernest Mandel and the University of Glasgow economist and Soviet specialist Alec Nove. While Mandel, basing himself on the classical texts of Engels, called for overcoming market relations through democratic planning,[24] Nove, referring to practical experience, insisted on the usefulness of the market.[25] Underlining the paradoxical nature of the discussion was the fact that the authors spoke in completely different theoretical languages, advancing arguments that in practice did not connect with one another. The upshot of this debate was the publication of an article by the British economist Diane Elson, who posed the question in fundamentally different fashion. While Nove came out in support of the market, and Mandel against it, Elson spoke of the mechanisms for the socialisation of markets that arose inescapably from the tasks of democratic planning.[26]

The question is not of whether the market itself is 'good' or 'bad', or even of how it is indispensable to a socialist economy as a mechanism enabling the rational use of resources and connecting producers with consumers. Instead it relates to the fact that the development of modern technologies and the formation of new needs (both individual and collective), along with the appearance of new problems, inevitably forces us to *go beyond the bounds of the market.* While not denying the necessity of the market, and not attempting to abolish or dismantle it, we find ourselves faced with tasks whose solution demands quite different approaches.

The market is irreplaceable if we are discussing the production of footwear or the need to improve the quality of service in restaurants, but we are far less able to rely on it for organising the supply of electrical energy to whole regions, or the financing of fundamental scientific research whose benefits are unlikely to be felt for twenty or thirty years. From this, the conclusion flows necessarily that the more massive and long-term the tasks that society sets itself, the less of a role the market will play in performing them, and the greater the need for planning. In this sense, the economic progress of humanity indeed requires going beyond the bounds of the market. In a certain sense, it even requires going outside the limits of the economy, as this is now understood.

Reflecting on the crisis of industrial civilisation and the growing importance of digital technologies, the Russian economist Vyacheslav Inozemtsev points to 'the impossibility of adequately calculating the value of information products and individualised goods, of determining the value of the most productive companies and of the human and social capital embodied in them'.[27] He sees a solution to the problem, however, only in the emergence of new statistical indicators that reflect the new reality more precisely. Meanwhile, the problem presented by changing productive forces cannot be solved without productive relations and social relations in a broader sense, including relations of power and property, being affected. By allowing productive activity to be regulated through direct agreements between interested collectives, communities and individuals, new technologies also pose the question of whether an objective need for market exchange even exists. For the same reason the technological bases for private property, no longer an essential element in the process of interaction between participants in economic processes, are disappearing or being restricted. In the twenty-first century a *multi-level economy* is spontaneously taking shape, and is inevitably demanding complex decisions that combine different approaches. The old does not disappear fully, merely yielding the predominant place to the new. This is still more cause to create a powerful public sector, working for the integration of different technological and social-domestic systems that are not only established historically within society, but that also continue to develop and interact within it.

On the one hand, the need to obtain the basic resources required for the reproduction of society as such creates a *flow economy* (as, for example, in the production of energy, basic raw materials and so forth, where the purchaser taken in isolation cannot freely choose just which barrel of oil best matches their tastes and passions), while on the other hand the need for strategic investments requires not only expenditures of public funds, but also their concentration under the control of organs responsible to society.

At the same time as the politics of neoliberalism have aimed to transform everything that can be produced or used by a human being into a commodity, the interests of society require *decommodification*, or in other words, that objects, actions and processes should have their original direct meaning restored to them, with access to them not limited by effective demand.[28]

The replacing of market exchange with direct relations between people and communities, where these relations are called into life by the actual development of technologies and of society, does not do away with the need for market mechanisms so long as what is involved is traditional forms of production and consumption. But the integration of these levels of economic activity is possible only on the basis of democratic planning. Consequently, the need for economic democracy flows out of the very process of the development of humanity.

14

From the Coalition of Resistance to the Coalition of Change

'The tradition of resistance', wrote Christian Laval, 'has long existed; it is renewed from generation to generation, and belonging to it, whether we like it or not, are both the best philosophers of political liberalism and the most ardent defenders of the Land of Soviets.'[1] Those who speak of resistance may include radical artists and trade union activists, representatives of oppressed minorities, philosophers and public figures. In each case the concept of resistance is lent a particular content. Importantly, the resistance may simply be to one aspect of the system, to a particular decision. Or, on the other hand, it may take the form of existential opposition to the dominant order.

It is an enormous shame that the system for the most part overcomes resistance, but even when opposition from the forces of society thwarts the plans of the ruling class, the fundamental relations of dominance remain unchanged. In the early twenty-first century protests organised by anti-globalist coalitions managed to unite various initiatives and movements, but this success did not prove long-lasting, and most importantly, did not lead to social changes.

Inevitably, the fact that one and the same situation has appeared repeatedly means that the question must be posed in a new fashion. The task is to *make the shift from supporting coalitions of resistance to forming coalitions of change*.

Mobilising civil society

The long-standing dominance of neoliberalism and the similarly drawn-out retreat by the left have created a sort of culture of despair, heightened by utopian illusions concerning catastrophic events that are supposed in some way to alter the situation and make the transition to a new society inevitable. This type of thinking has been described very aptly by Boris Kapustin:

Those despairing (former) leftists who suppose that there is nothing to be counted on in this situation, and nothing to be expected except a complete catastrophe that will occur at some point and change the world accordingly, are too optimistic. A catastrophe may occur in such a world – and the financial collapse of 2008 approximated to it closely enough, revealing in a general way what it might look like – but even a catastrophe will not change anything substantial, will not lead to a 'change of paradigm', if the present-day subjectivities of 'slave' and 'master' are preserved, and correspondingly, if the present-day shutdown of the dialectic remains.[2]

If the *potential of changes whose time has come* is to be transformed into a *process of social transformations*, practical actions are essential in order to unite and mobilise the forces that objectively have an interest in these changes. This practical work is in turn inseparable from an exact posing of the theoretical questions, and from a preparedness to answer them honestly and soberly. As Walter Benjamin stated, 'To be a dialectician means to catch the wind of history in your sails. These sails are concepts. However, it is not enough merely to have sails. What is decisive is the art of setting them correctly.'[3] This task cannot be fulfilled either by the endless repetition of truthful and radical slogans, or by attempts to mechanically subordinate mass movements to ready-made ideologies or organisations. The worst that members of the left can do is to divorce themselves from the everyday cares of the majority, from the majority's spontaneously formed and by no means always politically correct agenda, while motivating this on the basis of the 'immaturity of the masses'.

Analysing the mechanism of ideological hegemony employed by the ruling class, Slavoj Žižek has noted that hegemonic ideas are able to 'work' and to enjoy support among the lower orders of society only if in one way or another these ideas include an 'authentic popular content'.[4] In other words, the rulers cannot receive the support of the ruled unless at least in part, the interests, opinions, needs, wishes and fears of the ruled are taken into account. A revolution occurs at precisely the moment when the ideological self-exposure of the ruling class *necessarily* becomes complete and obvious, since beneath the impact of the social and economic crisis that class can no longer do anything in the interests of the majority.

In the mid-twentieth century, sociologists studying class conflicts on the local level came to the conclusion that the ability of the business elite to impose its will on society was determined not only and not so much by its own strength as by 'apathy on the part of the workers'.[5] In other words, the political, cultural and emotional demobilisation of the masses is an important factor in class rule, but in periods of crisis this situation is liable to change sharply. At the same time, the ruling classes themselves may discover that the passivity of the lower orders has become an obstacle to dealing with urgent tasks that require mass participation. The result is desperate efforts by the elites to 'arouse' the masses through patriotic propaganda, social campaigns and enforced mobilisations, but the ultimate results often prove completely different from those on which the rulers were counting (as Lenin noted accurately in his analysis of revolutionary situations).

At such moments the contradiction between the rhetoric of the authorities and the living practice of the masses becomes absolute, and the ruling class or stratum is no longer capable even of effective hypocrisy, instead revealing its genuine face to all society. In the place of ideological compromise there is open reaction, and the demand for resistance takes hold of broad layers that earlier had remained 'outside of politics'. Furthermore, the ideological formulae earlier implanted by the authorities in mass consciousness now begin to work against the ruling groups, which are forced either to reject these formulae or else, through their actions, to reveal their inability to adhere to them. In this case, it is completely unimportant how progressive or reactionary these ideas might be; the fundamental point is that *objectively* they have become subversive.

Unfortunately, the inability of the ruling classes to maintain mass belief in the official ideology by no means signifies the triumph of a progressive worldview. In a certain sense, the opposite is even true. In the first instance, the minds of the people begin to be taken over by the most superficial and murky ideas that are already circulating in society and that have not encountered systematic resistance, since from the point of view of the elites, they have not been considered dangerous. 'It may be said with certainty', Antonio Gramsci wrote, 'that economic crises in themselves do not give rise directly to major historical events; they are merely able to provide a more favourable soil for the spread of a particular method of thinking, for the posing and resolving of questions that encompass the whole subsequent process of development of the life of the state.'[6]

The crisis of hegemony of the ruling class creates the need for a new social bloc that must inevitably include many people whom the existing system had earlier suited well enough. These people come over to the new movement in part because they are driven by the logic of its ideas, in part to the degree that they recognise their own interests, and in part simply under the influence of growing emotional outrage at what is occurring. But in order for this protest to be transformed into a constructive, transformative force, it still needs to be worked on ideologically and politically.

Unfortunately, mass consciousness is by no means a 'clean slate'. Worse, the now-dysfunctional ideology of the ruling class still clutters people's consciousness even after these ideas cease to operate directly and are even rejected. In place of a picture of the world that is more or less coherent, even if reactionary in essence, there appears a trash-heap of ideological rubbish. This rubbish is accumulated over decades, by no means always deliberately.

Through adapting to the hegemony of neoliberalism, members of the left have made their own contribution to worsening the devastation within their heads (if we are to use the famous image of Mikhail Bulgakov). Typical of left discourse over many years has been an inclination to rename phenomena and people; instead of analysing social relations and trying to change them, there has been a substitution of concepts as a way of governing mass consciousness and at the same time, of adapting it to a politics of enforced fragmentation. Discussion is reduced to the advancing of various subjective evaluations that act in the capacity of *opinions*, but that have no connection whatsoever to the revealing of objective *truth*. In his time, Nikolay Bukharin recognised one of the signs of the degradation of bourgeois political economy in the attempts by Eugen Böhm-Bawerk and other authors of the 'Austrian School' to replace the objective logic of the law of value, employed by Adam Smith, David Ricardo and Karl Marx, with the subjectivist logic of 'marginal utility'.[7] Paradoxically, the radical (at first glance) critique of neoliberalism proceeds from the same subjective premises. Of course, it is by no means always true that an appeal to the subjective factor signifies an inability or lack of desire to analyse society adequately. But if what is involved is an attempt to substitute the subjective factor for a study of the objective course of events, then things are exactly as Bukharin stated.

The economically substantive concept of exploitation and the politically concrete idea of discrimination are being replaced by the concept of oppression, interpreted ever more broadly. In exactly the same way the concept of violence, that may now be 'non-physical', 'moral', 'verbal' or even 'emotional', is interpreted in endlessly expansive fashion. The total of those who are offended and in need of protection grows by the hour, so that everyone, regardless of their position in society and their attitude to the present socio-economic order, their practical activity or their place within the social system, is able to number themself among the victims or at least to proclaim themself as being among the defenders. The more widely each of these terms is applied, the greater the opportunities it provides for manipulation, and the more it works against those who are genuinely subject to *violence, exploitation and compulsion* in the narrow (and concrete) sense of these words.

The numerous new laws that relate specifically to isolated social sectors or topics are in essence reflections in the political sphere of market consumer abundance, or in the words of Baudrillard, 'democratic billboards of the consumer society'.[8] In practice, these politics not only reflect and perpetuate the logic of the market, but also reinforce it, turning what should be a self-evident recognition of objectively existing differences into a field of struggle over mutually recognised privileges that have not so much a class as a caste character. *Even while declaring some demands to be formally universal, their supporters, without themselves being aware of this, recognise the presence of a fundamental inequality, proclaimed as 'difference'.*

While there is no doubt that a multitude of people in various forms and for various reasons actually are offended or oppressed, or become victims of one or another kind of harassment, politicians who try to construct their projects on this basis either remain commonplace moralists or else attempt consciously to distract us from the *main* problems and contradictions of our epoch. At the same time, left groups that transform such verbal exercises into the basis of their ideological practice turn into subcultural talk-shops, at times even less attractive to the majority of 'ordinary' people than the various communities of Tolkien enthusiasts or consumers of organic foods.

The heterogeneous masses and democratic action

In the 1980s Ralph Miliband noted that although socialist ideology largely imagines working people as a uniform mass, in reality 'the working class is not a homogeneous bloc with one clear interest and one voice'. In his view, a socialist state should take on itself the task of politically integrating the worker masses, acting as a sort of 'mediator' between different groups and at the same time 'safeguarding the personal, civic and political freedoms which are intrinsic to the notion of socialist citizenship'.[9] The thesis concerning the extent to which this task should be carried out by the state power, possessing a certain autonomy with relation to the worker masses themselves (a topic that György Lukács addressed in a somewhat different form) inevitably prompts the question: is there not, hidden behind this, a justification of manipulative-bureaucratic rule, even if in a democratic form? Miliband, however, was obviously correct in pointing out that formulating and realising the democratic collective will of the majority, whether under a socialist or bourgeois system, requires conscious political work. Hence the *political* mission of the left is not to monitor the purity of theory, but on the basis of this theory, to work for a reconciliation of interests.

There is no doubt that since the 1980s, when Miliband published his thoughts, the social make-up of the worker masses has become even more heterogeneous. But precisely for this reason, there are no grounds to hope for the creation of a monolithic political organisation, united by a single, shared ideology. Even under the classical industrial capitalism of the nineteenth and twentieth centuries, upholding a *mechanical* unity that suppressed the natural differences arising from the social diversity of society was possible only at the cost of suppressing the freedom of the organisation's members.

Political unity under the conditions of a heterogeneous society inevitably takes on the form of a coalition, even if in technical terms the representatives of various social groups and currents can be kept within the framework of a single party. More often, however, several organisations are formed simultaneously and in parallel. The problem here lies not in pluralism as such, but in the fact that each of the groups that arises seeks to present its own views and principles as the only ones that are correct. Meanwhile, pluralism in no way negates the fact that certain strategic approaches actually do have better prospects than others from the point of view of the *overall interests of the cause*. Ultimately, respect for the views of others does not negate the objective truth or error of different judgements.

In *The Communist Manifesto* Marx and Engels noted the simultaneous existence of various proletarian and socialist parties, without seeing this as a particular problem. Describing the attitude of communists to democratic movements and to 'already established workers' parties', they called on their supporters to defend 'the future of the movement'.[10] What is involved, in other words, is the defence of the most general and long-term interests of the class, reflecting the objectively mature requirements for the development of society.

Trotsky came to the same conclusions when, in exile, he reconsidered the experience of the communist movement:

> In reality, classes are diverse, are riven by internal antagonisms, and come to the fulfilling of common tasks only through an internal struggle of tendencies, groups and parties. Within certain limits, it may be recognised that 'a party is a part of a class'. But since a class has many 'parts', some of which look ahead and others backward, one and the same class may include a number of parties. For the same reason, one party may rest on parts of different classes. In all of political history there has never been a case in which one single party has corresponded to a class, unless, of course, we take the police version for the actual situation.[11]

The trouble is that the reality of political struggle very often imposes its own demands, which by no means always coincide with the demands of democracy. Decisions need to be taken quickly, and must be fulfilled regardless of the degree to which all the participants in the discussion agree with their correctness. Especially under the conditions of crisis or revolution, real politics in essence compels a constant search for a balance between effective action and the democratic imperative that is the very heart of the socialist movement. The implementing of political decisions is in turn entrusted to an important degree to the governing apparatus, which acquires greater power and independence the more often it proves necessary to rely on its sense of duty regardless of how great the support from the masses might be for each decision adopted. As Trotsky observed, 'the living political process always carries out leaps, and at critical moments demands the same from revolutionary politics'.[12] To expect complete approval, detailed discussion and painstaking agreement on all the actions undertaken at moments when the fate of the country is being decided is naïve at the very least. For this precise reason outstanding revolutionists (and in general, the politicians heading the state during such 'fateful minutes') have been forced to act in authoritarian fashion, relying on their political apparatus. The fundamental question is not whether such a mode of action is permissible, but how to avoid transforming it into a constant, routine and self-reproducing practice, including during historical stages when quite different approaches are required.[13]

The critique of bureaucratism that has resounded constantly in the ranks of trade union organisations, in social-democratic parties, and then in communist parties as well has changed nothing, since no-one has succeeded in creating a stable political structure that has not featured at least a certain number of professional apparatus workers. The smothering of democracy, however, does not occur at the point where a bureaucratic apparatus arises, but when it starts taking *political decisions*, bypassing democratic procedures or reducing them to mere simulation. To use the terminology of Weber, what is required is the development of forms of democracy that, while reducing the role of political chiefs and of the party apparatus to a minimum, 'are characterised by a striving to *minimise the domination* of one individual over another'.[14] Just as we cannot demand of *practical* activity that it accord *ideally* with theoretical principles or with moral norms proclaimed in the form of a *general principle*, neither can we forget about these norms or postpone following them to some later point – that is, until the final victory of the new world. If the movement is going forward, it is inevitably making mistakes, but it is also correcting its errors. It is handing powers to its leaders, and is taking care to limit these powers; it is encountering problems, and it is solving them. Any other method will inevitably lead us into a dead end, the only exit from which will be another retreat.

'Good' theory and 'bad' reality

The transformation of society, as it becomes a practical matter, encounters the same contradictions as any other activity within the context of existing reality. This, however, is not an excuse for refraining from day-to-day work that requires not just decisiveness but also flexibility, within a framework that includes not only victories but also defeats. The political philosopher Grigory Vodolazov has noted 'the complex dialectical (that is, contradictory) unity of revolutionary strategy with revolutionary tactics', when in real life

> the strategic line of struggle under the influence of circumstances necessarily acquires bizarre tactical twists, and it may be that these twists do not contradict the strategic direction in any way. Further, the 'straightness' of a strategic line only ever exists in an ideal sense, that is, in people's heads. In real life, a strategic line cannot take any other form than tactical zigzags, and these zigzags are more complex and confused the more complex and confused the situation is itself.[15]

The counterposing of high and pure theory to 'vulgar' reality, and especially to the practice associated with it is a typical trait of left sectarianism, and especially of the particular form of left sectarianism that has become established during the years of the long retreat. Indeed, to maintain the purity of one's ideas against a background of universal pragmatism and constant ideological capitulations is an extremely worthy undertaking. But it is also completely lacking in prospects, and most importantly, has nothing in common with revolutionary action.

In connection with the Irish Uprising of 1916, Lenin mentioned that in the real world there cannot be a revolution without 'explosions by a section of the petty bourgeoisie with all its prejudices, without a movement of the unconscious proletarian and semi-proletarian masses'.[16] Hence the inevitable inconsistency of any revolutionary process and even, at times, the presence within it of reactionary trends that are always available to be used by fighters for the ideological purity of the movement as a sort of ideological alibi, justifying a refusal to take part in practical struggle.

Nikolay Berdyaev, recalling the works of György Lukács, wrote that this 'Hungarian writing in German, the cleverest of communist writers, who revealed a great subtlety of thought' understood revolution better than anyone as the moment when theory becomes combined organically with practice.[17] It must be recognised that Berdyaev, who did not consider himself a Marxist despite spending his whole life beneath the strong influence of Marx's ideas, understood the essence of the matter far better than many socialists and communists who refer to the 'laws of the materialist dialectic'. However, we shall let Lukács speak for himself. Evaluating the discussion between the revisionists who criticised Marxism and the dogmatists who defended Marx from any and all criticism, Lukács saw no special difference between them; the urge to safeguard ideological purity from the 'contamination' connected with searches for practical solutions could 'in the end spill over into just such contamination', leading to the very same departure from an apprehension of reality, from 'practical-critical activity', and to 'the same return to the utopian dualism of subject and object, of theory and practice' as revisionism had brought about.[18]

The hostile attitude of radical-left moralisers to real revolutions (which they counterpose endlessly to a sort of ideal revolution that is possible only in their imaginations) is explained by the fact that these groups exist and reproduce themselves outside of any link to mass politics, and so far as possible, to politics in general. Hence also their contemptuous attitude to 'bourgeois elections', an attitude that conceals their mistrust and disdain for the working masses who, whether from belief or compulsion, take part in these polls. Hence, too, their unending condemnation of mass demonstrations, behind which they see no more than 'consumer revolt', devoid of class consciousness, and their scornful criticism of other leftists who try to understand the questions that are in fact agitating the majority of people at a given stage of history.

Despite the constantly proclaimed cult of 'the working class' or 'the proletariat', for sectarian leftists the real worker is a synonym for a malignant opportunist. This is not just because the real worker does not share the sectarians' dogmas, but because working people have their own class interests of which they are perfectly aware, and which are not to be reduced to the immediate installation of a 'dictatorship of the proletariat' led by this or that left sect. Workers are guilty of wanting to live like human beings in the here and now, of wanting to receive decent pay, of wanting to be able to defend their rights and win improvements in their job conditions, and also to improve their domestic and cultural conditions without waiting for the final and complete victory of socialism. When people such as these – driven to extremes by exploitation and injustice – come out onto the streets, fight the police and take arms in their hands to win real and immediate improvements that are timely and essential regardless of what the slogans of ideologues might proclaim, the left moralisers not only hold aloof from fighting on their side, but also condemn them from the height of their eternal wisdom. In times of actual struggle left sectarians prefer a comfortable existence within a minuscule group, dangerous to no-one, to the terrors of real combat and the challenges of mass politics.

'Revolutions always have an ugly side,' Berdyaev wrote, 'and during revolutions, people who want to be particularly faithful to beauty cannot be too active.'[19] Like everything that is alive, reality is unfinished and incomplete, full of contradictions and thus fundamentally imperfect. People when they confront reality may well find that the body of theory they have embraced does not explain the facts they encounter. They then face a choice: they can either stick with the theory – or with ridiculous, philistine ideas about it – and curse the facts that do not coincide with it, or else they can turn to practice, in order to seek to *apply* the theory, and in the process, to lend it an *actual* social and historical meaning. In other words, theory like any tool is not meant for *evaluating* reality, but for *working* with it. This does not do away with the need to try to assess events in some fashion, but the conclusions that result are not the culmination of political thought; to the contrary, they merely initiate it.

'Anyone who waits for a "pure" socialist revolution,' Lenin wrote in 1916, 'will *never* see it happen. Such a person is a revolutionist only in words, and does not understand real revolution.'[20] Lenin in this case was drawing on the real experience of the events of 1905, which he evaluated without the slightest idealisation. This revolution, in his words,

> consisted of a series of battles involving all the dissatisfied classes, groups and elements of the population. Among them were masses of people with the most savage prejudices, struggling for the most unclear and fantastical goals. There were little groups that had taken Japanese money; there were speculators, adventurers, and so forth.[21]

But what was fundamentally important, Lenin continues, was the fact that *objectively* this was a movement of the masses, a movement that 'smashed tsarism and cleared the way for democracy'.[22]

In very much the same fashion the revolutionary upsurge of the masses in Kazakhstan in 2021, arising out of a spontaneous workers' protest, was accompanied by all sorts of provocations, by outbreaks of violence and looting. Nevertheless, it showed the power of the popular discontent that had accumulated during 30 years of capitalist restoration. Even if the participants in the events were remote from the left in ideological terms, they were quite able to spontaneously put forward class demands. These began with wage rises, the reinstatement of sacked enterprise workers and a lowering of the pension age, and extended to the legalisation of free trade unions and opposition parties (including those of the left); the right to strike; the nationalisation of enterprises; and free elections to organs of power. These demands were not invented by ideologues or 'planted' in mass consciousness by agitators, but arose as a result of striking workers making practical sense of their own experience.

Here we need to recall the words of Engels concerning the French revolutions of the nineteenth century. Each time when the demand for democracy became the slogan of the day, its implementation in practice depended on the development of social struggle. As a result,

> the proletariat, after paying for the victory with their blood, raised their own demands. These were more or less vague and even confused, depending in each case on the degree of development of the Parisian workers. Ultimately, however, all of these demands boiled down to doing away with the class opposition between capitalists and workers. How such a thing might occur – this, it is true, the workers did not know. But this very demand, for all its lack of definition, contained within itself a danger for the existing social system. The workers who were voicing this demand were still armed, and thus for the bourgeoisie, which was at the helm of the state, the first commandment was to disarm them. Hence, after every revolutionary victory achieved by the workers there followed a new struggle, which for the workers ended in defeat.[23]

Properly speaking, it is these repeated revolutions, reforms, counter-revolutions and new popular actions that in their totality make up the process of social transformation, the transition from the capitalist system to a new society.

The infantile urge to obtain everything immediately is in no way proof of radicalism. Rather, it speaks of an unpreparedness to follow the lengthy path in the course of which the political process will not only develop, passing through different phases that often negate each other, but will also *create* itself to the degree that the participants in events come to recognise their genuine historical mission, their place and their opportunities in this process.

Nikolay Berdyaev described the head of the Russian Provisional Government, Aleksandr Kerensky, as 'a man of the first stage of the revolution'.[24] This exquisite formulation conveys how the various phases of the movement require not only different ideas and slogans, but also different people. Only those who are capable of recognising the perspectives and possibilities of the process as a whole are able to traverse the whole path without losing their way and dissipating their political influence. Theory allows the *possibility* of such an understanding, but does not release people from personal responsibility, and does not free them of the need to make difficult decisions that cannot always be optimal and irreproachable. Whatever the case, it is only by turning our faces to history and accepting its logic that we can become part of it.

The socialist revolution in Europe, Lenin wrote in 1916,

cannot be other than a massive struggle of all the oppressed and dissatisfied of every kind. Sections of the petty bourgeoisie and of the backward workers will inevitably take part in it – without such participation mass struggle is impossible, and no revolution is possible – and just as inevitably, they will bring to the movement their prejudices, their reactionary fantasies, their weaknesses and errors. But *objectively* they will be attacking *capital*, and the conscious vanguard of the revolution, the advanced proletariat, voicing this objective truth to the heterogeneous and discordant, motley and outwardly fragmented mass struggle will be able to unite and direct this struggle, to conquer power, to seize the banks, to expropriate the trusts that are hated by all (though for different reasons!) and to carry out other dictatorial measures, in sum bringing about the overthrow of the bourgeoisie and the victory of socialism, a victory that will 'cleanse itself', though by no means immediately, of petty bourgeois dross.[25]

Today we can regard Lenin's practical activity, and also the results of the Bolshevik policies during the years from 1917 to 1920, in different ways. There is one thing, however, that we cannot doubt: the course of Lenin's life showed that he understood better than anyone else what revolutionary practice amounts to. He never sought to evade the challenge of history, and never hid from it behind a palisade of dogmatic formulae.

Conclusion

Critics of Marx have in retrospect directed two mutually exclusive accusations at him. One of these holds that his vision of the socialist future was utopian. The other charges that he failed to present his followers with a clear vision of the socialist future.

Observing the hopeless impasse in which economic policy has finished up since the crisis of 2008–10, Adam Tooze speaks bitterly of 'the center and the right having failed', and of the left being 'massively obstructed and self-obstructing'.[1] It is the latter characterisation that is the most important. After receiving a historic chance in the 2010s, the forces of the left not only failed to make any attempt to exploit it, but indeed, were assiduous in hiding from it. Fortunately, this chance has not yet been definitively squandered, and the collective life of society is not just providing us with new opportunities, but is also making increasingly harsh demands of us. If we do not meet these demands, we risk losing everything.

The 2008–10 crisis did not bring about radical systemic changes either on the global or national levels. Nevertheless, the price that capitalism paid for its conservative methods of overcoming the Great Recession included the rise of new, still more painful and catastrophic crises that devastated the system's mechanisms of reproduction. One element in this process was the Covid epidemic, which turned into a global medical crisis. Nor can the strengthening of authoritarianism experienced in Russia in 2020 and 2021, and the subsequent war with Ukraine, be regarded as isolated or chance developments born out of a ruler's morbid love for power, the corruption in his immediate entourage, or alarm at ripening natural changes. It would be more accurate to say that in Russia this alarm, which to one degree or another has gripped the elites of the entire world, has had specific consequences whose catastrophic nature is being exacerbated by the weakness of civil society and by a technical concentration of power without precedent in a developed society.

The systemic decay is giving rise to a crisis of such scope that once again, the question of revolution is inevitably being placed on the agenda. Only this time, there is no reason to hope that the question will be decided by the taking of another Bastille or Winter Palace.

Boris Kapustin has stated that in the early twenty-first century public life has seen 'an exclusion of revolution as a result of certain strategies, actions and relationships of forces, of the formation and collapse of various social institutions, of the adoption and rejection of various modes of thinking, and so forth.[2] Hence the question of revolution, which has been returned to the agenda in the 2020s by the course of events itself, requires both changes to our political practice and a radical rethinking of concepts and institutions that have become familiar over the past thirty years. Here too it is impossible not to agree with Kapustin, who insists on the need for a new 'theory of revolution, suited to modern neoliberal society'.[3] We can formulate such a theory, however, only in concert with the forging of a new political practice, and on the basis of understanding the experience already accumulated by socialist movements.

Here we encounter a major challenge that is not linked in any way to a rethinking of the moral foundations of socialism, or to the readiness of the left for social experimentation, or to the question of how accurately various thinkers assess the autonomy of different spheres of social life. This challenge lies in recognising the social content of practical activity, which not only reflects *objective interests and needs* (both of individual social groups and of society as a whole), but which also enables their *consolidation* on the basis of struggle for these interests.

Socialism arose as a generalisation of the collective practice of the workers' movement. With the change in the sociology of labour the original common identity of the proletariat, based on its role in industrial production, is also breaking down. At the same time, the class contradictions of capitalism are not just failing to disappear, but to a definite degree are growing even more acute. It is this that has brought about both the crisis of the positive programme of the socialist movement, and also the numerous and mostly unsuccessful attempts to reformulate the movement's social base and strategies (such as, for example, the sociologically weak but very strikingly presented 'multitudes' concept of Michael Hardt and Toni Negri).

Of course, the failures of our predecessors were not just the result of their mistakes, of a lack of radicalism or of inconsistency, any more than it would be correct to ascribe our probable future successes exclusively to our virtues and decisiveness. The objective relationship of forces creates the *possibility* of victory, or alternatively, makes achieving what we want improbable. Further, not a single historical possibility comes to pass in and of itself. Consequently, periods of retreat and failure also have their value – as times for the accumulation and interpretation of experience that will be irreplaceable at the moment of advance. The degree to which the opportunities that open up will be exploited depends in many ways on how well this experience is critically assimilated.

In society, the crisis of capitalism gives rise to an acute need for a *new hegemony*. What is important here is not only the state of culture or even politics, but the fact that the disorganisation and chaos that are becoming the constant companions of neoliberalism during the period of its drawn-out decline cannot be overcome on any other basis.

Charles Thorpe defines hegemony on the basis of the link between power and the dominant social order ('hegemony is power *as* order').[4] In other words, it is the ability of the ruling class or of some alternative force to impose order on society and to organise it that ensures the stability of the existing system or that creates the possibility of replacing it with something new. In the present case, however, what is involved is no longer the replacing of one social order with another, but the overcoming of chaos, the preservation and restoration of the bases of organised social being as such.

In Thorpe's view, the bourgeois system has outlived its potential in the historical sense, and while losing the ability to develop, has retained its capacity for the stable reproduction of instability:

> Capital is no longer capable of organizing society; nor does the ruling class care to. Globalization has extinguished the need of capital to organize society at the level of the nation-state and the bourgeoisie is incapable of organizing society at any higher level.[5]

A theoretical answer to the question of how to resolve this contradiction was provided many years ago by classical Marxism, which saw in the working class not simply the gravedigger of the bourgeoisie, but also a force able to construct a new social order on the basis of its own interests. It will be understood that in the early twenty-first century the structure of the working class, its composition and its interests in the broad sense have changed radically. The problem, however, does not lie only in this. The problem is how to convert the potential for a new hegemony into a political response to the crisis – that is, into practical social action. The retreat and capitulation by workers' organisations since the late twentieth century has by no means been solely the result of betrayal by their leaders, of sectarianism on the part of the radical left, of the opportunism of social-democratic leaders, and of the lack of principle of communist party or trade union apparatchiks. Rather, the fact that such people and political currents have dominated the left scene is itself a consequence of a more general and profound contradiction – between the global opportunities, and specific weaknesses that continue to exist here and now. As Thorpe surmises,

> the latent power of the working class as global collective rises in direct proportion to the also very real powerlessness and despair that the working class endures in its undefended condition as the former organizers of its power on the national level have turned against it and implemented the dictates of globally empowered capital.[6]

The contradiction noted by Thorpe is especially dramatic precisely because whether we like it or not, and despite the globalisation of capital, political life is developing within the framework of societies that have not in any way become global. To a substantial degree these societies retain their narrow national character, not to speak of the limitations of their corresponding political institutions. Will it be possible to organise social forces on a global level, and to mobilise the accumulated potential for change? This remains an open question, since as before society and political processes exist precisely within the context of the national state, and there is no other framework within which their *direct* mobilisation can proceed.

The global crisis thus develops in any case as the sum of national crises, developing in parallel and mutually interdependent, but nevertheless local. Meanwhile, a global alternative can be established only as the aggregate result of these processes and as the *cumulative effect* of a series of victories, each of which is in itself limited and local. In this sense any contemporary revolutionary action is by definition *insufficient*, but cannot be otherwise.

In essence, the reality of the capitalist crisis of the 2020s returns us to the question of permanent revolution, to the strategic issues that the socialists and communists of a century ago were unable to resolve. Beginning in one region of the planet, the process of transformation reaches its culmination or definitive form only when the revolutionary wave begins to engulf other countries. The revolutionary wave of the early twentieth century changed the world, but this occurred in a fashion different from what the revolutionists were expecting. In this regard the early socialist revolutions of the last century were doomed to failure, just like the first attempts to establish the principles of democracy and human rights in European societies that were still only exploring the possibilities of the bourgeois economy. The significance of the revolutions of the twentieth century was to pose tasks that in the terms of historical perspective were *already on the order of the day*, but that were *still insoluble* on the level of technological and cultural possibilities. In the first half of the twentieth century the political ripeness of the working class was defined to an important degree by the maturation of the productive forces and means of communication that were necessary for the socialist transformation. The situation now is in essence the mirror image of this. Today the main problem is on the left flank – where there is a shortage of politics.

Unfortunately there is no theoretical text, even the very best of them, that is able to solve these dilemmas, which are practical in nature. The task of thinkers is to discuss the problems honestly, while at the same time redirecting attention to a new, constructive political practice, the need for which is already more or less recognised. How and to what degree this need will be satisfied, the future is yet to show. For the present, however, it can only be stated that the growing scale of the crisis that the neoliberal model of capitalism confronts is providing the basis not only for a multitude of fears, but also for hope.

Observing how the development of capitalism was creating the conditions and premises for the socialist overturn, Marx and Engels saw the task of theory as being to explain, honestly and impartially, not only these premises but also what was happening to the worker masses themselves as the process of social change went ahead:

> To investigate historical conditions, and along with them, the very nature of this upheaval, and thus to explain to the now-oppressed class that is destined to carry out this heroic deed the nature of its own cause and the conditions that affect it – this is the task of scientific socialism, which is the theoretical expression of the proletarian movement.[7]

Since that time two centuries of class struggle, reforms, revolutions and restorations have made it possible not only to accumulate a vast historical experience, but also to recognise the contradictions of the socialist movement itself, contradictions whose victims have again and again been the seemingly most successful political forces of the left.

For the left movement, self-criticism is thus becoming a crucially important *practical* task, one that is incumbent on everyone who seriously shares the perspective of struggling for social changes that will lead us beyond the framework of neoliberal capitalism, and indeed, of capitalism in general. The scientific nature of socialist theory, on which Marx placed such great hopes, is defined precisely by the ability of socialists to look honestly and dispassionately at themselves and at the fruits of their activity, not in order to throw up their hands and repent, but taking account of the experience of earlier failures, to come up with radical answers to current questions.

As measured by the outcomes of almost half a century of neoliberal advance, the present crisis has paralysed social development. Overcoming it will require not only, and not so much, a theoretical effort to reformulate ethical and philosophical concepts as practical and political activity aimed at a new consolidation of the mass of working people under changed socio-economic and technological conditions. If this consolidation is to occur in reality, and not merely on the pages of books, then the task of expanding the sphere of social freedom will not be performed by theoreticians. It will be carried out by the people, millions of them, who take part in the practical transformation of society.

Over the 200-year history of industrial capitalism, the technological and cultural development of society has created an acute need for a new social order that provides scope for realising the potential of freedom and creativity – everyone's potential, not just that of a chosen few. As the Strugatsky brothers explain in their novel *Hard To Be a God*,

> you can persecute book-lovers as much as you like, you can ban science and eliminate art, but sooner or later you're going to correct yourself, and even if you do it with teeth clenched, you're going to open the way for everything that the power-hungry blockheads and ignoramuses find so hateful. However much these grey people who hold power despise knowledge, they can do nothing in the face of objective historical truth, they can only slow things down, they can't stop them. Even though they despise and fear knowledge, they inevitably finish up having to encourage it, so as to maintain their positions. Sooner or later they have to permit universities and scientific societies, establish research centres, observatories and laboratories, create a staff of thoughtful, knowledgeable people, of people they are no longer able to control, people with a quite different psychology, with quite different requirements, and these people cannot exist, much less function, in the earlier atmosphere of low-life greed, of banal domestic interests, of dull-witted self-satisfaction and exclusively sensual needs. These people need a new atmosphere, an atmosphere of universal and all-encompassing cognition, imbued with creative tension, they need writers, artists, composers, and the grey people who hold power are forced to make concessions to this. Anyone who balks at this will be replaced in the struggle for power by more cunning rivals, but inevitably though paradoxically, and against their own will, whoever makes these concessions will through their actions be digging a grave for themself. This is because the growth of the people's culture, across its whole range

from research in the natural sciences to the ability to take delight in great music, is lethal to know-nothing egoists and fanatics [...] Then comes the epoch of gigantic social upheavals, accompanied by an unprecedented development of science, and connected with it, an exceptionally broad process of the intellectualisation of society, an epoch when the greyness wages its last battles that in their ferocity return humanity to the Middle Ages, but in which it suffers defeat, and in a society now free from class oppression, disappears forever as a real force.[8]

The twenty-first century, which we met with optimism and enthusiasm just as we meet any new epoch, has brought us exactly the kind of battle that the fantasy writers predicted. This battle is now being fought out. All of us, regardless of our wishes or intentions, are participants in it.

Attempts to evade it will not work.

But we can, with dignity and assurance, play our roles.

Notes

Foreword

1. Kagarlitsky B. My Trip to Syktyvkar. *CounterPunch*, 18 January 2024: https://www.counterpunch.org/2024/01/18/my-trip-to-syktyvkar/.
2. Ibid.
3. President of Russia. Valdai International Discussion Club meeting. Sochi, 5 October 2023: http://en.kremlin.ru/events/president/news/72444.
4. Weissman, S Freedom for Boris Kagarlitksy: Solidarity is Stronger than Repression! *Links*, 22 February 2024. https://links.org.au/freedom-boris-kagarlitsky-solidarity-stronger-repression.
5. Amnesty International, Russia: Anti-terrorism legislation misused to punish activist Boris Kagarlitsky. London, 15 February 2024. https://www.amnesty.org/en/latest/news/2024/02/russia-anti-terrorism-legislation-misused-to-punish-activist-boris-kagarlitsky/.
6. The 'Post Globalization Initiative' was Boris's vehicle: https://www.youtube.com/ @pglobalinitiative/videos.
7. Kagarlitsky B. Yalta Conference Got the Name Conference of Resistance. Post Globalization Initiative, 13 October 2014: https://www.youtube.com/watch?v=eRvZOok2wpc.
8. Kagarlitsky B. Eastern Ukraine People's Republics between Militias and Oligarchs. *Links*, 16 August 2014: https://links.org.au/boris-kagarlitsky-eastern-ukraine-peoples-republics-between-militias-and-oligarchs.
9. Kagarlitsky B. and fuentes f. Russian Socialist Dissident Boris Kagarlitsky on Putin's Growing Domestic Crisis: 'People will not fight for this regime.' *Links*, 1 August 2022: https://links.org.au/russian-socialist-dissident-boris-kagarlitsky-putins-growing-domestic-crisis-people-will-not-fight.
10. Objectives of Israel's and Russia's Wars 'Nearly Identical' – Did Lavrov Shift Position on Gaza? *Palestine Chronicle*, 28 December 2023: https://www.
11. Kagarlitsky B. Letter from Prison. CounterPunch, 17 August 2023: https://www.counterpunch.org/2023/08/17/letter-from-prison/.

Preface

1. Klausevits K.S. *O voyne*. Moscow: EKSMO, St Petersburg: Midgard, 2007, p. 542.
2. Ibid., p. 543.
3. Gramshi A. *Izbrannye proizvedeniya*. Moscow: Inostrannaya literatura, 1957–1959, vol. 3, p. 197.

4. Kagarlitsky B. *The Dialectic of Change*. London: Verso, 1989.
5. Gramshi A. *Izbrannye proizvedeniya*, vol. 1, p. 35.
6. Mlynarzh Z. *Moroz udaril iz Kremlya*. Moscow: Respublika, 1992, p. 9.

Chapter 1

1. See: Fukuyama F. *The End of History and the Last Man*. New York—London etc.: Free Press, 1992. Russian translation: Fukuyama F. *Konets istorii i posledniy chelovek*. Moscow: AST, 2015.
2. Zombart V. *Izbrannye raboty*. Moscow: Territoriya budushchego, 2005, p. 226.
3. A detailed analysis of the political crisis of social democracy can be found in an article by the German political scientist Frank Bandau. See: Bandau F. The Electoral Crisis of Social Democracy: Postindustrial Dilemmas or Neoliberal Contamination? *Political Studies Review*, vol. 20, no. 3, August 2022. Russian translation: Rabkor 27 August 2022, https://rabkor.ru/columns/analysis/2022/08/27/social_democracy_crysis/.
4. Vasilyev M. and Budraytskis I. (eds) *Antologiya pozdnego Trotskogo*. Moscow: Algoritm, 2007, p. 5.
5. Bregman R. *Utopiya dlya realistov: Kak postroit' ideal'nyy mir*. Moscow: Al'pina Pablisher, 2018, p. 27. English edition: Bregman R. *Utopia for Realists: How We Can Build the Ideal World*. Little, Brown and Company/Hachette Book Group USA, 2017.
6. Mangeym K. *Diagnoz nashego vremeni*. Moscow: Yurist, 1994, pp. 167–168.
7. Ibid., p. 168.
8. Ibid., p. 164.
9. Chalikova V.A. (ed.) *Utopiya i utopicheskoe myshlenie*. Moscow: Progress, 1991, p. 50.
10. Marks K. and Engel's F. *Sochineniya*. Moscow: Politizdat, 1975–2004, vol. 19, p. 201.
11. Dyurkgeym E. *O razdelelnii obshchestvennogo truda*. Moscow: Kanon, 1966, p. 52.
12. Platon. *Dialogi*. St Petersburg: Azbuka, 2021, p. 406.
13. Ibid., p. 407.
14. Strugatskiy A.N. and Strugatskiy B.N. *Trudno byt' bogom. Ponedel'nik nachinaetsya v subbotu. Piknik na obochine. Za milliard let do kontsa sveta*. Moscow: AST, 2008, p. 342.
15. Bauman Z. *Does the Richness of the Few Benefit Us All?* Cambridge—Maiden MA: Polity Press, 2013, pp. 73–74.
16. Kautskiy K. *Ekonomicheskaya uchenie Karla Marksa*. Moscow: AST, 2021, pp. 288–289.
17. Marks K. and Engel's F. *Sochineniya*, vol. 19, p. 209.
18. Chalikova V.A. (ed.) *Utopiya i utopicheskoe myshlenie*, p. 53.
19. Lukach G. *Istoriya i klassovoe soznanie*. Moscow: Logos-Al'tera, 2003, p. 123.

Chapter 2

1. Lukach G. *Lenin i klassovaya bor'ba*. Moscow: Algoritm, 2008, pp. 54, 55.
2. Ibid., p. 55.
3. *Roza Lyuksemburg: aktual'nye aspekty politicheskoy i nauchnoy deyatel'nosti*. Moscow: Pamyatniki istoricheskoy mysli, 2004, p. 223.
4. Cited in: Bri M. *Otkryt' Rozu Lyuksemburg snova*. Moscow: Logos/Rosa Luxemburg Stiftung, 2020, p. 145.
5. *Roza Lyuksemburg*, p. 227.
6. Stepun F.A. *Sochineniya*. Moscow: ROSSPEN, 2000, p. 233.
7. Berdyaev N. *Maloe sobranie sochineniy*. St Petersburg: Azbuka, 2018, p. 116.
8. It is interesting that the choice by Lukács in favour of Bolshevism was very abrupt, and unexpected both by those in his circle and by the Hungarian communists. A.S. Stykalin in his biography of the thinker testifies that 'the turn by Lukács to the new faith occurred literally in the interval between two Sundays'. Nevertheless, Lukács 'demonstrated with all his subsequent political, philosophical and scholarly activity that his convergence with the communist movement, unexpected by his former co-thinkers, was not for him a brief, casual enthusiasm' (Stykalin A.S. *D'erd' Lukach—myslitel' i politik*. Moscow: LENAND, 2021, p. 48).
9. The well-known Russian political scientist I.K. Pantin regards Lenin as the initiator of 'the proletarian-Jacobin tendency in the Russian liberation movement' (*Filosofiya politicheskogo deystviya. Iz istorii levoy politicheskoy mysli XX veka*. Moscow: Ideya-Press, 2010, p. 93). This characterisation rests on the words of Lenin himself: 'Jacobins, connected indissolubly to the organisation of the proletariat and conscious of their class interests – these are the social democrats' (Lenin V.I. *Polnoe sobranie sochineniy*. 5th edition. Moscow: Politizdat, 1975–1978, vol. 8, p. 370). Lenin returned to this theme repeatedly. In 1905, for example, he wrote that socialists should take as their example the Jacobins, who 'consistently defended the interests of the progressive class of the eighteenth century, just as the revolutionary social democrats consistently defend the interests of the progressive class of the twentieth century' (ibid., vol. 9, p. 308), at the same time as he compared the Mensheviks to the Girondists. In conversations with comrades he more than once repeated this comparison, stressing that the Bolsheviks should become the Russian Jacobins (see: Valentinov N. *Vstrechi s Leninym*. New York: Chalidze Publications, 1981). It is true, as Pantin notes, that in the early days of the revolution Lenin hoped that the Bolsheviks would be 'Jacobins without the guillotine' (*Filosofiya politicheskogo deystviya*, p. 93).
10. Robespierre M. *Oeuvres complètes*. Paris: E. Leroux, 1910–1967, vol. 10, p. 353.
11. Lenin V.I. *Polnoe sobranie sochineniy*, vol. 35, p. 214.

12. A comparison of the Bolsheviks and Jacobins is also characteristic of the works of Trotsky (see: Trotskiy L. *Predannaya revolyutsiya. Chto takoe SSSR i kuda on idet?* Moscow: Marksistskaya tendentsiya, 2021, pp. 95, 97).

13. Lenin V.I. *Polnoe sobranie sochineniy*, vol. 35, p. 185.

14. Bri M. *Otkryt' Lenina snova.* Moscow: Logos/Rosa Luxemburg Stiftung, 2017, p. 76.

15. See: Trotskiy L. *Predannaya revolyutsiya*, p. 56.

16. Ibid., p. 90.

17. Manfred A.Z. *Velikaya Frantsuzskaya revolyutsiya.* Moscow: Nauka, 1983, p. 337.

18. Bri M. *Otkryt' Lenina snova*, p. 77.

19. Ibid.

20. Marks K. and Engel's F. *Sochineniya.* Moscow: Politizdat, 1975–2004, vol. 33, p. 45.

21. Trotskiy L. *Predannaya revolyutsiya*, pp. 89–90.

22. Ibid., p. 90.

23. Ibid.

24. Ibid.

25. Lenin V.I. *Polnoe sobranie sochineniy*, vol. 37, p. 220.

26. *Sotsialisticheskiy vestnik*, 4 April 1927. Cited in: Mosunov A. *Partiya men'shevikov v 1923–27 gg.* Petrozavodsk: Kopistar, 2014, p. 10.

27. Lenin V.I. *Polnoe sobranie sochineniy*, vol. 37, p. 220.

28. *Sotsialisticheskiy vestnik*, 4 April 1927. Cited in: Mosunov A., *Partiya men'shevikov v 1923–27 gg*, p. 12.

29. Lenin V.I. *Polnoe sobranie sochineniy*, vol. 44, p. 53.

30. Ibid., vol. 45, p. 357.

31. Veber M. *Politika kak prizvanie i professiya.* Kharkov: Litera Nova, 2018, p. 221.

32. Trotskiy L. *Predannaya revolyutsiya*, pp. 89–97.

33. Gramsci A. *Quaderni del carcere.* Torino: Einaudi, 1975, vol. 2, p. 800.

34. Gramshi A. *Izbrannye proizvedeniya.* Moscow: Inostrannaya literatura, 1957–1959, vol. 2, p. 127.

35. Kautskiy K. *Diktatura proletariata. Ot demokratii k gosudarstvennomu rabstvu. Bol'shevizm v tupike.* Moscow: Antidor, 2002, p. 63.

36. Ibid., p. 64.

37. Shumpeter Y.A. *Teoriya ekonomicheskogo razvitiya. Kapitalizm, sotsializm i demokratiya.* Moscow: Eksmo, 2007, p. 773. English edition: Schumpeter J.A. *Capitalism, Socialism and Democracy.* London–New York: Routledge, 1994, p. 361.

38. Mlynarzh Z. *Moroz udaril iz Kremlya.* Moscow: Respublika, 1992, p. 8.

39. Leongard V. *Revolyutsiya otvergaet svoikh detey.* Karlsruhe: Condor Verlag, 1960, p. 349.

40. Ibid., p. 351.

41. Stalin I.V. *Rech' ha XIX s''ezde partii.* Moscow: Politizdat, 1953, p. 7.

42. Mlynarzh Z. *Moroz udaril iz Kremlya*, p. 8.

43. Trotskiy L. *Predannaya revolyutsiya*, p. 93.

44. Shumpeter Y.A. *Teoriya ekonomicheskogo razvitiya*, p. 774. English edition: Schumpeter J.A. *Capitalism, Socialism and Democracy*, p. 361.

Chapter 3

1. Kamyu A. *Buntuyushchiy chelovek. Mif o Sizife.* Moscow: AST, 2021, p. 236.
2. Ibid., p. 238.
3. Ibid., p. 239.
4. Shumpeter Y.A. *Teoriya ekonomicheskogo razvitiya. Kapitalizm, sotsializm i demokratiya.* Moscow: Eksmo, 2007, p. 534. English edition: Schumpeter J.A. *Capitalism, Socialism and Democracy.* London–New York: Routledge, 1994, p. 150. It was not without a certain cynicism that the Austrian thinker observed how bourgeois dictatorships were crueller to protesting workers than to intellectuals, since the existence of intellectual freedom was part of the capitalist 'way of life' (ibid.). Schumpeter's remark in this case clearly contradicts most of the political experience of recent decades, when a vital task of the repressive apparatus of bourgeois regimes, in Russia and many other countries, has become the suppression (including through relatively moderate forms of authoritarianism) not only of particular intellectuals, but of intellectual activity in general.
5. Veber M. *O Rossii. Izbrannoe.* Moscow: ROSSPEN, 2007, p. 49.
6. Veber M. *Khozyaystvo i obshchestvo.* Moscow: Izdatel'skiy dom Vysshey shkoly ekonomiki, 2016, vol. 1, p. 262.
7. Weber M. *Gesamtausgabe*, Tübingen, Bd. 10, Hb. 2, S. 986.
8. Ibid., p. 800.
9. Ibid., p. 961.
10. *Sotsiologicheskoe obozrenie*, vol. 16, no. 3, 2017, pp. 90–91.
11. Ibid., p. 91.
12. See: Keynes J.M. *A Short View of Russia.* London: Hogarth Press, 1925. Russian edition in: Keyns Dzh.M. *Vpechatleniya o Sovetskoy Rossii. Dolzhno li gosudarstvo upravlyat' ekonomikoy.* Moscow: Algoritm, 2015.
13. Cited in: V.L. Barnett. Keyns i Rossiya: v dolgosrochnoy perspektive ekonomicheskaya teoriya vsegda nakhoditsya v sostoyanii perekhoda. *Vestnik Sankt-Peterburgskogo universiteta*, 2007, Ser. 5, Vypusk 1, p. 17.
14. Skochpol T. *Gosudarstva i sotsial'nye revolyutsii. Sravnitel'nyy analiz Frantsii, Rossii i Kitaya.* Moscow: Izdatel'stvo Instituta Gaydara, 2017, p. 25. English edition: Skocpol T. *States and Social Revolutions: A Comparative Analysis of France, Russia and China.* Cambridge: Cambridge University Press, 1999, p. 4. Skocpol focuses not so much on national states as on the influence regimes that come to power in one country exert on other countries. The American scholar backs up her ideas by quoting from the Japanese historian Elbaki Hermassi. See: Hermassi E. Toward a Comparative Study of Revolutions. *Comparative Studies in Society and History*, vol. 18, no. 2, April 1976, p. 214.
15. On the influence that the Bolshevik Revolution had on the development of the welfare state in Western countries, see: Rasmussen M. and Knutsen S. *Reforming to Survive: The Bolshevik Origins of Social Policies.* Cambridge: Cambridge University Press, 2021.

16. The extent to which the Stalinist modernisation was perceived as an indispensable progressive phenomenon even by people who themselves were among its victims is particularly evident in the memoirs of the German communist Wolfgang Leonhard, written after his flight from East Germany. As Leonhard notes, the sons and daughters of kulaks whom he met in Karaganda in 1941 'with the passage of time had turned into Stalinists' (Leongard V. *Revolyutsiya otvergaet svoikh detey*. Karlsruhe: Condor Verlag, 1960, p. 151). These were the same young people who personally related to the author whole volumes on the horrors of collectivisation and exile. 'Of course, it is quite possible that some of them were concealing their real feelings and speaking hypocritically when they professed their loyalty to the Stalin regime and their love for it. Nevertheless, the majority of my fellow students there thought as I did, and as did many of the friends of my youth in Moscow, young people whose parents had fallen victim to the purges of 1936–1938. They considered that the fate of particular families had been tragic, and of course unjust, but that fundamentally, the Soviet regime had to be supported, and that as a result, all its measures had to be defended' (ibid., p. 152).

17. Nove A. *The Economics of Feasible Socialism Revisited*. London: Harper Collins Academic, 1991, p. vi.

18. Lenin V.I. *Polnoe sobranie sochineniy*. 5th edition. Moscow: Politizdat, 1975–1978, vol. 45, p. 380.

19. Kautsky K. *Diktatura proletariata. Ot demokratii k gosudarstvennomu rabstvu. Bol'shevizm v tupike*. Moscow: Antidor, 2002, p. 77.

Chapter 4

1. *Avanstsena. Memuarnyy roman*. Moscow: Slovo, 1997, p. 80.

2. Djilas M. *The New Class: An Analysis of the Communist System*. New York: Frederick A. Praeger, 1961.

3. Voslenskiy M. *Nomenklatura. Gospodstvuyushchiy klass Sovetskogo Soyuza*. Moscow—Berlin: Direkt-Media, 2019.

4. See: Gelbreyt Dzh.K. *Novoe industrial'noe obshchestvo*. Moscow: AST, 2004. English edition: Galbraith J.K. *The New Industrial State*. Boston: Houghton Mifflin Company, 1967.

5. See: Glushchenko I., Kagarlitskiy B. and Kurennyy V. (eds) *SSSR. Zhizn' posle smerti*. Moscow: Vysshaya Shkola Ekonomiki, 2012.

6. Mlynarzh Z. *Moroz udaril iz Kremlya*. Moscow: Respublika, 1992, p. 86.

7. Ibid.

8. Ibid., p. 87.

9. See: Fisera V. The Workers Councils: The Second Prague Spring. *New Left Review*, vol. 1, no. 105, September–October 1977.

10. Mlynarzh Z. *Moroz udaril iz Kremlya*, p. 87.

11. Djilas M. *The New Class*, pp. 68, 69.

12. An analysis of the intersectoral redistribution of resources, and of the struggle for them, was provided by the academician Yuriy Yaremenko. See: Yaremko Yu. V. *Strukturnye izmeneniya v sotsialisticheskoy ekonomike*. Moscow: Mysl', 1981. For a popular account of Yaremenko's views, see: Belanovskiy S. Yuriy Vasilyevich Yaremenko (1935–1996). *Segodnya*, 20 September 1996.

13. Shubin A.V. *Zolotaya osen' ili Period zastoya. SSSR v 1975–1985 gg.* Moscow: Veche, 2008, p. 96.

14. Nove A. *The Economics of Feasible Socialism Revisited*. London: Harper Collins Academic, 1991, p. 4.

15. Veber M. *O Rossii. Izbrannoe*. Moscow: ROSSPEN, 2007, p. 49.

16. Kapustin B. *Rassyzhdeniya o "kontse revolyutsii"*. Moscow: Izdatel'stvo Instituta Gaydara, 2019, p. 126.

17. *Vestnik Sankt-Peterburgskogo universiteta*, 2007, Ser. 5, Vypusk 1, p. 19.

18. Veber M. *Politika kak prizvanie i professiya*. Kharkov: Litera Nova, 2018, p. 166.

Chapter 5

1. Zimmel' G. *Bol'shie goroda i dukhovnaya zhizn'*. Moscow: Strelka Press, 2018, p. 87.

2. Marks K. and Engel's F. *Sochineniya*. Moscow: Politizdat, 1975–2004, vol. 22, p. 233.

3. Bodriyyar Zh. *Obshchestvo potrebleniya*. Moscow: AST, 2020, p. 28.

4. Ibid., p. 29.

5. Carmona Báez G.A. *Global Trends and the Remnants of Socialism: Social, Political and Economic Restructuring in Cuba*. Amsterdam: Academisch proefschrift, 2002, p. 41.

6. See: Krugman P. *The Conscience of a Liberal*. New York—London: W.W. Norton & Co., 2007. Russian edition: Krugman P. *Kredo liberala*. Moscow: Evropa, 2009.

7. This radically differentiates bourgeois from feudal society, as well as from traditional society in the broader sense. Even if in these earlier societies individual achievements and feats (for example, acts of valour) were celebrated, these were never perceived outside the context of their *belonging to a collectivity* – to a social estate, locality, faith, order, family and so forth.

8. See: Brenner R. *The Economics of Global Turbulence: The Advanced Capitalist Economies from Long Boom to Long Downturn, 1945–2005*. New York—London: Verso, 2006. Russian edition: Brenner R. *Ekonomika global'noy turbulentnosti: razvitye kapitalisticheskie ekonomiki v period ot dolgogo buma do dolgogo spada, 1945–2005*. Moscow: Izdatel'skiy dom Vysshey shkoly ekonomiki, 2014.

9. Bukharin N.I. *Izbrannye proizvedeniya*. Moscow: Politizdat, 1988, p. 395.

10. Marks K. and Engel's F. *Sochineniya*, vol. 25, part 1, p. 268.

11. Shmitt K. *Gosudarstvo: pravo i politika*. Moscow: Izdatel'skiy dom 'Territoriya budushchego', 2013, p. 303.

12. See: Mazzucato M. *The Entrepreneurial State: Debunking Public vs. Private Sector Myths*. London—New York: Anthem Press, 2013.

13. Bek U. *Vlast' i ee opponenty v epokhu globalizma. Novaya vsemirno-politicheskaya ekonomiya.* Moscow: Izdatel'skiy dom 'Territoriya budushchego', 2007, p. 180.

14. Zimmel' G. *Bol'shie goroda i dukhovnaya zhizn'*, p. 99.

15. Kharrington B. *Kapital bez granits: upravlyayushchie chastnym kapitalom i odin protsent.* Moscow: Izdatels'stvo Instituta Gaydara, 2022, p. 269. English edition: Harrington B. *Capital without Borders: Wealth Managers and the One Percent.* Cambridge, MA: Harvard University Press, 2016, pp. 257–258.

16. The expression is that of Ruslan Dzarasov. See: Dzarasov R. and D. Novozhenov. *Krupnyy biznes i nakoplenie kapitala v sovremennoy Rossii.* 2nd edition. Moscow: 2009.

17. See: ibid., p. 287.

18. Bodriyyar Zh. *Obshchestvo potrebleniya*, p. 21.

19. Ibid., p. 22.

20. Lukach G. *Istoriya i klassovoe soznanie.* Moscow: Logos-Al'tera, 2003, p. 113; *Lenin i klassovaya voyna.* Moscow: Algoritm, 2008, p. 86.

21. Lukach G. *Istoriya i klassovoe soznanie*, p. 321.

22. Marks K. and Engel's F. *Sochineniya*, vol. 23, p. 655.

23. Lukach G. *Istoriya i klassovoe soznanie*, p. 322.

24. Ibid.

Chapter 6

1. *International Socialism*, vol. 172, Autumn 2021, p. 19. See also: Gills B. and Morgan J. (eds) *Economics and Climate Emergency.* London: Routledge, 2022.

2. *Union Magazine. Zhurnal o budushchem*, vol. 1, 2021, p. 69.

3. See: ibid., p. 70.

4. Ibid., p. 71.

5. Ibid., p. 70.

6. Cited in: *International Socialism*, vol. 173, Winter 2022, p. 3. It is noteworthy that a song of the Canadian truckers who in 2022 organised a 'freedom convoy' in protest at the Covid restrictions began literally with the same words: 'We're not gonna take it any more'. See: https://www.youtube.com/watch?v=8wh3QJ24jbo.

7. Srnicek N. and Williams A. *Inventing the Future: Postcapitalism and a World without Work.* London: Verso, 2016, p. 2.

8. *Das Denknetz*, vol. 11, April 2022, p. 8.

9. Ibid., p. 12.

10. See: Rekvits A. *Obshchestvo singulyarnostey. O strukturnykh izmeneniyakh epokhi moderna.* Moscow—Berlin: Direktmedia Pablishing, 2022, pp. 222, 221–282. German edition: *Die Gesellschaft der Singularitäten. Zum Strukturwandel der Moderne.* Berlin: Suhrkamp, 2017.

11. Ibid., p. 149.

12. Genkin A.S. and Frumkin K.S. (eds) *Koronaekonomika. Khronika ekonomicheskikh posledstviyakh pandemii 2020 goda.* Moscow: Izdatel'skie resheniya, p. 243.

13. *International Socialism*, vol. 173, Winter 2022, p. 9.

14. Gaaze K., Danilov V., Dudenkova I., Kralechkin D. and Safronov P. (eds) *Proshchay kovid?* Moscow: Izdatel'stvo Instituta Gaydara, 2020, p. 325.

15. Ibid., p. 302.

16. *New Left Review*, vol. 208, November–December 1994, p. 48.

17. In this case we can turn to the earlier-mentioned work by Paul Krugman, *The Conscience of a Liberal*, which shows particularly well how the welfare state, through the non-commercial nature of its activity, has allowed households to save and to redistribute their resources, receiving additional freedom for working out their life strategies and economic plans. It was on this basis that the modern middle class, whose existence the market reforms are placing under threat, first became established.

18. Bodriyyar Zh. *Obshchestvo potrebleniya.* Moscow: AST, 2020, p. 66.

19. In the context of this discussion it is worth recalling the idea of the *social dividend*, as expounded by the Polish economist Oskar Lange. This dividend would be paid to all members of a socialist society out of the revenues accruing to the state from the incomes of enterprises. The main difference between a social dividend and UBI is that in the first instance the social dividend is *earned*, though not on an individual basis but through the efforts of the whole society, while second, its implementation and functioning would be bound up inextricably with the *socialised economy* or with one or another of its parts. In this way, a direct *economic* connection would be established between society and the state sector of the economy.

20. In the present book, discussion and criticism of the concept of UBI has been kept to a minimum, since this topic is addressed at length in another of the author's texts: Kagarlitskiy B. *Mezhdu klassom i diskursom, Levye intellektualy na strazhe kapitalizma.* Moscow: Izdatel'skiy dom Vysshey shkoly ekonomiki, 2017. English edition: Kagarlitsky B. *Between Class and Discourse: Left Intellectuals in Defence of Capitalism.* London: Routledge, 2020.

21. *Proshchay kovid?*, p. 319.

22. Kelton S. *The Deficit Myth: Modern Monetary Theory and the Birth of the People's Economy.* New York: Public Affairs, 2020, p. 2.

23. Wray L.R. *Modern Money Theory: A Primer on Macroeconomics for Sovereign Monetary Systems.* University of Missouri–Kansas City, 2015, p. 49.

24. Ibid., p. 146.

25. Ibid., p. 149.

26. Godley W. *Seven Unsustainable Processes.* New York: The Jerome Levi Economics Institute, 1999, p. 4.

27. Ibid.

28. Ibid.

29. Wray L.R. *Modern Money Theory*, p. 221.

30. It is noteworthy that the policy of 'qualitative easing' (in other words, expanding the money supply) enacted by the US Federal Reserve System has sparked a rapid growth of financial speculation and increased demand for financial instruments of all kinds, including bitcoins and other cryptocurrencies, that are viewed as a private alternative to state money. Nevertheless, as soon as the Federal Reserve and then other central banks switched in 2022 to tighter policies in an attempt to restrain the inflation they had themselves stimulated, the price of bitcoins began falling.

31. Although none of the supporters of MMT assert outright that the measures they propose represent a panacea, one gains that impression from reading the well-known book by Stephanie Kelton *The Deficit Myth*. For a Marxist critique of Kelton's work, see: Roberts M. The Deficit Myth. *Michael Roberts Blog*, 16 June 2020: https://thenextrecession.wordpress.com/2020/06/16/the-deficit-myth/.

32. *Das Denknetz*, vol. 10, November 2021, p. 33.

33. See: Shene M. *Permanentnyy krizis. Rost finansovoy aristokratii i porazhenie demokratii*. Moscow: Izdatel'skiy dom Vysshey shkoly ekonomiki, 2017.

34. Tuz A. *Krakh. Kak desyatiletie finansovykh krizisov izmenilo mir*. Moscow: Izdatel'stvo Instituta Gaydara, 2020, p. 39. English edition: Tooze A. *Crashed: How a Decade of Financial Crises Changed the World*. New York: Viking, 2018.

Chapter 7

1. Shene M. *Permanentnyy krizis. Rost finansovoy aristokratii i porazhenie demokratii*. Moscow: Izdatel'skiy dom Vysshey shkoly ekonomiki, 2017, p. 115.

2. Tuz A. *Krakh. Kak desyatiletie finansovykh krizisov izmenilo mir*. Moscow: Izdatel'stvo Instituta Gaydara, 2020, p. 20. English edition: Tooze A. *Crashed: How a Decade of Financial Crises Changed the World*. New York: Viking, 2018.

3. Ibid.

4. See: ibid., p. 23.

5. Ibid., p. 24.

6. Ibid.

7. See: Genkin A.S. and Frumkin K.S. (eds) *Koronaekonomika. Khronika ekonomicheskikh posledstviyakh pandemii 2020 goda*. Moscow: Izdatel'skie resheniya, p. 28.

8. *Indian Journal of Politics and International Relations*, vol. 12, no. 2 and vol. 13, no. 1 (2019–2020), p. 70.

9. Ibid., p. 71.

10. Ibid., p. 73.

11. See: *Socialist Review*, May 2020, p. 17.

12. See: Gaaze K., Danilov V., Dudenkova I., Kralechkin D. and Safronov P. (eds) *Proshchay kovid?* Moscow: Izdatel'stvo Instituta Gaydara, 2020, pp. 236–237.

13. *Revolutionary Marxism: A Journal of Theory and Politics* (Devrimci Marksizm). Special annual English edition 2021, p. 136.
14. See: *Proshchay kovid?*, p. 241.
15. Thorpe C. *Sociology in Post-Normal Times*. New York—London: Lexington Books, 2022, p. 2.
16. *Union Magazine. Zhurnal o budushchem* no. 1, 2021, p. 14.
17. Ibid., p. 15.
18. Ibid., pp. 13–14.
19. Ibid.
20. See: Agamben Dzh. *Kuda my prishli? Epidemiya kak politika.* Moscow: Nookratiya, 2022.
21. See: Malm A. *Korona, klimat, khronicheskaya chrezvychaynaya situatsiya.* Moscow: Gorodets, 2023. English edition: Malm A. *Corona, Climate, Chronic Emergency: War Communism in the Twenty-First Century.* London: Verso Books, 2020.
22. *Koronaekonomika*, p. 29.
23. *Union Magazine. Zhurnal o budushchem*, vol. 1, 2021, p. 12.
24. Ibid., p. 13.
25. For a more detailed treatment, see: Kagarlitskiy B. *Vosstanie srednogo klassa.* Moscow: Ul'tra.kul'tura, 2003. English edition: Kagarlitsky B. *The Revolt of the Middle Class.* Moscow: Kulturnaya revolutsiya, 2006.
26. *Das Denknetz*, vol. 10, November 2021, p. 47.
27. *Proshchay kovid?*, p. 319.
28. Ibid., p. 324.
29. Ibid., p. 325.
30. Ibid., p. 55.
31. *Das Denknetz*, vol. 10, November 2021, p. 7.
32. Lenin V.I. *Polnoe sobranie sochineniy.* 5th edition. Moscow: Politizdat, 1975–1978, vol. 26, p. 218.
33. Yablokov's book has appeared in both Russian and English. The comparison between Russia and the US appears in the foreword to the English edition: Yablokov I. *Fortress Russia: Conspiracy Theories in the Post-Soviet World.* Cambridge: Polity Press, 2018, p. 3. In the Russian edition it is also stressed that 'the Russian and American societies are similar in their desire to find conspiracies everywhere'. See: Yablokov I. *Russkaya kul'tura zagovora. Konspirologicheskie teorii na postsovetskom prostranstve.* Moscow: Al'pina non-fikshn, 2020, p. 19.

Chapter 8

1. Robinson W. *The Global Police State.* London: Pluto Press, 2020, p. 77.
2. Ibid., p. 78.
3. Engel's F. *Izbrannye voennye proizvedeniya.* Moscow: Voenizdat, 1956, p. 695.
4. *International Socialism*, vol. 174, Spring 2022, p. 24.
5. *The Times*, 27 Dec. 1915, p. 3.

6. Potemkin V.P. (ed.) *Istoriya diplomatii*. Moscow: Politizdat, 1945, vol. 2, p. 246.
7. Ibid., p. 258.
8. Ibid.
9. Faynberg I. *1914-y. Dokumental'nyy pamflet*. Moscow: MTP, 1934, p. 52.
10. Potemkin V.P. *Istoriya diplomatii*, vol. 2, p. 261.
11. Klein M.C. and Pettis M. *Trade Wars Are Class Wars: How Rising Inequality Distorts the Global Economy and Threatens International Peace*. New Haven: Yale University Press, 2020, p. 225.
12. Engel's F. *Izbrannye voennye proizvedeniya*, pp. 611–612.
13. Lenin V.I. *Polnoe sobranie sochineniy*, vol. 26, p. 212.
14. See: ibid.
15. Ibid., p. 319.
16. Quoted in: Urilov I.Kh. *Yu. I. Martov. Politik i istorik*. Moscow: Nauka, 1997, p. 200.
17. *Istoriya Vtorogo Internatsionala*. Moscow: Nauka, 1966, vol. 2, p. 407.
18. Sukhanov N.N. *Zapiski o revolyutsii*. Moscow: Izdatel'stvo politicheskoy literatury, 1991, vol. 1, p. 51.
19. Krom M. *Patriotizm ili Dym otechestva*. St Petersburg: Izdatel'stvo Evropeyskogo universiteta v Sankt-Peterburge, 2020, p. 116.
20. M.I. Tugan-Baranovskiy (ed.) *Velikaya voyna. Sbornik statey*. Petrograd: Izdanie yuridicheskogo knizhnogo sklada 'Pravo', 1915, p. 276.
21. Milanović B. The Novelty of Technologically Regressive Import Substitution. *Globalinequality*, 30 April 2022: https://glineq.blogspot.com/2022/04/the-novelty-of-technologically.html?m=1.
22. On the ties between the Green New Deal and the mobilisation economy that arose out of the military events, see: Hart-Landsberg M. The Planning and Politics of Transformation: World War II Lessons for a Green New Deal. *New Politics*, vol. 18, no. 4, Winter 2022, and by the same author: The Green New Deal and the State: Lessons from World War II. *Against the Current*, vol. 207, July–August 2020.
23. Kharvi D. *Sostoyanie postmoderna. Issledovanie istokov kul'turnykh izmeneniy*. D. Kharvi—Vysshaya Shkola Ekonomiki (VShE), 1989, p. 268. English edition: Harvey D. *The Condition of Postmodernity: An Enquiry into the Origins of Cultural Change*. Cambridge, MA—Oxford: Blackwell, 1992, p. 336.
24. Simon R. *Gramsci's Political Thought: An Introduction*. London: Lawrence & Wishart, 1985, p. 39.
25. Ibid.
26. *Das Denknetz*, vol. 11, April 2022, p. 7.
27. Cited in: Sarabeev V. *Trotskiy, Stalin, kommunizm*. St Petersburg: Piter, 2021, p. 34.
28. Cited ibid., p. 34.
29. For more on this point, see: Kagarlitskiy B. Proiskhozhdenie revolyutsionnykh partiy. *Levaya politika*, vol. 16, 2011.

Chapter 9

1. See: Khardt M. and Negri A. *Mnozhestovo: voyna i demokratiya v epokhu imperii.* Moscow: Kul'turnaya revolyutsiya, 2006. English edition: Negri A. and Hardt M. *Multitude: War and Democracy in the Age of Empire.* Penguin Books, 2009.
2. Rekvits A. *Obshchestvo singulyarnostey. O strukturnykh izmeneniyakh epokhi moderna.* Moscow—Berlin: Direktmedia Publishing, 2022, p. 148. German edition: *Die Gesellschaft der Singularitäten. Zum Strukturwandel der Moderne.* Berlin: Suhrkamp, 2017.
3. Inozemtsev V.L. *Za predelami ekonomicheskogo obshchestva.* Moscow: Academia–Nauka, 1998, p. 244.
4. Ibid., p. 246.
5. Gramshi A. *Izbrannye proizvedeniya.* Moscow: Inostrannaya literatura, 1957–1959, vol. 3, p. 198.
6. Gramshi A. *Izbrannye proizvedeniya*, vol. 3, p. 136.
7. The term 'culture wars' was introduced into wide circulation in 1991 by the American sociologist James Davison Hunter, in connection with the reformatting of political debates in the US. See: Hunter J.D. *Culture Wars: The Struggle to Define America.* New York: BasicBooks, 1991.
8. Shmitt K. *Gosudarstvo: pravo i politika.* Moscow: Izdatel'skiy dom 'Territoriya budushchego', 2013, p. 257.
9. Ibid.
10. Ibid.
11. *New Left Review*, no. 217, May–June 1996, p. 41.
12. Laval' K. *Chelovek ekonomicheskiy. Esse o proiskhozhdenii neoliberalizma.* Moscow: Novoe literaturnoe obozrenie, 2010, p. 374.
13. The term 'cultural Marxism', originally associated by a number of American sociologists with the heritage of the Frankfurt School (see: Schroyer T. *The Critique of Domination: The Origins and Development of Critical Theory.* Boston: Beacon Press, 1975), later came to be used aggressively by conservative commentators in the US to characterise their opponents in the 'culture wars'.
14. Chris Cutrone (ed.) *Marxism in the Age of Trump: Articles from Platypus Review 2015-2017.* Ann Arbor, MI: Platypus Publishing, 2018, p. 136.
15. Cutrone notes that in 2016 such charges were being levelled by BLM supporters against Bernie Sanders and his group. See: ibid.
16. See: Žižek S. Multiculturalism, or, The Cultural Logic of Multinational Capitalism. *New Left Review*, no. 225, 1997, p. 44.
17. Frank T. *What's the Matter with Kansas? How Conservatives Won the Heart of America.* New York: Metropolitan Books, 2004, p. 8.
18. Ibid., p. 243.
19. Zombart V. *Izbrannye raboty.* Moscow: Territoriya budushchego, 2005, p. 214.
20. Ibid., p. 216.
21. Ibid., p. 320.

22. Bermudo J.M. Prologue. In: del Turia J. *Temática del marxismo: síntesis conceptual del pensamiento de sus fundadores y de sus realizadores*. Barcelona: Editorial Cinc D'Oros, 1977, p. xiv.

23. Rekvits A. *Obshchestvo singulyarnostey. O strukturnykh izmeneniyakh epokhi moderna*. Moscow—Berlin: Direktmedia Pablishing, 2022, p. 226. German edition: *Die Gesellschaft der Singularitäten. Zum Strukturwandel der Moderne*. Berlin: Suhrkamp, 2017. The 'culturalization of inequality', as Reckwitz observes, is perfectly compatible with a positive evaluation of particular groups that are conveniently included in the general logic of multiculturalism: 'In the context of extolling cultural diversity particular elements of the culture of the lower classes, for example, the culture of the working class or of blacks and migrants, may take on a certain attractiveness' (pp. 294–295). The oppressed communities, however, are regarded not as social or economic but precisely as cultural groups. 'Ethnic collectives (migrants, indigenous population groups, cultural minorities and so forth) are often viewed from the point of view of "culture" in an essentialised sense (and not from the position of class or other criteria)' (p. 323). Meanwhile, they are 'presented as homogeneous communities', so that no significance is assigned to social differentiation or even conflicts within them (ibid).

24. Stending G. *Prekariat: Novyy opasnyy klass*. Moscow: Ad Marginem Press, 2014, p. 10. English edition: Standing G. *The Precariat: The New Dangerous Class*. London–New York: Bloomsbury Academic, 2011, p. 1.

25. Ibid., p. 11. English edition: ibid., p. 1.

26. Lukach G. *Lenin i klassovaya bor'ba*. Moscow: Algoritm, 2008, p. 64.

27. Simon R. *Gramsci's Political Thought: An Introduction*. London: Lawrence & Wishart, 1985, p. 28.

28. Thorpe C. *Sociology in Post-Normal Times*. New York—London: Lexington Books, 2022, p. 6.

29. *Das Denknetz*, no. 10, November 2021, p. 5.

30. Simon R. *Gramsci's Political Thought*, p. 25.

31. See: Veber M. *Politika kak prizvanie i professiya*. Kharkov: Litera Nova, 2018, pp. 167–168.

32. Ibid., p. 222.

33. Ibid., pp. 222–223.

34. On left populism in Latin America, see: Rusakova T.Yu. Populizm kak sotsial'no-politicheskoe yavlenie i ego novoe zvuchanie. *Latinskaya Amerika*, no. 11, 2006.

35. Veber M. *Politika kak prizvanie i professiya*, p. 176.

36. Batkin L.M. *Ital'yanskoe Vozrozhdenie: problem i lyudi*. Moscow: RGGY, 1995, pp. 361–362.

37. See: Makiavelli N. *Gosudar'*. Moscow: Planeta, 1990, p. 74. In setting out Machiavelli's concept, Batkin refers also to Machiavelli's correspondence with Piero Soderini, which is cited according to: Machiavelli N. *Opere. Vol VI: Lettere/A cura di F. Gaeta*. Milano, 1961. See: Batkin L.M. *Ital'yanskoe Vozrozhdenie*, pp. 353–354.

38. Veber M. *Khozyaystvo i obshchestvo*. Moscow: Izdatel'skiy dom Vysshey shkoly ekonomiki, 2016, vol. 4, p. 189.

39. Trotskiy L. *Predannaya revolyutsiya. Chto takoe SSSR i kuda on idet?* Moscow: Marksistskaya tendentsiya, 2021, p. 53.

40. Ivanovskiy Z.V. (ed.) *Latinskaya Amerika: politicheskiy landshaft na fone turbulentnosti*. Moscow: ILA RAN, 2022, p. 339.

41. The logic of polarisation was also evident in the elections of 2022 in France. The coalition of incumbent president Emmanuel Macron (the 'Ensemble' electoral bloc) received 245 seats in the National Assembly and fell short of an absolute majority. The left, which went to the polls as part of the 'New Popular Ecological and Social Union' (NUPES) headed by Jean-Luc Mélenchon, gained 131 deputies' mandates. At the same time, the National Rally (Rassemblement National, formerly Front National) of Marine Le Pen scored a breakthrough result. This was not simply a record for Le Pen's party, but also a qualitative leap.

42. Ivanovskiy Z.V. (ed.) *Latinskaya Amerika: politicheskiy landshaft ha fone turbulentnosti*, pp. 330–331.

Chapter 10

1. Bri M. *Otkryt' Rozu Lyuksemburg snova*. Moscow: Logos/Rosa Luxemburg Stiftung, 2020, p. 86.

2. For a more detailed discussion, see: Kagarlitskiy B. *Mezhdu klassom i diskursom, Levye intellektualy na strazhe kapitalizma*. Moscow: Izdatel'skiy dom Vysshey shkoly ekonomiki, 2017. English edition: Kagarlitsky B. *Between Class and Discourse: Left Intellectuals in Defence of Capitalism*. London: Routledge, 2020.

3. Marcuse H. *One-Dimensional Man: Studies in the Ideology of Advanced Industrial Society*. London—New York: Routledge, 2002, p. 4.

4. Gramshi A. *Izbrannye proizvedeniya*. Moscow: Inostrannaya literatura, 1957–1959, vol. 3, p. 174.

5. Ibid., p. 176.

6. Zuboff S. *The Age of Surveillance Capitalism: The Fight for a Human Future at the New Frontier of Power*. New York: PublicAffairs, 2018.

7. Ibid., p. 10.

8. See: Fuko M. *Nadzirat' i nakazyvat'. Rozhdenie tyur'my*. Moscow: Ad Marginem, 2018.

9. Veber M. *Politika kak prizvanie i professiya*. Kharkov: Litera Nova, 2018, p. 95.

10. Debor G. *Obshchestvo spektaklya*. Moscow: Izdatel'stvo 'Logos', 2000, p. 24.

11. An instructive example here is the purchase by Elon Musk in 2022 of the Twitter network. In the name of freedom of speech, restrictions preventing the publication of offensive statements were removed, but at the same time the new managers of the network tightened controls on its employees and provoked a mass exit of users who did not agree with the new policies. As can be seen, the ending of corporate censorship in its most primitive form not only failed to limit corporate control as such, but did not make the network more democratic either.

12. Srnicek N. *Platform Capitalism*. New York—Cambridge: Polity Press, 2016, p. 3.
13. See: Cheshkov M. *Kritika predstavleniy o pravyashchikh gruppakh razvivayushchikhsya stran*. Moscow: Nauka, 1979.
14. See: Castells M. *The Rise of the Network Society*, The Information Age: Economy, Society and Culture vol. 1. Cambridge, MA—Oxford: Blackwell, 1996; Castells M. *The Power of Identity*, The Information Age: Economy, Society and Culture vol. 2. Cambridge, MA—Oxford: Blackwell, 1997; Castells M. *End of Millennium*, The Information Age: Economy, Society and Culture vol. 3. Cambridge, MA—Oxford: Blackwell, 1998.
15. See: Srnichek N. *Platform Capitalism*, p. 9.
16. Fuko M. *Nadzirat' i nakazyvat'*, p. 174.
17. De Serto M. *Izobretenie povsednevnosti. 1. Iskusstvo delat'*. St Petersburg: Izdatel'stvo Evropeyskogo universiteta v Sankt-Peterburge, 2013, p. 129. On the views of de Certeau, see also: Volkov V.V. and Kharkhordin O.V. *Teoriya praktik*. St Petersburg: Izdatel'stvo Evropeyskogo universiteta v Sankt-Peterburge, 2008.
18. De Serto M. *Izobretenie povsednevnosti*, p. 97.
19. Debor G. *Obshchestvo spektaklya*, p. 15.
20. De Serto M. *Izobretenie povsednevnosti*, pp. 116–117.
21. Ibid., p. 111.

Chapter 11

1. Lyuksemburg R. *Sotisal'naya reforma ili revolyutsiya*. Moscow: Politizdat, 1959, p. 40.
2. Ibid., p. 37.
3. Ibid.
4. Ibid., p. 40.
5. Ibid., p. 42.
6. See: Marcuse H. *Counterrevolution and Revolt*. Boston: Beacon Press, 1972.
7. Marks K. and Engel's F. *Sochineniya*. Moscow: Politizdat, 1975–2004, vol. 19, p. 305.
8. Vodolazov G. *Ot Chernishevskogo k Plekhanovu (ob osobennostyakh razvitiya sotsialisticheskoy mysli v Rossii)*. Moscow: MGU, 1969, p. 7.
9. Marks K. and Engel's F. *Sochineniya*, vol. 13, p. 7.
10. Ibid., vol. 19, p. 223.
11. Ibid., p. 214.
12. The fragmentary and discrete nature of the market is defined particularly well by Max Weber: 'The market as a site of exchange is a place marked by a succession of rational generalisations, each of which is so transient that it fades out with the exchanging of the goods that are its object' (Veber M. *Khozyaystvo i obshchestvo*. Kharkov: Litera Nova, 2018, vol. 2, p. 269). Commenting on this, Pierre Bourdieu notes that for Weber what is important is not the price of the commodity, which is determined by the relationship between supply

and demand, but the instantaneous nature of the acts of exchange, which occur in constantly changing circumstances – that is, the fact that 'the market is the site of a multitude of momentary social relationships that have neither preconditions nor consequences' (Bourdieu P. *Ekonomicheskaya antropologiya. Kurs lektsiy v Kollezh de Frans (1992–1993)*. Moscow: Delo, 2019, p. 254). It is thus obvious that the fragmentation of the cultural field that has accompanied the triumph of postmodernism in the social sciences and arts is a perfectly natural continuation of the more general process through which the market is absorbing science and art.

13. The concept of social capital is embedded in the sociology of Pierre Bourdieu, who along with this employs the term 'symbolic capital', defined among other ways as 'the criteria of years of service and of reputation' (Bourdieu P. *Ekonomicheskaya antropologiya*, p. 227). It is important to reflect that social capital is *exclusively a group resource*. In the late nineteenth and early twentieth centuries sporadic examples occurred of renegacy (in the form of a 'recognition' of conservative values, coming with age and status). The reward received was precisely for the *shift* of the individual from one political camp to another. Around the turn of the twenty-first century we encounter a collective phenomenon that in essence amounts to a collective shift of the *entire* camp. In such a situation the value of an individual act of apostasy is not especially great from the point of view of the political establishment, but the importance of a *general* shift to the right of the intellectual community and its discourse is huge. The individual value of a 'matured' intellectual journalist is in proportion to their ability to 'stay in formation' with former and current co-thinkers who have shifted to new positions. On the other hand additional sanctions, including from the 'left' intellectual community, are imposed on those who do not change their views, instead refusing to move with the general trend of the discourse and continuing to defend and develop the ideas that this camp formulated in the past and that represented the point of its existence.

Chapter 12

1. De Serto M. *Izobretenie povsednevnosti. 1. Iskusstvo delat'*. St Petersburg: Izdatel'stvo Evropeyskogo universiteta v Sankt-Peterburge, 2013, p. 110.
2. Gramshi A. *Izbrannye proizvedeniya*. Moscow: Inostrannaya literatura, 1957–1959, vol. 3, p. 160.
3. Schumpeter J.A. *Capitalism, Socialism and Democracy*. London–New York: Routledge, 1994, p. 317.
4. Marks K. and Engel's F. *Sochineniya*. Moscow: Politizdat, 1975–2004, vol. 4, p. 446.
5. Ibid.
6. Vasilyev M. and Budraytskis I. (eds) *Antologiya pozdnego Trotskogo*. Moscow: Algoritm, 2007, p. 302.

7. Ibid., p. 299.
8. Ibid., p. 304.
9. Marks K. and Engel's F. *Sochineniya*, vol. 19, p. 222.
10. Trotskiy L. *Predannaya revolyutsiya. Chto takoe SSSR i kuda on idet?* Moscow: Marksistskaya tendentsiya, 2021, p. 51.
11. Marks K. and Engel's F. *Sochineniya*, vol. 19, p. 223.
12. Trotskiy L. *Predannaya revolyutsiya*, p. 198.
13. Kautskiy K. *Diktatura proletariata. Ot demokratii k gosudarstvennomu rabstvu. Bol'shevizm v tupike.* Moscow: Antidor, 2002, p. 245.
14. Trotskiy L. *Predannaya revolyutsiya*, p. 198.
15. See: Veber M. *Khozyaystvo i obshchestvo*. Kharkov: Litera Nova, 2018, vol. 1, p. 158.
16. Shubin A.V. *Mirovaya revolyutsionnaya volna (1918–1923). Priliv.* Moscow: Akademicheskiy proekt, 2020, p. 762.
17. Ibid., p. 761.
18. Keyns Dzh.M. *Obshchaya teoriya zanyatosti, protsenta i deneg. Izbrannoe.* Moscow: EKSMO, 2007, p. 336.
19. See: Lange O. Economics of Socialism. *Journal of Political Economy*, vol. 50, no. 2, 1942.
20. Weber M. *Khozyaystvo i obshchestvo*, vol. 1, p. 152.
21. On the experience of corporate planning during the 'golden epoch' of the welfare state, see: Galbraith J.K. *The New Industrial State*. Boston: Houghton Mifflin Company, 1967. On the planning conducted by corporations in the twenty-first century, see: Phillips L. and Rozworski M. *The People's Republic of Walmart: How the World's Biggest Corporations are Laying the Foundation for Socialism*. London: Verso, 2019.
22. Levchenko S. *Usilienie planovykh nachal v upravlenii sotsial'no-ekonomicheskim razvitiem regionov Rossiyskoy Federatsii*. Moscow—Irkutsk: RAEN, 2021, p. 112.
23. See: Gorshenina A.V. Finlyandiya: strategiya i taktika razvitiya. *Byudzhet*, no. 7, July 2010. Information on the work of the Sitra company can be found on its website: https://www.sitra.fi/en/.
24. Bodriyyar Zh. *Obshchestvo potrebleniya*. Moscow: AST, 2020, p. 66.
25. The communist principles proclaimed in the USSR were merely one of the forms of compulsory ideology. In this regard the multiculturalism that has triumphed in the West in the early twenty-first century fits this concept no less well.

Chapter 13

1. *Financial Times*, 4 Sept. 2017.
2. In the English-language literature, the discussion on how to calculate resources for the purposes of socialist planning came to be known as the 'socialist calculation debate'. It was conducted between the representatives of the Austrian School Ludwig von Mises and Friedrich von Hayek on the one hand, and a group of Marxist economists of whom the best known was Oskar Lange, on the other.

See: Lange O. *Theories of Reproduction and Accumulation*. Oxford: Pergamon Press, 1977. See also: Lange O. Letter to F.A. Hayek, translated by Thadeusz Kowalik. *Journal of Political Economy*, vol. 50, no. 2, 1942. Collaborating with Lange in this discussion was Abba Lerner. See: Lerner A. Statics and Dynamics in Socialist Economics. *The Economic Journal*, vol. 47, no. 186, 1937. For an overview of the discussion, see: Adaman F. and Devine P. The Economic Calculation Debate: Lessons for Socialists. *Cambridge Journal of Economics*, vol. 20, 1996.

3. Marks K. and Engel's F. *Sochineniya*. Moscow: Politizdat, 1975–2004, vol. 19, p. 224.
4. Ibid., p. 227.
5. Ibid., p. 221.
6. Ibid., vol. 22, p. 234.
7. Veber M. *Khozyaystvo i obshchestvo*. Kharkov: Litera Nova, 2018, vol. 1, p. 152.
8. Ibid., p. 153.
9. Ibid.
10. Ibid., p. 151.
11. Lenin V.I. *Polnoe sobranie sochineniy*. 5th edition. Moscow: Politizdat, 1975–1978, vol. 37, p. 219.
12. Trotskiy L. *Predannaya revolyutsiya. Chto takoe SSSR i kuda on idet?* Moscow: Marksistskaya tendentsiya, 2021, p. 68.
13. Ibid., p. 69.
14. Rogovin V. *Stalinskiy neonep*. Moscow: B.I., 1995, p. 21.
15. Stalin I.V. *Sochineniya*, vol. 13, p. 341.
16. On the Stalinist ideology of 'abundance' in the 1930s, see: Glushchenko I. *Obshchepit. Mikoyan i sovetskaya kukhnya*. Moscow: Izdatel'skiy dom Vysshey shkoly ekonomiki, 2015.
17. Rogovin V. *Stalinskiy neonep*, p. 23.
18. Stalin I.V. *Ekonomicheskie problemy sotsializma v SSSR*. Moscow: Gospolitizdat, 1952, pp. 16–17.
19. See: Šik O. *Plan and Market under Socialism*. London: Routledge, 2017.
20. The official beginning of the discussion is usually considered to have been the publication, in the newspaper *Pravda* on 9 September 1962, of an article by the Kharkov economist Evsey Liberman entitled 'Plan, Profit and Reward'. The main ideas of the radical-democratic reformers were formulated in 1967 by the Czech economist Ota Šik, and in a more moderate variant, by the Hungarian economist Rezső Nyers. See: Šik O. *Plan and Market under Socialism*; N'ersh R. Reforma khozyaystvennogo mekhanizma. *Kommunist*, vol. 16, 1967.
21. Here we may recall the well-known 'Kornai paradox'. In studying the operations of light industry, the Hungarian economist János Kornai found that the planning organs brought to the organisations implementing the plan their idea of the expected result, in the form of a collection of various indicators, after which the lower-level structures no longer worked to secure the results, but to fulfil

these indicators. The final outcome was completely in line with these planning targets, but might differ strikingly from what the authors of the plan intended. See: Kornai J. *Overcentralization in Economic Administration.* Oxford: Oxford University Press, 1959.

22. In the late 1960s Włodzimierz Brus developed his own theory of the transition to socialism, stressing that the statisation of property was an essential but insufficient condition for the rise of a socialist economy, while bureaucratisation was a consequence of the gap, inevitable in the transition process, between formal and real collectivisation. From this followed the need for a new stage of socialist transformations aimed at overcoming this gap. See: Brus W. *Socialist Ownership and Political Systems.* London—Boston: Routledge & Kegan Paul, 1975.

23. Khonnet A. *Idea sotsializma. Popytka aktualizatsii.* Moscow–Berlin: Direktmedia Pablishing, 2022, p. 102.

24. See: Mandel E. The Myth of Market Socialism. *New Left Review,* vol. 169, May–June 1988.

25. See: Nove A. Markets and Socialism. *New Left Review,* vol. 161, January–February 1987.

26. Elson D. Market Socialism or Socialization of the Market? *New Left Review,* vol. 172, November–December 1988.

27. Inozemtsev V.L. Raskolotaya tsivilizatsiya. Moscow: Academia–Nauka, 1999, p. 191.

28. In his works, the South African scholar Patrick Bond develops the idea of decommodification. An example is provided by his article 'Decentralization, Privatization and Countervailing Popular Pressure: South African Water Commodification and Decommodification', in the collection: Beard V.A., Miraftab F. and Silver C. (eds) *Planning and Decentralization: Contested Spaces for Public Action in the Global South.* London: Routledge, 2008. See also: Bond P. Globalisation/Commodification or Deglobalisation/Decommodification in Urban South Africa. *Policy Studies,* vol. 26, nos. 3/4, 2005.

Chapter 14

1. Laval' K. *Chelovek ekonomicheskiy. Esse o proiskhozhdenii neoliberalizma.* Moscow: Novoe literaturnoe obozrenie, 2010, p. 376.

2. Kapustin B. *Rassyzhdeniya o "kontse revolyutsii".* Moscow: Izdatel'stvo Instituta Gaydara, 2019, p. 15.

3. Cited in: Bri M. *Otkryt' Lenina snova.* Moscow: Logos/Rosa Luxemburg Stiftung, 2017, p. 52.

4. *New Left Review,* vol. 225, September–October 1997, p. 31.

5. Ledyaev V.G. *Sotsiologiya vlasti. Teoriya i opyt empiricheskogo issledovaniya vlasti v gorodskikh soobshchestvakh.* Moscow: Izdatel'skiy dom Vysshey shkoly ekonomiki, 2012, p. 26.

6. Gramshi A. *Izbrannye proizvedeniya.* Moscow: Inostrannaya literatura, 1957–1959, vol. 3, p. 172.

7. See: Bukharin N.I. *Politicheskaya ekonomiya rant'e: Teoriya tsennosti i pribyli avstriyskoy shkoly.* Moscow: Orbita, 1988.

8. Bodriyyar Zh. *Obshchestvo potrebleniya.* Moscow: AST, 2020, p. 66.

9. Miliband R. *Class Power and State Power.* London: Verso, 1983, p. 77.

10. Marks K. and Engel's F. *Sochineniya.* Moscow: Politizdat, 1975–2004, vol. 4, p. 458.

11. Trotskiy L. *Predannaya revolyutsiya. Chto takoe SSSR i kuda on idet?* Moscow: Marksistskaya tendentsiya, 2021, pp. 221–222.

12. Trotskiy L. *Permanentnaya revolyutsiya.* St Petersburg: Azbuka-klassika, 2009, p. 164.

13. It may be noted that Machiavelli took up the same question in the twenty-fifth chapter of *The Prince,* when he observed that acting in one and the same fashion might have completely different results depending on the situation.

14. Veber M. *Khozyaystvo i obshchestvo.* Kharkov: Litera Nova, 2018, vol. 1, p. 305.

15. Vodolazov G. *Ot Chernishevskogo k Plekhanovu.* Moscow: MGU, 1969, pp. 13–14.

16. Lenin V.I. *Polnoe sobranie sochineniy.* 5th edition. Moscow: Politizdat, 1975–1978, vol. 30, p. 54.

17. Berdyaev N. *Maloe sobranie sochineniy.* St Petersburg: Azbuka, 2018, p. 87.

18. Lukach G. *Istoriya i klassovoe soznanie.* Moscow: Logos-Al'tera, 2003, p. 124.

19. Berdyaev N. *Maloe sobranie sochineniy,* p. 114.

20. Lenin V.I. *Polnoe sobranie sochineniy,* vol. 30, p. 54.

21. Ibid.

22. Ibid.

23. Marks K. and Engel's F. *Sochineniya,* vol. 22, pp. 190–191.

24. Berdyaev N. *Maloe sobranie sochineniy,* p. 116.

25. Lenin V.I. *Polnoe sobranie sochineniy,* vol. 30, p. 54.

Conclusion

1. Tuz A. *Krakh. Kak desyatiletie finansovykh krizisov izmenilo mir.* Moscow: Izdatel'stvo Instituta Gaydara, 2020, p. 39. English edition: Tooze A. *Crashed: How a Decade of Financial Crises Changed the World.* New York: Viking, 2018.

2. Kapustin B. *Rassyzhdeniya o "kontse revolyutsii".* Moscow: Izdatel'stvo Instituta Gaydara, 2019, p. 16.

3. Ibid., p. 18.

4. Thorpe C. *Sociology in Post-Normal Times.* New York—London: Lexington Books, 2022, p. 9.

5. Ibid., p. 111.

6. Ibid., p. 113.

7. Marks K. and Engel's F. *Sochineniya.* Moscow: Politizdat, 1975–2004, vol. 19, p. 230.

8. Strugatskiy A.N. and Strugatskiy B.N. *Trudno byt' bogom. Ponedel'nik nachinaetsya v subbotu. Piknik na obochine. Za milliard let do kontsa sveta.* Moscow: AST, 2008, pp. 120–121.

Index

Thanks to our Patreon subscriber:

Ciaran Kane

Who has shown generosity and
comradeship in support of our publishing.

The Pluto Press Newsletter

Hello friend of Pluto!

Want to stay on top of the best radical books
we publish?

Then sign up to be the first to hear about our
new books, as well as special events,
podcasts and videos.

You'll also get 50% off your first order with us
when you sign up.

Come and join us!

Go to bit.ly/PlutoNewsletter